WEIGHT WATCHERS®
NEW PROGRAM COOKBOOK

WEIGHT WATCHERS®
NEW PROGRAM COOKBOOK

by

JEAN NIDETCH

NEW AMERICAN LIBRARY
TIMES MIRROR

WEIGHT WATCHERS is a registered trademark of Weight Watchers International, Inc.

Acknowledgments

Without the cooperation of our publishers, New American Library, and some of our staff who were involved in this project, it would not have been possible to bring this book to fruition.

We, therefore, express our special thanks to Patty Barnett, Anne Hosansky, Mary-Lynn Mondich, Franco Palumbo, Eileen Pregosin, and Isabel Sobol.

A special indebtedness to Felice Lippert, Vice President and Director of Food Research, for the invaluable part she played in the creation and formulation of the recipes contained in this book.

CONTENTS

v

FOREWORD

Imagine eating delicious meals and snacks without paying for them in pounds.

These weight-conscious days, there's an increasing interest in losing weight—or maintaining it—while, at the same time, enjoying satisfying and nutritious foods. The Weight Watchers Organization understands this and understands, also, that one of the most important ingredients in a successful eating plan is *variety*.

In 1977, the Weight Watchers Food Plan, which had already been so successful, was made even more rewarding. It became more flexible and easier to follow, with portion *ranges* and the interchanging of meals permitted. And with more "dos" and fewer "don'ts," a lot of the guilt has gone! As for variety . . . ! Imagine eating juicy cheeseburgers, cocoa milk shakes, lox and bagels, hot dogs on a roll, tortillas, yogurt, and so many other favorites—in proper quantities, of course—while enjoying the "dessert" of weight loss! It's a Food Plan that allows "legal" to fit into any life-style. ("Legal" means foods that are acceptable for use on the Weight Watchers Food Plan.)

Of course, the aim is not only to reach goal weight but to *stay* there! So our Program also includes a revised Maintenance Plan, which brings back forbidden "goodies" within expert, easy-to-follow, portion-controlled guidelines.

You'll find both the weight reduction Food Plan and the Maintenance Plan—for men, women, and youths—in this book. It's a Program that combines food expertise with the on-the-spot knowledge gained from our millions of hours of worldwide classroom experience.

"*Millions of hours* . . ." That's an awe-inspiring statistic, isn't it? I'd like to share with you what it reflects, for those "millions" began with *one*.

Yes, we began with one Weight Watchers class, back in 1963. It met each week in a small loft in Little Neck, Queens. By unbelievable contrast, *hundreds of thousands* of men, women, and teen-agers now attend weekly classes, not just in a corner of one city but in thousands of cities—and villages—in all fifty of the States and throughout most of western Europe, as well as Canada, Mexico, Brazil, the Caribbean, South Africa, Israel, Japan, Australia, New Zealand, Hong Kong. And the list is constantly growing. Truly, the "sun never sets" on Weight Watchers classes!

Perhaps the major reason we have grown into the largest and—I am proud to say—most respected weight control organization in the world is that we are not content to stand still. Under the leadership of our dedicated Chairman of the Board and President, Albert Lippert, we have unceasingly searched for ever-better ways to help over-weight individuals.

This means helping people not only to lose weight but also to learn to eat properly. A professional Food Research Department, headed by Felice Lippert, includes a medical director and a staff of nu-tritionists who supervise the Food Plan, making certain it is well-balanced and geared to optimum nutrition. It was this department that researched and created the new Program.

Our concern, however, extends beyond teaching people *what* to eat, to include *how*—and *why*—we turn to food. One of our most exciting developments has been a behavior modification program, aimed at helping Weight Watchers members learn to cope with problem times in non-food ways, and to *un*learn self-destructive eating habits. For only by developing new eating patterns can weight loss be *maintained!*

Our global classes provide invaluable empathy and support, and they are staffed with lecturers who have traveled that same route from FAT to SLIM. To me, these classes are the roots of our Organization, but our *branches* now reach in a multitude of other directions as well. Walk into almost any supermarket and you'll find us, for we have Weight Watchers preportioned frozen luncheons and dinners, as well as a wide range of foods and beverages.

We also have Weight Watchers restaurants, camps, magazines, and books, which brings me to the book you are now holding in your hand.

The popular 1973 edition of the *Weight Watchers Program Cook-*

book remained on the best-seller lists for months and sold over a million copies!

Why, then, you may ask, is there a *new* cookbook?

The revisions in the Food Plan opened the door to a host of palatable possibilities. So the talented chefs and home economists, who also staff our Food Research Department, busied themselves in our test kitchen for many months. The result? They have "celebrated" the revised Program by creating some of the newest, most delectable dishes we have ever tasted! You'll find the recipes in this book.

We've also selected 71 of your favorite recipes from the previous edition and gathered these "old favorites" together in one appetizing chapter. As an additional guide, we've included sample menus.

What this all adds up to is a book for every weight-conscious person who wants to enjoy tasty, tempting meals and, at the same time, learn about portion control. So whether or not you are on our Program, the *Weight Watchers Program Cookbook* provides you and your family with a nutritious pattern for streamlined eating.

I'm confident you'll enjoy the delicious results.

Jean Nidetch

FOUNDER
WEIGHT WATCHERS INTERNATIONAL

WEIGHT WATCHERS FOOD PROGRAM, INCLUDING MENU PLANS

This chapter has been designed to help you understand the Food Plan. Please read it carefully before you proceed.

Remember to eat only the foods listed on your Menu Plan—in the quantities and weights specified. Never, never skip a meal. As you will learn from these pages, there is a wide range of approved foods. They may be combined in varied ways, as described in our recipes, but remember to count all ingredients. Keeping a daily food diary, as outlined on page 14, will help you do this.

The word "serving" appears throughout the Food Plan. A serving may be defined as *a portion of food which equates to the amount of food allowed on Program.*

1. FRUITS

A list of fruits and serving sizes is given on page 20. You may use fresh, canned, or frozen fruit, with no sugar added. This is true of approved fruit juices, too. Fruits rich in Vitamin C are marked with an asterisk, and one of these fruits must be taken daily.

2. EGGS AND CHEESE

Select 4 medium eggs a week, cooked in the shell, poached, scrambled without fat, made into omelets or soufflés, or used in other ways in other dishes. See page 36 for further details.

CHEESE: Pot cheese, cottage cheese (skim milk type preferred), and skim milk ricotta cheese are approved soft cheeses. Use in the amounts indicated on your Menu Plan.

SEMISOFT AND HARD CHEESES are limited to 4 ounces weekly. Examples of semisoft cheeses are Bleu, Brie, and Camembert. Hard cheeses include American, Cheddar, Jarlsburg, Muenster, and Swiss.

3. BREAD, CEREAL, CHOICE GROUP

Use enriched or whole grain bread, rolls, or buns. Use packaged, presliced bread or packaged rolls; approximately 1 ounce per serving. See page 79 for further details.

CEREAL may be selected up to 3 times weekly, if desired. When cereal is taken, bread may be taken at the Morning Meal or another meal. You may have 1 ounce (or cup measure equivalent) of ready-to-eat (not presweetened) or uncooked cereal, with at least ½ milk serving. See page 95 for further details.

You may substitute a CHOICE GROUP item up to 3 times a week by omitting 1 serving of bread each time you make this selection. See page 98 for additional information.

4. MILK

Select servings from this group daily, at any time, in the amount allowed on your Menu Plan.

A serving of SKIM MILK is 1 cup (8 fluid ounces). The skim milk may be made from nonfat dry milk, or it may be commercially prepared liquid skim milk. Do not use a commercially prepared liquid skimmed milk product, or liquid skim milk with whole milk solids added.

A serving of EVAPORATED SKIMMED MILK is ½ cup (4 fluid ounces).

A serving of BUTTERMILK is ¾ cup (6 fluid ounces).

A serving of plain unflavored YOGURT is ½ cup (4 fluid ounces).

5. POULTRY, MEAT, FISH, AND LEGUMES

Your Menu Plan gives net cooked weight (fat, skin, and bones trimmed away from fish, meat, and poultry; cooking liquid drained from legumes). See individual sections for further explanations. A ½ serving of poultry, meat, or fish may be combined with cheese, egg, or legumes.

POULTRY, VEAL, GAME: Select chicken, turkey, or other poultry (not duck or goose), veal, or wild game. Serve poultry with skin removed.

"BEEF" GROUP: This includes beef, ham, lamb, pork, and tongue.

Select up to 3 times a week, if desired. Use lean meats and remove all visible fat before eating. Once a week, if desired, in place of 1 "Beef" Group selection, you may use bologna, frankfurters, knockwurst, beef sausages, or organ meats (such as gizzards, hearts, kidneys, sweetbreads, and tripe).

LIVER: Select once a week, in the amounts specified on your Menu Plan. All liver is legal. See section beginning on page 189 for details.

FISH: Select any fish in the marketplace at least 3 to 5 times weekly. Vary selections. Use fresh, frozen, canned, or smoked fish. All canned fish must be well drained. It is strongly recommended that 5 fish meals be eaten weekly. However, if fish is selected 3 or 4 times per week, chicken must be substituted for the 1 or 2 omitted fish meals. See page 203 for more details.

LEGUMES: Legumes are dried beans, lentils, and peas. They are available canned, frozen, or packaged. Select up to 3 times weekly, if desired. For further details, see page 232.

6. VEGETABLES

Select reasonable amounts of all but the "limited vegetables." You must select at least 2 servings daily. Vegetables must be eaten at both the Midday and Evening Meals. They may also be eaten at any other time. Vary your selections, using both raw and cooked vegetables throughout the week. Each serving is ½ cup or 1 medium (e.g., tomato, cucumber, etc.). See page 249 for more details.

LIMITED VEGETABLES: These are optional and must be weighed. Do not exceed a combined total of 4 ounces, drained weight, daily, of the vegetables listed on page 249–50.

7. FATS

Select 3 servings daily, at mealtime only, of the fats listed on page 294. The fat may be used in a spread, salad dressing, or sauce, or it may be used in cooking, if you follow the methods on page 295.

8. OPTIONAL

Many juices, beverages, condiments, seasonings, and other foods are permitted on the Weight Watchers Food Plan. They are not required. Use them only if you wish, but do not exceed the prescribed amounts. The section beginning on page 313 has full details.

Menu Plan for Women

Morning Meal:
  Fruit, 1 serving
  Choice of
    Egg, 1
      or
    Cheese, soft, ⅓ cup
      or
    2½ ounces
      or
    Cheese, semisoft
      or hard, 1 ounce
      or
    Cereal, 1 ounce with
      ½ milk serving
      or
    Fish, cooked, 2 ounces
      or
    Poultry or Meat, cooked,
      1 ounce
  Bread, 1 serving
  Beverage, if desired

Midday Meal:
  Choice of
    Poultry, Meat, or Fish,
      cooked, 3 to 4 ounces
      or
    Eggs, 2

      or
    Cheese, soft, ⅔ cup
      or 5 ounces
      or
    Cheese, semisoft
      or hard, 2 ounces
      or
    Legumes, cooked, 6 ounces
  Vegetables
  Bread, 1 serving, if desired
  Beverage, if desired

Evening Meal:
  Choice of
    Poultry, Meat, or Fish,
      cooked, 4 to 6 ounces
      or
    Legumes, cooked, 8 ounces
  Vegetables
  Bread, 1 serving (if not eaten
    at Midday Meal)
  Beverage, if desired

Daily:
  Milk, 2 servings, at any time
  Fats, 3 servings, at mealtime
  Fruits, 3 servings (1 at Morn-
    ing Meal, 2 at any time)

Note: The Midday Meal may be interchanged with the Evening Meal.

Menu Plan for Men

Morning Meal:
    Fruit, 1 serving
    Choice of
        Egg, 1
            or
        Cheese, soft, ⅓ cup
            or 2½ ounces
            or
        Cheese, semisoft
            or hard, 1 ounce
            or
        Cereal, 1 ounce with
            ½ milk serving
            or
        Fish, cooked, 2 ounces
            or
        Poultry or Meat, cooked,
            1 ounce
    Bread, 1 serving
    Beverage, if desired

Midday Meal:
    Choice of
        Poultry, Meat, or Fish,
            cooked, 3 to 4 ounces
            or
        Eggs, 2
            or

Cheese, soft, ⅔ cup
    or 5 ounces
    or
Cheese, semisoft
    or hard, 2 ounces
    or
Legumes, cooked, 6 ounces
Vegetables
Bread, 2 servings
Beverage, if desired

Evening Meal:
    Choice of
        Poultry, Meat, or Fish,
            cooked, 6 to 8 ounces
            or
        Legumes, cooked, 12
            ounces
    Vegetables
    Bread, 1 serving
    Beverage, if desired

Daily:
    Milk, 2 servings, at any time
    Fats, 3 servings, at mealtime
    Fruits, 3 to 5 servings (1 at
        Morning Meal, 2 to 4 at
        any time)

Note: The Midday Meal may be interchanged with the Evening Meal.

Menu Plan for Youth

Morning Meal:
  Fruit, 1 serving
  Choice of
    Egg, 1
      or
    Cheese, soft, ⅓ cup
      or 2½ ounces
      or
    Cheese, semisoft
      or hard, 1 ounce
      or
    Cereal, 1 ounce with
      ½ milk serving
      or
    Fish, cooked, 2 ounces
      or
    Poultry or Meat, cooked,
      1 ounce
  Bread, 1 serving
  Beverage, if desired

Midday Meal:
  Choice of
    Poultry, Meat, or Fish,
      cooked, 3 to 4 ounces
      or
    Eggs, 2
      or
    Cheese, soft, ⅔ cup
      or 5 ounces
      or
    Cheese, semisoft
      or hard, 2 ounces
      or
    Legumes, cooked, 6 ounces
  Vegetables
  Bread, 2 servings
  Beverage, if desired

Evening Meal:
  Choice of
    Poultry, Meat, or Fish,
      cooked, 4 to 6 ounces
      or
    Legumes, cooked, 8 ounces
  Vegetables
  Bread, 1 serving
  Beverage, if desired

Daily:
  Milk, 3 to 4 servings, at any
    time
  Fats, 3 servings, at mealtime
  Fruits, 3 to 5 servings (1 at
    Morning Meal, 2 to 4 at
    any time)

Note: The Midday Meal may be interchanged with the Evening Meal.

Menu Suggestions for One Week

Follow your Menu Plan as to amount permitted; complete program requirements where necessary. (See page 13.)

Morning Meal

Monday Vegetable juice, ½ serving; Blueberry Muffins (see page 87; beverage

Tuesday Orange, 1 serving; Cooked Cereal with Fruit (see page 95); beverage

Wednesday Ginger Figs (see page 27); Not-So-Danish Pastry (see page 323); beverage

Thursday Grapefruit juice, 1 serving; Raisin French Toast (see page 46); beverage

Friday Berry "Cream" (see page 26); Cheese Toast (see page 81); beverage

Saturday Prune Bread Custard (see page 88); beverage

Sunday Honeydew, 1 serving; 1 ounce ready-to-eat cereal with ½ serving skim milk; raisin bread, 1 serving; beverage

Midday Meal

Monday California Orange Chicken Salad (see page 142); Carrot and Pineapple Mold (see page 260); Brandylike Alexander (see page 123)

Tuesday Instant "Pizza" (see page 86); Tossed Salad with Lemony Mayonnaise (see page 300); strawberries, ¾ serving; Hot Chocolate (see page 123)

Wednesday Split Pea Soup (see page 246); Oriental Vegetable Mix (see page 290); cantaloupe, 1 serving; beverage

Thursday Seafood Salad (see page 225); pumpernickel bread, 1 serving; Apple-Strawberry Chiffon (see page 126); Cappuccino Chiller (see page 123)

Friday   Sweet-and-Sour Tongue with Water Chestnuts (see page 188); Sliced Tomatoes with Rémoulade Sauce (see page 300); rye bread, ½ serving; Pineapple Sherbet (see page 34); beverage

Saturday   Zucchini Soup (see page 131); Baltimore Crab Cakes (see page 217); Hearts of Lettuce with Pimento Dressing (see page 336); Mint Sherbet (see page 341); beverage

Sunday   Cheese Soufflé (see page 67); Cooked Mushrooms (see page 272); Baked Apple (see page 23); Lemonade (see page 346)

Evening Meal

Monday   Grapefruit, 1 serving; Lemon-Broiled Trout (see page 214); Baked Eggplant Casserole (see page 263); Boiled Corn (see page 100); beverage

Tuesday   Sauerbraten (see page 166); Sauerkraut with Prunes (see page 282); green beans, 1 serving; Coffee "Brandy" (see page 340)

Wednesday   Veal-Stuffed Manicotti (see page 157); Green Salad with Basic French or Vinaigrette Dressing (see page 302); Cinnamon Peach Creme (see page 127); beverage

Thursday   Hot Tomato Bouillon (see page 321); Chicken Livers in Orange Sauce (see page 28); cauliflower, 1 serving; Tossed Salad with Tangy French Dressing (see page 337); Hot Mint Tea (see page 347)

Friday   Skinny Devil (see page 345); Baked Fish Creole (see page 211); Currants, 1 serving with Easy Whipped Topping (see page 340); Chocolate Milk Shake (see page 124)

Saturday   Tomato juice, 1 serving; Quick-and-Easy Lamb Dinner (see page 176); Minty Hot Cucumber (see page 263); Cooked Celery (see page 261); orange and grapefruit sections, 1 serving; beverage

Sunday   Steamed Fish Chinese Style (see page 251); cooked enriched rice, ½ cup; Mexi-Cauliflower Romaine and Pepper Salad (see page 289); Rhubarb-Strawberry Dessert (see page 34); beverage

Additional Program Requirements To Complete Menu Plan on Page 11-12*

Monday

Add: ¼ serving Fat
            ½ serving Milk (½ cup skim milk)

Tuesday

Add: ½ serving Milk (½ cup skim milk)
            1½ servings Fat

Wednesday

Add: 1 serving Milk (1 cup skim milk)

Thursday

Add: ¹¹/₁₆ serving Milk (½ cup plus 3 tablespoons skim milk)

Friday

Add: ¼ serving Milk (¼ cup skim milk)
            ½ serving Fat

Saturday

Add: 1 serving Milk (1 cup skim milk)

Sunday

Add: 1 serving Milk (1 cup skim milk)

*Note: *Men and Youth*—Add additional foods—bread, fruits, milk, and additional amounts of meat, fish, poultry, and legumes as allowed on the Program daily (see page 9-10).

GENERAL INFORMATION

1. Wherever specific amounts are given, they relate to the Women's Menu Plan. Adapt for Men and Youth.
2. The herbs used in these recipes are dried unless otherwise indicated.
3. When combining two recipes (e.g., pie crust and pie filling), be sure to include *both* equivalencies in your day's food allotment.
4. Nonstick pans make it possible for you to cook without fat. Use pans manufactured with a nonstick surface, or spray an ordinary pan with a release agent (nonstick cooking spray), following directions on the aerosol can. Release agents (nonstick cooking sprays) with less than 2 calories per spray are acceptable.
5. Recipe directions may sometimes look as if they're taking the long way around, but remember, they're all shortcuts to your goal weight! Never try to "get away with" using one pan when we call for two (you may have one less pot to wash, but you'll still have that pot around your middle). Always take the trouble to measure and weigh—don't think you can judge portions by eye.

WEIGHT WATCHERS STRONGLY ADVISES YOU TO CONSULT YOUR PHYSICIAN WHILE PARTICIPATING IN THE PROGRAM.

Daily Food Record

To help you keep track of your daily and weekly use of foods, rule a notebook page into eight columns. List the following headings across the page:

Food   Mon.   Tues.   Wed.   Thurs.   Fri.   Sat.   Sun.

List the following headings down the page, in the Food column:

Fruit (*)
Fruit
Eggs
Soft Cheese
Hard Cheese
Bread
Bread (once-a-week selection)
Cereal
Choice Group
Milk
Poultry, Veal, and Game
"Beef" Group

"Beef" Group (once-a-week selection)
Liver
Fish
Legumes
Vegetables
Limited Vegetables
Fats
Bonus
Something Extra
Specialty Foods (15 calories)

Oven Heats

If your oven does not have a thermostat or regulator, the following chart will give you an idea of the equivalent amount of heat required for each temperature range in degrees Fahrenheit.

250° to 275°F.   Very slow oven
300° to 325°F.   Slow oven
350° to 375°F.   Moderate oven
400° to 425°F.   Hot oven
450° to 475°F.   Very hot oven
500° to 525°F.   Extremely hot oven

Oven thermostats should be checked at least once a year. If your oven does not have a thermostat, an oven thermometer can be purchased and placed in the oven to help determine the degree of heat.

Since foods bake faster in heat-resistant glass than in shiny metal pans, lowering the temperature 25°F. is generally recommended when baking in glass.

Your Microwave Oven

Many of our recipes can be done in your microwave oven. You will have to experiment with your unit and follow manufacturer's advice for timing, since there is no one standard that applies to all, but generally, you should allow about ¼ of the cooking time. That is, if our recipe suggests 16 minutes, allow 4 minutes in your microwave oven (or slightly less, since it's wiser to undercook than overcook). Please also note that our roasting procedures for beef, ham, lamb, and pork require the use of a rack, so that during cooking the fat drains off into the pan. A plastic rack is available for use in a microwave oven.

Our kitchens tested a number of basic foods and have the following timing tips for you:

Baked Apple (1 medium): Set in custard cup, cook 3 minutes; let stand several minutes. Makes 1 serving.

Each serving is equivalent to: 1 serving Fruit

Baked Fish Fillets (1 pound): Cook 7 minutes; let stand several minutes. Divide evenly. Makes 2 evening meal servings.

Each serving is equivalent to: 6 ounces Fish

Baked Potato (1 3-ounce): Make crosswise cut, cook 4 minutes; let stand 2 to 3 minutes. Makes 1 serving. Serve at mealtime only.

Each serving is equivalent to: 1 serving Choice Group

Roast Beef (1 pound boneless): On plastic rack set in baking dish, cook 4 minutes; turn, cook 4 minutes more; let stand 10 to 15 minutes. Divide evenly. Makes 2 evening meal servings.

Each serving is equivalent to: 6 ounces "Beef" Group

Hamburger Patty (6 ounces, 4-inch diameter): Coat with browning sauce. Place on plastic rack set in baking dish. Cover with paper towel. Cook 2 minutes; turn patty, cook 1 minute. Makes 1 midday meal serving.

Each serving is equivalent to: 4 ounces "Beef" Group

Roast Chicken (4 to 4½ pounds): Place breastside down on plastic rack set in baking dish. Cook 7 minutes; turn breastside up, cook 7 minutes; turn dish, cook another 7 minutes. Let stand 10 to 15 minutes. Remove skin. Weigh portions. Makes about 6 evening meal servings.

Each serving is equivalent to: 6 ounces Poultry

Roast Pork (1 pound boned and rolled): Place on plastic rack set in baking dish, cook 6 minutes. Turn roast, cook 6 minutes more. Turn roast, cook 4 minutes. Let stand 10 to 15 minutes. Divide evenly. Makes 2 evening meal servings.

Each serving is equivalent to: 6 ounces "Beef" Group

Acorn Squash (1¼ pounds): Pierce skin in several places. Cook 4 to 6 minutes. Scoop out pulp and weigh 8 ounces. Divide evenly. Makes 2 servings.

Each serving is equivalent to: 4 ounces Limited Vegetable

Slow Cookers

If you enjoy using this appliance, there's no reason why you can't adapt many of our recipes. We're giving you a head start on your own experiments with the following guidelines from our kitchen. (See index for the recipes.)

Portuguese Style Pinto Bean Soup: Combine all ingredients except salt and pepper in slow cooker; cook covered on low for 6 to 8 hours. Season.

Poached Liver: Combine all ingredients in slow cooker. Add water to cover. Cook covered on low for 6 to 8 hours.

"Old-Fashioned" Pot Roast: Combine cooked beef and remaining ingredients in slow cooker; cook covered on high for 6 to 9 hours.

Chicken Stock: Combine all ingredients in slow cooker; cover and cook on low for 12 hours. Strain.

Chicken Italian Style (Cacciatore): After browning the chicken in skillet, combine in slow cooker with remaining ingredients. Cook covered on low for 6 to 8 hours.

Minestrone (Vegetable Soup Italian Style): Combine all ingredients except macaroni in slow cooker; cook covered on low for 6 to 8 hours. Add macaroni, cook 15 to 20 minutes longer.

Artificial Sweeteners

The use of artificial sweeteners on the Weight Watchers Food Program has always been optional. Natural sweetness is available in the form of fruits, which we do permit on our eating plan. Your use of artificial sweeteners is completely optional; and we believe that the decision about using them should be made by you and your physician. If you decide against these products, we hope you'll enjoy the more than 600 sweetener-free recipes included in this book.

FRUITS

Apples, peaches, plums, berries, and dozens of other fruits are listed in the first category in the Program. You may enjoy them fresh, canned, or in prepared desserts, such as Apple-Raisin Brown Betty, Apricot Almondine Mousse, Banana Pudding, Pineapple Sherbet, and Orange Gelatin "Cream." However you use your allotted fruits, they are a satisfying and nutritious component of our Food Program.

Rules for Using Fruits

1. Amounts
Women:	3 servings daily
Men:	3 to 5 servings daily
Youth:	3 to 5 servings daily
2. One serving must be taken at the Morning Meal.
3. Use fresh, frozen, or canned fruit or fruit juices, with no sugar added.
4. Fruits must be measured frozen, not thawed.
5. Each day, select at least one fruit marked with an asterisk (*).
6. Fruits marked with an asterisk (*) are rich sources of Vitamin C. If these fruits are heated, the Vitamin C is affected. Therefore, an additional fruit marked with an asterisk (*) must be consumed that day.
7. Dried prunes are the only dried fruits permitted.

Fruit Servings

Juices

*grapefruit, ½ cup (4 fluid ounces)
*orange, ½ cup (4 fluid ounces)
*orange and grapefruit, ½ cup (4 fluid ounces)
  prune, ⅓ cup
  tangerine, ½ cup (4 fluid ounces)
*tomato or mixed vegetable juice, 1 cup (8 fluid ounces)

Fruits

  apple, 1 medium or 1 cup cored and sliced
    canned, ¾ cup
  applesauce, ½ cup
  apricots, fresh, 2 medium
    canned, 4 halves with 2 tablespoons juice
  banana, ½ medium
  berries
    blackberries, ½ cup
    blueberries, ½ cup
    boysenberries, ½ cup
    cranberries, 1 cup
    elderberries, ½ cup
    loganberries, ½ cup
    raspberries, ½ cup
*strawberries, 1 cup whole or ¾ cup sliced
*cantaloupe, ½ medium or 1 cup chunks or balls
  carambola, 1 medium
  cherries, fresh, 10 large or 15 small
    canned, ½ cup
*currants, fresh, ¾ cup
  figs, fresh, 2 small
  fruit cocktail or salad, ½ cup
*grapefruit, ½ medium
*grapefruit sections, ½ cup
  grapes, 12 medium or 20 small

*honeydew or similar melon, 2-inch wedge or
  1 cup chunks or balls
*kiwi, 1 medium
  kumquats, fresh, 3 medium
  loquats, 10 pitted
  mandarin orange, 1 large
  mandarin orange sections, canned, ½ cup
*mango, ½ small
  murcot, 1 medium
  nectarine, 1 medium
*orange, 1 small
*orange sections, ½ cup
*papaya, ½ medium
  peach, fresh, 1 medium
    canned, 2 halves with 2 tablespoons juice,
    or ½ cup sliced
  pear, fresh, 1 small
    canned, 2 halves with 2 tablespoons juice
  persimmon, 1 medium
  pineapple, fresh, ¼ medium
    canned: chunks, crushed, tidbits, ½ cup
            sliced, 2 slices with 2 tablespoons juice
  plums, fresh, 2 medium
    canned, whole, 2 with 2 tablespoons juice
  prunes, dried, 4 medium or 3 large
  quince, 1 medium
  rhubarb, 2 cups raw or 1 cup cooked
  tangerine, 1 large
*ugli fruit, 1 medium
  watermelon, triangle, 3 x 1½ inches, or 1 cup cubed

Apple and Pear Pie

3 medium Delicious apples, pared,
  cored, and sliced
3 small pears, pared, cored, and
  sliced
½ teaspoon cinnamon

1 tablespoon cornstarch dissolved
  in 1 tablespoon water
2 tablespoons magarine, melted
  (optional)
9-inch Pie Crust (see page 84)

In medium saucepan combine fruit, cinnamon, and enough water to cover. Cook over medium heat for 7 minutes. Add cornstarch, stirring constantly. Cook until thickened. Remove from heat. Stir in margarine if desired. Pour fruit mixture into crust. Bake at 350°F. about 40 minutes or until fruit is tender. Serve warm or chilled. Divide evenly. Makes 6 servings. Serve at mealtime only.

Each serving is equivalent to: 1 serving Fruit; ½ serving Something Extra (½ teaspoon cornstarch); 1 serving Fat (optional); 9-inch Pie Crust (see page 84)

Apple–Raisin Brown Betty

4 medium Delicious apples, pared,
  cored, and sliced
½ cup water
1 tablespoon cornstarch

½ teaspoon cinnamon
2 slices raisin bread, made into
  crumbs
1 tablespoon margarine

Layer apples in an 8x8x2-inch nonstick baking pan. Combine water, cornstarch, and cinnamon in a measuring cup; stir to dissolve cornstarch; pour over apples. In bowl combine bread crumbs and margarine, mixing with hands until particles are the size of peas. Sprinkle over apples. Bake at 350°F. for 40 to 45 minutes. Divide evenly. Serve warm or cool. Makes 4 servings. Serve at mealtime only.

Each serving is equivalent to: 1 serving Fruit; ¾ serving Something Extra (¾ teaspoon cornstarch); ½ serving Bread; ¾ serving Fat

Applesauce Home-Style

Apples are often waxed before they are shipped. Be sure to wash them well to remove the coating.

6 medium Delicious apples, cored
  and sliced
⅓ cup water

Small piece lemon rind
Cinnamon and nutmeg to taste
  (optional)

Combine apples, water, and lemon rind in saucepan. Cover and simmer 10 minutes, or until apples are very soft. Stir in spices, if desired, and serve as is; or put through food mill. The pureed sauce can be cooked in a saucepan until thickened, if desired. Serve hot or cold. Divide evenly. Makes 6 servings.

Each serving is equivalent to: 1 serving Fruit

Note: Delicious apples are naturally sweet enough to be cooked without artificial sweeteners. If other varieties are used, you may wish to add artificial sweetener to taste.

Baked Apples

Bake apples at the same time you are cooking an oven meal.

4 medium Red Delicious apples, cored
½ cup water

1 teaspoon lemon juice
½ teaspoon vanilla extract
½ teaspoon cinnamon

Pare apples halfway down. Place in shallow casserole. Add water, lemon juice, and vanilla. Sprinkle apples with cinnamon. Cover; bake at 400°F. for 20 minutes or until apples are tender. Divide evenly. Makes 4 servings.

Each serving is equivalent to: 1 serving Fruit

Apricot Almandine Mousse

With fast-setting recipes like this one, it's a good procedure to set out all the measured ingredients beforehand.

8 canned apricot halves, with ¼ cup juice, no sugar added
1 envelope unflavored gelatin
¼ cup boiling water
⅔ cup nonfat dry milk

Artificial sweetener to equal 2 teaspoons sugar (optional)
1 teaspoon lemon juice
¼ teaspoon almond extract
3 to 4 ice cubes

Pour apricot juice into blender container. Sprinkle gelatin over juice and let stand a few minutes to soften. Add boiling water and process until gelatin is dissolved. Add 6 apricot halves, milk, sweetener if desired, lemon juice, and extract. Process until combined. Add ice cubes, one at a time, processing after each addition, until smooth. Pour mousse immediately into 2 large dessert cups, dividing evenly. Garnish each serving with 1 apricot half, diced or sliced. Makes 2 servings.

Each serving is equivalent to: 1 serving Fruit; 1 serving Something Extra (½ envelope gelatin); 1 serving Milk (1 cup skim milk)

Note: The season for apricots is short—from late May to early August—so eat them fresh while you can, or buy them frozen or canned, no sugar added.

Apricot Tarts

12 canned apricot halves with ¼ cup plus 2 tablespoons juice, no sugar added

3 tablespoons frozen orange juice concentrate

1 tablespoon lemon juice

2 teaspoons cornstarch, dissolved in 2 teaspoons water

6 Toast Cups II (see page 84)

In medium saucepan combine first 4 ingredients. Cook, stirring often until thickened. Divide evenly into 6 toast cups. Chill until firm. Makes 3 servings, 2 tarts each. Serve at mealtime only.

Each serving is equivalent to: 1½ servings Fruit; ⅔ serving Something Extra (⅔ teaspoon cornstarch); Toast Cups II (see page 84)

Banana Mousse

1 envelope unflavored gelatin

¼ cup cold water

½ cup boiling water

1 ripe medium banana, diced, divided

⅔ cup nonfat dry milk

Artificial sweetener to equal 2 teaspoons sugar (optional)

1 teaspoon lemon juice

6 to 7 drops yellow food coloring

4 to 6 ice cubes

In blender container sprinkle gelatin over cold water to soften; add boiling water. Process to dissolve. Add ¾ of diced banana, milk, sweetener if desired, lemon juice, and food coloring. Process until smooth. Add ice cubes, one at a time, processing after each addition.

Pour into bowl. Fold in remaining banana. Evenly divide mousse into 2 dessert glasses. Makes 2 servings.

Each serving is equivalent to: 1 serving Something Extra (½ envelope gelatin); 1 serving Fruit; 1 serving Milk (1 cup skim milk)

Banana Pudding

4 medium eggs, separated
4 ripe medium bananas
½ cup skim milk

1 tablespoon vanilla extract, divided
¼ teaspoon cream of tartar
Dash salt

Preheat oven to 350°F. In medium bowl beat egg yolks until lemon-colored. Slice and add 3 bananas, milk, and 2 teaspoons vanilla. Pour into an 8-inch round baking dish or pie pan. In large bowl, combine egg whites, cream of tartar, and salt; beat until stiff but not dry. Mash remaining banana. Fold banana and 1 teaspoon vanilla into beaten whites. Pile on top of banana-yolk mixture. Bake 30 minutes or until pudding is set and meringue is golden brown. Divide evenly. Makes 4 morning or midday meal servings. Supplement as required.

Each serving is equivalent to: 1 Egg; 2 servings Fruit; ¹/₈ serving Milk (2 tablespoons skim milk)

Old-Fashioned Berry Pudding

2 cups huckleberries or blueberries
1 tablespoon cornstarch
Dash salt
¼ cup water
Artificial sweetener to equal ¼ cup sugar, or to taste
1 teaspoon lemon juice

Dash ground cloves
2 tablespoons plus 2 teaspoons margarine
8 slices raisin bread
2 recipes Best Whipped Topping (8 servings, see page 340), or 1 cup plain unflavored yogurt

In a medium saucepan, toss berries with cornstarch and salt. Add water and sweetener; simmer, stirring constantly, until berries are cooked, but still whole, about 5 minutes. Add lemon juice and cloves.

Remove from heat, cool slightly. Spread 1 teaspoon of margarine on each slice of bread. Arrange 4 slices, margarine side up, in an 8x8x2-inch serving dish. Spread half of the berry mixture over the bread. Top with remaining 4 slices of bread, margarine-side up. Spread with remaining berry mixture. Cover and refrigerate several hours or overnight. Serve with Whipped Topping or yogurt. Divide evenly. Makes 8 servings. Serve at mealtime only.

Each serving is equivalent to: ½ serving Fruit; ⅜ serving Something Extra (⅜ teaspoon cornstarch); 1 serving Fat; 1 serving Bread; Best Whipped Topping (see page 340) or ¼ serving Milk (2 tablespoons yogurt)

Berry "Cream"

Good way to serve blackberries, boysenberries, loganberries, or raspberries.

For each serving put ½ cup ripe, fresh berries in a stemmed dessert glass. Spoon ¼ cup plain unflavored yogurt over the mounded fruit. Makes 1 serving.

Each serving is equivalent to: 1 serving Fruit; ½ serving Milk (¼ cup yogurt)

Cherry Torte

1 cup prune juice
2 tablespoons cornstarch
  dissolved in 2 tablespoons water
½ teaspoon almond extract
¼ teaspoon grated lemon rind

Dash salt
3 cups canned cherries, no sugar
  added
9-inch Pie Crust (see page 84)

In medium saucepan combine first 5 ingredients. Cook over medium heat stirring until thickened. Add cherries. Pour into pie crust. Bake at 400°F. for about 15 minutes. Cool and serve. Divide evenly. Makes 6 servings. Serve at mealtime only.

Each serving is equivalent to: 1½ servings Fruit; 1 serving Something Extra (1 teaspoon cornstarch); 9-inch Pie Crust (see page 84)

Ginger Figs

4 small fresh figs   **1 teaspoon lemon juice**
½ cup water   **1 slice fresh ginger root**

Combine all ingredients in saucepan, cover; cook over low heat about 15 minutes or until figs are tender. Remove ginger and discard. Serve with juice, warm or chilled. Divide evenly. Makes 2 servings.

Each serving is equivalent to: 1 serving Fruit

Kiwi Fruit

This fruit with the light brown skin is the size of a hen's egg, comes from New Zealand, and has bright green flesh that tastes something like watermelon with a hint of strawberry. It is soft when ripe. Cut it in half, sprinkle with lemon juice, and eat it out of the shell with a teaspoon. Or peel, slice thin, and serve it with cheese and plain unflavored yogurt at your morning or midday meal. One medium kiwi fruit is equivalent to 1 serving Fruit.

Lemon Tricks

1. You get more juice from a lemon if it's at room temperature. Roll it on the counter before squeezing.
2. For a small amount of juice, poke a hole in the lemon with a toothpick. Remove the toothpick and squeeze out juice. Replace the toothpick in the hole; refrigerate the lemon for future use.
3. Freeze lemon shells to use as decorative containers for salad dressing, parsley sprigs, or other foods.
4. *"Candy" Basket*—Freeze a serving of ripe bing cherries or seedless green grapes. Serve frozen in lemon or orange shells.

Orange Gelatin "Cream"

2 envelopes unflavored gelatin	1 teaspoon lemon juice
1 cup water	1 cup evaporated skimmed milk,
½ cup frozen orange juice	chilled
concentrate	Dash nutmeg (optional)

In saucepan soften gelatin in water. Heat, stirring until gelatin is dissolved. Stir in orange juice concentrate and lemon juice. Chill until syrupy. In bowl whip milk until peaks form, fold into gelatin mixture. Transfer to 6-cup mold or 4 individual 1½-cup molds. Chill until firm. Unmold and sprinkle with nutmeg if desired. Divide evenly. Makes 4 servings.

Each serving is equivalent to: 1 serving Something Extra (½ envelope gelatin); 1 serving Fruit; ½ serving Milk (¼ cup evaporated skimmed milk)

Variation: For a tart flavor, fold 2 cups plain unflavored yogurt into gelatin mixture instead of whipped evaporated skimmed milk. Use a 4-cup mold. Change equivalent listing from ½ serving Milk to 1 serving Milk (½ cup yogurt).

Orange Sauce

Delicious with poultry or veal.

¼ cup cider vinegar	½ teaspoon cherry extract
2 tablespoons frozen orange juice	2 slices fresh ginger root
concentrate	1 cup orange sections, no sugar
1 tablespoon soy sauce	added
1½ teaspoons cornstarch,	
dissolved in 2 teaspoons water	

In small saucepan combine all ingredients except orange sections. Cook, stirring often, until thickened. Remove ginger root. Add orange sections. Divide evenly. Makes 3 servings.

Each serving is equivalent to: 1 serving Fruit; ½ serving Something Extra (½ teaspoon cornstarch)

Broiled Spiced Peaches

A quickie . . . delicious too. Serve with broiled chicken or liver, as a garnish for ham after it is baked, or as a dessert.

8 canned peach halves, with ½ cup juice, no sugar added
1 teaspoon lemon juice
½ cinnamon stick
1 clove

2 teaspoons cornstarch, dissolved in 2 teaspoons water
2 teaspoons imitation (or diet) margarine

In a shallow broiling pan, broil peach halves cut side up, about 4 inches from source of heat, for 5 minutes or until peaches begin to brown. While peaches are broiling, combine peach juice, lemon juice, cinnamon stick, and clove in a small saucepan. Bring to a boil. Lower heat, simmer 2 to 3 minutes. Discard cinnamon stick and clove. Add cornstarch and cook, stirring until thickened. Remove from heat, stir in margarine. Divide juice mixture evenly into peach cavities; broil 1 minute longer. Makes 4 servings, 2 peach halves each. Serve at mealtime only.

Each serving is equivalent to: 1 serving Fruit; ½ serving Something Extra (½ teaspoon cornstarch); ¼ serving Fat

Peach Custard

1 slice raisin bread, torn into small pieces
1 medium peach, peeled and sliced
1 cup skim milk

1 medium egg
½ teaspoon vanilla extract
Dash cinnamon

Make a layer of bread in a 1-pint baking dish. Arrange peach slices over bread. Combine remaining ingredients in blender container and process; pour over peach slices and bread. Bake at 325°F. for about 30 minutes or until custard is set. Makes 1 morning or midday meal serving. Supplement as required.

Each serving is equivalent to: 1 serving Bread; 1 serving Fruit; 1 serving Milk (1 cup skim milk); 1 Egg

Compote of Pears and Prunes

16 dried medium prunes
1 cup hot tea
2 ripe small pears, pared, cored, and quartered

1 lemon, sliced
½ teaspoon vanilla extract
¼ cup plain unflavored yogurt

In medium bowl combine prunes and tea. Let stand 8 hours or overnight. Remove prunes from liquid; pit and set aside. In medium saucepan combine prune liquid, pears, and lemon slices. Bring to boil. Reduce heat. Simmer, basting pears often until fruit is tender. Stir in vanilla, add prunes, and chill. Divide prunes, pears, and liquid evenly into 4 dessert dishes. Top each serving with 1 tablespoon of yogurt. Makes 4 servings.

Each serving is equivalent to: 1½ servings Fruit; ⅛ serving Milk (1 tablespoon yogurt)

Spiced Pear Salad

6 canned pear halves, with ¼ cup plus 2 tablespoons juice, no sugar added
¼ cup red wine vinegar
¼ cinnamon stick

1 clove
2 cups shredded lettuce
¼ cup plus 2 tablespoons imitation mayonnaise

Combine pear juice with vinegar, cinnamon stick, and clove in a medium saucepan. Bring to a boil; cook until mixture is reduced to about ¼ cup. Place pear halves in a medium bowl. Pour hot juice over pears and chill for several hours, turning fruit occasionally. Drain pears; strain and reserve liquid. Arrange pear halves on shredded lettuce. Combine liquid with mayonnaise and serve over pears as a salad dressing. Divide evenly. Makes 6 servings. Serve at mealtime only.

Each serving is equivalent to: ½ serving Fruit; ⅓ cup Vegetables; 1½ servings Fat

Preparing Pineapple

Select a ripe medium pineapple with a showy crown of leaves and prepare it in one of the following ways:

1. *Pineapple Quarters:* Cut the pineapple from the crown through the bottom, first in half, then in quarters. Using a small paring knife, cut away the hard, fibrous core, leaving the crown attached. Loosen fruit by cutting close to the rind with a sharp straight or curved serrated knife. Cut crosswise through the loosened fruit, then cut lengthwise once or twice to make bite-size pieces. Serve each quarter section of pineapple on a bed of parsley, watercress, mint, or other greens. Makes 4 servings.

2. *Sliced Fresh Pineapple:* Cut off the crown. Hold fruit upright on cutting board and, with a long, sharp knife, cut away the rind in strips, working from top to bottom. With a small, pointed knife, remove the "eyes." Cut out the center core. Cut the fruit in slices about ½ inch thick. Place in bowl and cover with foil or plastic wrap. Chill several hours or until ready to serve. Divide evenly. Makes 4 servings.

3. *Pineapple Container:* Cut off crown about 2 inches from the top and set aside. Hold the fruit upright and with a long, sharp knife remove the pineapple pulp, cutting close to the rind. Don't pierce through the rind, or it will leak. Refrigerate the rind and crown to use as a container. Dice pulp and serve in pineapple rind. Divide evenly. Makes 4 servings. Pulp may also be used for Pineapple Sherbet (see page 34), fruit cup, or other desserts.

Each serving is equivalent to: 1 serving Fruit

Pickled Pineapple-Pepper Relish Mold

Delicious with curries and colorful too.

2 cups canned crushed pineapple, no sugar added

1 medium green pepper, seeded and minced

1 medium red pepper, seeded and minced

½ cup minced celery

¼ cup cider vinegar

1 envelope unflavored gelatin

Combine all ingredients, except gelatin, in a large bowl. Marinate for 2 hours. Drain liquid into a small saucepan. Sprinkle gelatin over liquid to soften. Heat, stirring to dissolve. Combine with pineapple mixture. Spoon into a 1-quart mold. Chill until set. Unmold. Divide evenly. Makes 8 servings.

Each serving is equivalent to: ½ serving Fruit; 3 tablespoons Vegetables; ¼ serving Something Extra (⅛ envelope gelatin)

Pineapple-Cherry Parfait with Whipped Topping

2 cups canned crushed pineapple, no sugar added, divided
1 cup frozen, pitted, sweet cherries, no sugar added, partially thawed
½ teaspoon cherry extract

½ teaspoon pineapple extract
Artificial sweetener to equal 4 teaspoons sugar
Whipped Topping (see following recipe)

Place 1½ cups pineapple in blender container; process until smooth. Pour into a 1½-quart bowl. Cut all but 6 cherries into quarters over bowl to catch juice. Combine cut cherries and remaining pineapple with pureed pineapple. Stir in extracts and sweetener. Divide evenly into 6 parfait glasses. Top each with 1 serving of Whipped Topping and 1 cherry. Refrigerate or serve immediately. Makes 6 servings.

Whipped Topping

1 envelope unflavored gelatin
¼ cup cold water
½ cup boiling water
⅔ cup nonfat dry milk

Artificial sweetener to equal 4 teaspoons sugar
1 teaspoon vanilla extract
6 to 8 ice cubes

Sprinkle gelatin over cold water in blender container, to soften. Add boiling water. Process until dissolved. Add remaining ingredients, except ice cubes. Process until smooth. Add ice cubes, one at a time, processing after each addition, until topping sets. Divide evenly. Makes 6 servings.

Each serving is equivalent to: 1 serving Fruit; ⅓ serving Something Extra (¹/₆ envelope gelatin); ⅓ serving Milk (⅓ cup skim milk)

Pineapple-Peach Sherbet

You can create dozens of different sherbets by varying the basic ingredients. Use fruit, water, fruit juice, skim milk, evaporated skimmed milk, buttermilk, yogurt, artificial sweetener, and flavoring extracts. This one is sure to be a favorite!

1 medium peach, peeled and quartered
2 slices canned pineapple, with 2 tablespoons juice, no sugar added

½ cup plain unflavored yogurt
1 teaspoon raspberry extract

Combine all ingredients in blender container. Process until smooth. Place in freezer container and freeze until firm, about 20 minutes. Remove from freezer and beat with a rotary beater. Refreeze until icy. Divide evenly into 2 sherbet glasses. Makes 2 servings.

Each serving is equivalent to: 1 serving Fruit; ½ serving Milk (¼ cup yogurt)

Variation: A very small amount of unflavored gelatin is often added to sherbet to keep its texture smooth. In a small saucepan soften ½ teaspoon of unflavored gelatin in ¼ cup of water. Heat, stirring to dissolve. Add to ingredients in blender container and follow above recipe. Add ¹/₆ serving Something Extra (¼ teaspoon gelatin) to equivalent listing.

Pineapple Sherbet

This is brought to the table in a pineapple shell for an attractive presentation.

1 ripe medium pineapple   **1 tablespoon lemon juice**
1 cup water

Prepare pineapple container according to directions on page 31 and set aside. In medium saucepan combine diced pineapple, water, and lemon juice. Cook about 5 minutes. Place in food processor or blender container and process, in 2 batches if necessary, until smooth. Place in freezer container. Freeze until firm. Remove from freezer and beat until fluffy. Spoon into pineapple shell and freeze until ready to serve. Divide evenly. Makes 4 servings.

   Each serving is equivalent to: 1 serving Fruit

Oven-Stewed Prunes

To conserve energy put this dish in the oven when baking a casserole or other food.

16 dried medium prunes   **½ lemon, thinly sliced**
1 cup water   **Small piece cinnamon stick**

Place all ingredients in 2-cup ovenproof dish; cover. Bake at 350°F. for 1 hour or until prunes are very tender. Remove cinnamon stick. Divide evenly. Makes 4 servings.

   Each serving is equivalent to: 1 serving Fruit

Rhubarb-Strawberry Dessert

4 cups rhubarb   **Artificial sweetener to equal 6**
2 cups strawberries   **   teaspoons sugar**

Combine rhubarb and strawberries in a 1½-quart casserole. Cover and bake at 300°F. for 1 hour or until rhubarb is tender. Remove from oven; cool. Add sweetener, mix well; chill, if desired. Divide evenly. Makes 4 servings.

Each serving is equivalent to: 1 serving Fruit

Watermelon Froth

1 cup cubed, seeded watermelon
¼ medium pineapple, pared and diced, or ½ cup canned crushed pineapple, no sugar added

3 ice cubes (optional)
2 mint sprigs

Process fruit in blender container until pureed. If desired add ice cubes, one at a time, processing after each addition until all ice is crushed. Divide evenly into 2 glasses. Garnish with mint sprigs. Makes 2 servings.

Each serving is equivalent to: 1 serving Fruit

Minted Summer Delight

1 medium cantaloupe
2 cups mint sprigs, divided
1 cup cubed, seeded watermelon

1 cup strawberries
1 cup honeydew melon balls
½ cup blueberries

Cut cantaloupe in half. Remove seeds. Cut skin from fruit, keeping pulp intact. Cut each cantaloupe half lengthwise into about 9 crescent-shaped slices. Place ¾ of the mint on serving platter. Arrange cantaloupe slices over mint, with the points of the melon slices meeting in the center of the platter, like spokes of a wheel. Arrange remaining fruit between cantaloupe slices. Chop remaining mint and sprinkle over fruit. Divide evenly. Makes 6 servings.

Each serving is equivalent to: 1 serving Fruit

EGGS

The egg is nature's marvel, and our test kitchen staff has hatched some marvelous ideas for using it. Make our famous French toast . . . our fluffy soufflés and filling frittatas. We show you how to fill an omelet with everything from spinach or mushrooms to prunes or cheese. Best of all, we show you how to make a two-part meal, or desserts like custard and meringues, from one egg!

Rules for Using Eggs

1. Amounts
   Women, Men, and Youth: 1 egg at the Morning Meal
                            2 eggs at the Midday Meal
2. Select 4 medium eggs a week. They may be cooked over direct heat, without fat; or in the shell. Raw eggs are "legal."
3. Egg whites and egg yolks may be prepared in separate recipes, provided that both whites and yolks are consumed as part of the same meal.

Hard-Cooked Eggs

If possible, bring eggs to room temperature before cooking. Put medium eggs in saucepan and add enough water to cover eggs by at least 1 inch. Cover; bring rapidly just to boiling. Turn off heat; if necessary, remove pan from burner to prevent further boiling. Let stand in the hot water 12 to 15 minutes. Cool immediately and thoroughly in cold water—shells are easier to remove and it is less likely you will have a dark surface on yolks. To remove shell: Crackle it by tapping gently all over. Roll egg between hands to loosen shell; then peel, starting at large end. Hold egg under running cold water or dip in bowl of water to help ease off shell.

Poached Eggs

Pour about 1 inch of water in a shallow pan or skillet. Add 1 to 2 teaspoons white vinegar if desired and ½ to 1 teaspoon salt, depending on the size of the pan. Bring water to a boil. Break 1 medium egg into a small cup. Reduce heat to simmer; gently slide egg into water. Repeat with remaining eggs, but be sure not to crowd them. Cook for 2 to 3 minutes or until done to taste. Remove eggs from water with a slotted spoon. If eggs are to be served cold, gently place them in cold water. If they are to be served hot, serve them at once or slightly undercook them and reheat in simmering water for about 30 seconds. For a more decorative effect, the edges of the egg whites can be trimmed and combined with minced herbs and served over the eggs.

Variation: Reheat 1 poached egg in ½ cup simmering tomato juice or chicken bouillon, seasoned to taste. Serve egg and liquid in soup bowl. Makes 1 morning or midday meal serving. Supplement as required.

Each serving is equivalent to: 1 Egg; ½ serving Bonus (½ cup tomato juice) or ⅔ serving Something Extra (½ cup bouillon)

Scrambled Eggs

Beat 1 medium egg in a bowl. For a lighter product, add up to 1 tablespoon water before beating. Pour into a preheated nonstick skillet. When the egg begins to firm, stir, scraping mixture from bottom and sides of pan, until done to taste. Season as desired. Makes 1 morning meal serving.

Soft-Cooked or Coddled Eggs

Follow procedure for hard-cooked eggs but let eggs stand in hot water only 1 to 4 minutes, depending on desired degree of doneness. Cool for a few seconds in cold water.

Sunnyside Up

Use a heated nonstick or heavy iron skillet. Break 1 medium egg into a cup, slide it into the skillet, and cook until done to taste. To firm the top without turning egg, cover skillet. Makes 1 morning meal serving.

Poached Egg in Rice

½ cup cooked enriched rice　　**1 teaspoon margarine (optional)**
1 medium egg, poached

If rice is cold, heat by placing in strainer and steaming over boiling water. Transfer to breakfast bowl and top with egg. Dot with margarine if desired and allow to melt. Makes 1 morning meal serving.

　　Each serving is equivalent to: 1 serving Choice Group; 1 Egg; 1 serving Fat (optional)

Double-Boiler Scrambled Egg and Potato

This method enables you to scramble eggs with fat and to reheat cold fillings without using a second pan. Also, eggs stay moist and creamy.

2 tablespoons margarine　　　　**1 teaspoon chopped fresh parsley**
6 ounces peeled cooked potato,　　**or chives**
**　diced**　　　　　　　　　　　　**½ teaspoon salt**
4 medium eggs, beaten　　　　　**Pepper to taste**
3 tablespoons liquid (water or
**　potato liquid)**

Melt margarine in top of double boiler over boiling water. Add potato and heat. Combine eggs with liquid, parsley or chives, salt, and pepper. Add to margarine-potato mixture. Cook, stirring frequently, until done to taste. Divide evenly. Makes 2 midday meal servings.

Each serving is equivalent to: 3 servings Fat; 1 serving Choice Group; 2 Eggs

Variations:

Rice Scramble—Use 1 cup cooked enriched rice instead of potato in basic recipe and season with hot sauce to taste before adding eggs.

Mexican Scramble—Following preceding method, cook ½ medium green pepper, diced, in the melted margarine until tender. Add 1 tablespoon diced pimento and a dash of cumin. Replace potato with 1 cup canned, whole kernel corn. Add 2½ tablespoons Vegetables to equivalent listing.

Lox Scramble

2 tablespoons margarine
4 ounces diced onion or scallion
1 medium green pepper, seeded
  and diced

6 ounces lox, diced
4 medium eggs, beaten

Melt margarine in top of double boiler over boiling water. Add onion and green pepper. Cover and cook until soft. Add lox and mix well. Pour in eggs; cook, stirring occasionally, until eggs are done to taste. Divide evenly. Makes 4 midday meal servings.

Each serving is equivalent to: 1½ servings Fat; 1 ounce Limited Vegetable; 2 tablespoons Vegetables; 1½ ounces Smoked Fish; 1 Egg

Variation: Omit lox. Sprinkle lemon juice over 8 ounces drained, canned tuna or other flaked, cooked fish and use in preceding recipe. In equivalent listing, substitute 2 ounces Fish for the 1½ ounces Smoked Fish.

Scrambled Eggs in a Skillet

6 ounces peeled cooked potato,
  diced
4 medium eggs, beaten
3 tablespoons liquid (water or
  potato liquid)

1 teaspoon chopped fresh parsley
½ teaspoon salt
Pepper to taste

Brown potato in preheated nonstick skillet. Turn to brown all sides. Combine remaining ingredients and add to skillet. Scramble with a fork until done to taste. Divide evenly. Makes 2 midday meal servings.

Each serving is equivalent to: 1 serving Choice Group; 2 Eggs

Baked Herb Omelet

4 medium eggs, separated
¼ cup water
1 teaspoon chopped fresh parsley
¼ teaspoon chives
¼ teaspoon marjoram

¼ teaspoon chervil
¼ teaspoon tarragon
¼ teaspoon thyme
¼ teaspoon salt
⅛ teaspoon pepper

Preheat oven to 350°F. In a large bowl, beat egg whites until stiff, but not dry. In another large bowl, beat egg yolks with remaining ingredients until thick. Fold whites into yolk mixture. Transfer to a preheated nonstick omelet pan with ovenproof handle. Cook until brown on bottom. Transfer pan to oven and bake for 15 minutes or until brown on top. Serve at once on a hot platter. Divide evenly into 4 wedges. Makes 4 morning or midday meal servings. Supplement as required.

Each serving is equivalent to: 1 Egg

Bread Omelet

1 slice enriched white bread,
  cubed
¼ cup skim milk
2 medium eggs, separated

Dash salt and pepper
Watercress or parsley sprigs to
  garnish

Combine bread and milk in a medium bowl. Add beaten egg yolks, salt, and pepper; stir to combine. In a separate bowl beat egg whites until stiff but not dry; fold into yolk mixture. Transfer to a preheated 8-inch nonstick skillet with flameproof handle, and cook until bottom is brown. Place under preheated broiler, as close to heat source as possible, until lightly browned and puffy. Remove from broiler, fold omelet in half, and garnish with watercress or parsley. Serve immediately. Makes 1 midday meal serving.

Each serving is equivalent to: 1 serving Bread; ¼ serving Milk (¼ cup skim milk); 2 Eggs

Creamy Skillet Omelet

1 medium egg   Dash celery salt
1 tablespoon plain unflavored
   yogurt

In a small bowl beat egg, yogurt, and celery salt until blended. Pour into a preheated nonstick skillet and cook over medium heat. As edges and bottom begin to set, lift edges of egg mixture so that the uncooked portion flows underneath. When dry on top, fold in half and serve on a warm plate. Makes 1 morning or midday meal serving. Supplement as required.

Each serving is equivalent to: 1 Egg; ⅛ serving Milk (1 tablespoon yogurt)

Creole Omelet

¼ medium green pepper, diced   Salt and pepper to taste
⅛ medium tomato, diced   Curry powder to taste (optional)
2 tablespoons diced pimento   1 medium egg, beaten
1 ounce diced onion

In a nonstick skillet combine green pepper, tomato, pimento, and onion. Season with salt and pepper. Add curry powder, if desired. Cook, stirring occasionally, until vegetables are tender and mixture is almost dry. Add egg; stir quickly to combine. Cook until egg is brown on bottom. Turn with spatula to brown other side. Makes 1 morning or midday meal serving. Supplement as required.

Each serving is equivalent to: ¼ cup plus 1 tablespoon Vegetables; 1 ounce Limited Vegetable; 1 Egg

Variation:
Ratatouille Omelet—Serve omelet with 1 serving hot Ratatouille (see page 291). Add equivalents to preceding equivalent listing.

Frittata (Italian Omelet)

2 medium eggs, separated
1 cup cooked, diced zucchini
1½ ounces grated Mozzarella
   cheese

½ ounce grated Parmesan cheese
Salt and pepper to taste
½ cup tomato sauce, no sugar
   added (optional)

In bowl beat egg whites until stiff but not dry. In separate bowl beat yolks until frothy. Add zucchini, cheeses, salt, and pepper. Fold in whites. Pour into a nonstick skillet with flameproof handle. Cook until bottom is brown; then place skillet under broiler as close to heat source as possible. Cook until omelet is browned and puffy. Serve with tomato sauce if desired. Divide evenly. Makes 2 midday meal servings.

Each serving is equivalent to: 1 Egg; ½ cup Vegetables; 1 ounce Hard Cheese; ½ serving Bonus (¼ cup tomato sauce) (optional)

Variations:
1. Add 2 teaspoons chopped fresh mint leaves and 1 teaspoon basil to beaten eggs and zucchini before folding in whites.
2. Omit cheese. Makes 2 morning meal servings. Eliminate cheese from equivalent listing.

Luncheon Cheese Omelet

1 medium egg, beaten

1 ounce grated Swiss or Cheddar
   cheese, divided

In a small bowl combine egg with ½ ounce cheese. Pour into a preheated nonstick skillet or omelet pan with flameproof handle. Cook until almost solid on top; sprinkle with remaining cheese. Place under broiler as close to heat source as possible. Broil until cheese is melted. Makes 1 midday meal serving.

Each serving is equivalent to: 1 Egg; 1 ounce Hard Cheese

Variation:
Luncheon Fish Omelet—Omit cheese. Combine 2 ounces drained, canned tuna, flaked, or 2 ounces diced cooked mussels with egg. Add a dash of lemon juice. Cook in nonstick skillet until done to taste. Brown under broiler, if desired.

Substitute 2 ounces Fish for 1 ounce Hard Cheese in equivalent listing.

Prune-Filled Omelet

4 dried medium prunes   ½ **teaspoon vanilla extract**
1 medium egg, beaten

Place prunes in a small saucepan and add enough water to cover. Bring to a boil, lower heat, and cook until prunes are soft. Drain and reserve liquid. Pit prunes; puree in blender container or food processor and set aside. Combine egg, 1 tablespoon reserved liquid, and vanilla. Pour mixture into a preheated nonstick skillet or omelet pan. Cook until bottom is brown. Top with prune puree and fold omelet in half. Serve at once on a heated serving plate. Makes 1 morning or midday meal serving. Supplement as required.

Each serving is equivalent to: 1 serving Fruit; 1 Egg

Variation: Prepare omelet as in preceding recipe, using a skillet with a flameproof handle. If desired, other fruits may be substituted for prunes in the preceding recipe. See page 20 for "Fruit Servings." After omelet is folded, top with ½ cup strawberries, sliced. Dot with 1 teaspoon margarine. Broil for 1 minute, close to heat source, to melt margarine. Remove from broiler and serve at once. Add ½ serving Fruit and 1 serving Fat to equivalent listing.

Puffy Omelet

4 medium eggs, separated　　　**¼ teaspoon salt**
¼ cup water　　　**¼ teaspoon cream of tartar**

Preheat oven to 350°F. In bowl beat egg yolks until thick and lemon-colored, about 5 minutes. In separate bowl combine egg whites with water, salt, and cream of tartar. Beat until stiff but not dry. Fold whites into yolks. Heat a 10-inch nonstick skillet with ovenproof handle. Pour in omelet mixture, smooth surface with spatula. Reduce heat to medium; cook until lightly browned on bottom. Transfer to oven and bake for 12 to 15 minutes or until top is firm and dry. Fold and turn onto warm platter. Divide evenly. Makes 2 midday meal servings.

　　Each serving is equivalent to: 2 Eggs

Vegetable Omelets

Omelets bursting with savory fillings are yours for the making. For a morning or midday meal, allow about ¼ cup vegetable filling for a one-egg omelet. The filling may be mixed into the batter, added to the partly cooked egg, added just before the omelet is folded, or spooned on top of the folded omelet as a hot sauce. Vary flavors by adding small amounts of extract to taste. Use a heavy iron omelet pan or skillet, a nonstick pan, or a pan sprayed with a release agent. Spraying the pan with a release agent before adding the egg mixture makes it easier to slide the omelet out of the pan. Keep in mind that omelets continue to cook by retained heat after they are removed from the range.

1 medium egg　　　**Salt, pepper, and seasonings to**
1 tablespoon water or vegetable　　　**taste**
**　liquid**　　　**Batter filling from following list**

In bowl combine egg, water, and seasonings, and beat. Add a batter filling from list below. Mix well and pour into preheated pan. Cook at moderate heat. When edges are firm, lift so uncooked portion flows underneath. Repeat as necessary. When bottom is set and inside almost done to your taste, fold in half. Serve on heated plate. Makes 1 morning or midday meal serving. Supplement as required.

Mushroom-Peas Omelet—Combine 2 tablespoons cooked diced mushrooms, 2 ounces cooked peas, and 1 teaspoon chives. Mix into batter. Serve omelet with watercress garnish.

Each serving is equivalent to: 1 Egg; 2 tablespoons Vegetables; 2 ounces Limited Vegetable

Herb-Asparagus Omelet—Add 2 teaspoons minced fresh herbs such as parsley or marjoram and ¼ teaspoon dried herbs such as tarragon or chervil to batter. Layer 3 hot, cooked asparagus spears lengthwise on cooked omelet before folding it over to serve; ¼ cup cooked zucchini fingers may be substituted for the asparagus.

Each serving is equivalent to: 1 Egg; ¼ cup Vegetables

Artichoke Omelet—Combine 2 ounces cooked, diced artichoke hearts and 1 teaspoon tomato paste. Season with ⅛ teaspoon instant chicken broth and seasoning mix. Mix well and add to batter.

Each serving is equivalent to: 1 Egg; 2 ounces Limited Vegetable; $1/_{12}$ serving Bonus (1 teaspoon tomato paste); ⅛ serving Something Extra (⅛ teaspoon broth mix)

Variation: Prepare any of the preceding omelets. After they are cooked, cool, dice, and serve over mixed greens.

Western Omelet

2 medium eggs, separated
Salt and pepper to taste
3 ounces ham, diced
1 ounce diced onion
2 tablespoons diced green pepper
2 tablespoons diced celery
2 tablespoons skim milk
½ cup tomato sauce, no sugar added (optional)

In bowl beat egg whites until stiff but not dry. Set aside. In separate bowl beat egg yolks until frothy. Season with salt and pepper. Add ham, onion, green pepper, celery, and skim milk to egg yolks. Fold in whites. Pour into a nonstick skillet with a flameproof handle. Cook until bottom is brown; then place skillet under broiler, as close to heat source as possible. Cook until omelet is browned and puffy. Serve with tomato sauce if desired. Divide evenly. Makes 2 midday meal servings.

Each serving is equivalent to: 1 Egg; 1½ ounces "Beef" Group (cured); ½ ounce Limited Vegetable; 2 tablespoons Vegetables; ¹/₁₆ serving Milk (1 tablespoon skim milk); ½ serving Bonus (¼ cup tomato sauce) (optional)

Baked French Toast with Fruit

For a company treat, you can make two elegant dishes from your morning egg. Serve the French Toast with either of the two meringue-topped fruits. Toast and fruit can be baked at the same time. If you are making more than 3 servings, the baking time may need to be increased. Watch closely to avoid underbaking or overbaking.

Baked French Toast

1 medium egg yolk*
1 teaspoon water
Dash salt

Dash vanilla extract
1 slice raisin bread

In a shallow bowl, combine egg yolk, water, salt, and vanilla. Soak bread in mixture, turning at least once. Let stand until all liquid is absorbed. Place bread on baking sheet; bake at 350°F. for 10 to 12 minutes or until lightly browned. Makes 1 morning meal serving. Supplement as required.*

Each serving is equivalent to: 1 Egg Yolk*; 1 serving Bread

*Baked French Toast must be consumed at the same meal as either Grapefruit with Meringue Topping or Pineapple with Meringue Topping, which contains remaining egg white.

Grapefruit with Meringue Topping

½ medium grapefruit
1 medium egg white*

⅛ teaspoon cream of tartar
Dash salt

With a knife, loosen the pulp from grapefruit; discard seeds and tough center membrane. In a medium bowl beat egg white with cream of tartar and salt until it stands in peaks. Pile mixture on top of grape-fruit. Place in small foil pan. Bake at 350°F. for 10 to 12 minutes or until topping begins to brown. Makes 1 morning meal serving. Supplement as required.*

Each serving is equivalent to: 1 serving Fruit; 1 Egg White*

Pineapple with Meringue Topping

½ cup canned pineapple chunks, no sugar added
Few drops each, orange and coconut extracts
1 medium egg white*

Artificial sweetener to equal 2 teaspoons sugar
⅛ teaspoon cream of tartar
Dash salt

Arrange pineapple chunks in an individual oven-to-table casserole. Sprinkle with extracts. In a medium bowl, beat egg white with sweetener, cream of tartar, and salt until it stands in peaks. Pile mixture on top of pineapple. Bake at 350°F. for 10 to 12 minutes or until topping begins to brown. Makes 1 morning meal serving. Supplement as required.*

Each serving is equivalent to: 1 serving Fruit; 1 Egg White*

*Grapefruit with Meringue Topping or Pineapple with Meringue Topping must be consumed at the same meal as Baked French Toast which contains remaining egg yolk.

Raisin French Toast

Whole wheat or enriched white bread may replace raisin bread.

1 medium egg, beaten
1 tablespoon skim milk
¼ teaspoon vanilla extract

Dash salt
1 slice raisin bread

In a shallow bowl, combine egg, milk, vanilla, and salt. Soak bread in mixture, turning at least once. Let stand until as much liquid as possible is absorbed. Place in preheated nonstick skillet or on griddle treated with a release agent. Pour any remaining egg mixture over bread. Cook until brown on one side; turn to brown other side. Serve hot. Makes 1 morning or midday meal serving. Supplement as required.

Each serving is equivalent to: 1 Egg; $^1/_{16}$ serving Milk (1 tablespoon skim milk); 1 serving Bread

Variations:

1. Follow preceding directions but let bread stand in batter overnight in refrigerator. In the morning, slip the bread onto a nonstick baking sheet. Pour any remaining egg mixture over bread; bake at 400°F. for 12 minutes or until top is puffy and brown. This is an easy way to get a lot of puffy toast for a big family or company without last-minute fuss.

2. For the midday meal, top French Toast with a 1-ounce slice of hard cheese and broil until cheese is bubbly hot and melted. Makes 1 midday meal serving. Add 1 ounce Hard Cheese to equivalent listing.

Baked Pancake

2 medium eggs, beaten
2 tablespoons evaporated
   skimmed milk
2 tablespoons margarine, melted

1 tablespoon flour
¼ teaspoon vanilla extract
1 tablespoon lemon juice
   (optional)

Combine all ingredients except lemon juice in a small bowl. Beat until smooth. Pour into a preheated nonstick skillet with ovenproof handle. Bake at 425°F. for 15 minutes or until browned on top. Sprinkle with lemon juice, if desired. Divide evenly. Makes 2 morning or midday meal servings. Supplement as required.

Each serving is equivalent to: 1 Egg; ⅛ serving Milk (1 tablespoon evaporated skimmed milk); 3 servings Fat; 1½ servings Something Extra (1½ teaspoons flour)

Cottage Cheese Pancakes

2 medium eggs, separated
⅔ cup cottage cheese
2 tablespoons flour

1 teaspoon baking powder
¼ teaspoon salt
½ cup plain unflavored yogurt
(optional)

In a medium bowl, combine egg yolks, cottage cheese, flour, baking powder, and salt. Beat egg whites, in a small bowl, until stiff but not dry. Fold into yolk mixture. Drop batter from mixing spoon onto a preheated nonstick griddle. Brown pancakes on both sides, turning once with a spatula. Divide evenly. Serve ¼ cup yogurt as topping on each portion if desired. Makes 2 midday meal servings.

Each serving is equivalent to: 1 Egg; ⅓ cup Soft Cheese; 3 servings Something Extra (1 tablespoon flour); ½ serving Milk (¼ cup yogurt) (optional)

Variation:

Banana Cheese Pancakes—Do not separate eggs. Combine all ingredients except yogurt in blender container. Add 1 medium banana, sliced. Process until smooth. Proceed as in basic recipe. Add 1 serving Fruit to equivalent listing.

Yogurt Pancakes

1 medium egg, beaten
1 teaspoon flour

1 tablespoon plain unflavored
yogurt
Dash salt

In a bowl combine egg and flour. Add yogurt and salt, and beat again. Drop by spoonfuls onto preheated nonstick griddle. Cook, turning once to brown both sides. Makes 2 large or 4 small pancakes; 1 morning or midday meal serving. Supplement as required.

Each serving is equivalent to: 1 Egg; 1 serving Something Extra (1 teaspoon flour); ⅛ serving Milk (1 tablespoon yogurt)

Russian Egg Salad

⅓ cup finely diced carrots
⅓ cup finely diced celery
2 ounces cooked peas

4 medium eggs, hard-cooked and
   diced
Lettuce leaves
Russian Mayonnaise (see page 300)

In bowl combine first 4 ingredients. Chill. Serve on lettuce leaves with Russian Mayonnaise. Divide evenly. Makes 2 midday meal servings.

Each serving is equivalent to: ⅓ cup Vegetables; 1 ounce Limited Vegetable; 2 Eggs; Russian Mayonnaise (see page 300)

Tuna-Stuffed Egg Platter

4 medium eggs, hard-cooked
8 ounces drained, canned tuna,
   flaked, divided
2 tablespoons plus 2 teaspoons
   vegetable oil, divided
14 capers

¼ teaspoon dry mustard
Dash allspice
Freshly ground pepper to taste
4 medium tomatoes, sliced
2 cups chilled cooked green beans
2 tablespoons red wine vinegar

Cut eggs in half lengthwise. Remove yolks; place in medium bowl; mash. Add 1 ounce tuna, 2 teaspoons oil, 6 minced capers, mustard, allspice, and pepper. Mix well. Divide evenly and fill egg whites, mounding mixture in the center. Top each with 1 caper. On each of 4 salad plates arrange 1 sliced tomato, ½ cup green beans, and 2 filled egg halves. Divide remaining tuna evenly and arrange one portion on each plate. Combine remaining oil with vinegar and sprinkle equal amounts over the green beans and tomato on each plate. Makes 4 midday meal servings.

Each serving is equivalent to: 1 Egg; 2 ounces Fish; 2 servings Fat; 1 cup Vegetables

Custard

1 medium egg, beaten
1 cup skim milk
Artificial sweetener to equal 4
   teaspoons sugar

½ teaspoon vanilla extract
Dash salt
Dash cinnamon

Combine all ingredients in blender container. Process until blended. Pour into a 1½-cup custard cup. Set cup in baking pan and pour in ½ inch hot water. Bake at 325°F. for 1 hour or until knife inserted in center comes out clean. Serve warm or chilled. Makes 1 morning or midday meal serving. Supplement as required.

Each serving is equivalent to: 1 Egg; 1 serving Milk (1 cup skim milk)

Variations:

Mocha Custard—Substitute ½ cup hot coffee for ½ cup skim milk, and add 1 teaspoon cocoa. Prepare as in basic recipe. Sprinkle instant coffee lightly over chilled custard before serving. Makes 1 morning or midday meal serving. Supplement as required.

Each serving is equivalent to: 1 Egg; ½ serving Milk (½ cup skim milk); 1 serving Something Extra (1 teaspoon cocoa)

Cheese Custard—Omit vanilla extract and add ¼ teaspoon dehydrated onion flakes, reconstituted in water, and 1 ounce grated Swiss or Cheddar cheese. Makes 1 midday meal serving. Add 1 ounce Hard Cheese to equivalent listing.

Apricot Custard—Put 2 canned apricot halves, no sugar added, in bottom of the custard cup before adding custard mixture. Serve 1 tablespoon apricot juice over custard. Garnish with grated orange rind. Add ½ serving Fruit to equivalent listing.

SOUFFLÉS

Soufflés made with vegetables and a creamy sauce are pretty and scrumptious-tasting midday meal dishes. They are easy to manage if you handle the whites properly.

1. For best results start with eggs at room temperature, about 70°F. The whites will then beat to a maximum volume.
2. Separate eggs carefully so no yolk mixes with the whites.
3. Beat egg yolks, with or without other ingredients according to recipe directions.

4. Beat whites in a clean dry bowl. For stability, add a pinch of cream of tartar to egg whites after they have been whipped until they are foamy. Beat until they stand in stiff peaks and are glossy, not dry.
5. Fold in egg whites gently so they don't lose volume.
6. Be sure to preheat the oven when making soufflés.
7. To make a soufflé with a crown, use a rubber spatula and make a groove 1 inch from the edge of the dish and 1½ inches deep.

Basic Vegetable Soufflé

3 tablespoons margarine
3 tablespoons flour
½ cup evaporated skimmed milk
½ cup Chicken Stock (see page 140), vegetable liquid, or tomato juice

2 cups cooked finely diced vegetables (see following list)
Seasonings (see following list)
4 medium eggs, separated
¼ teaspoon cream of tartar (optional)

Preheat oven to 350°F. Melt margarine in top of double boiler, over boiling water. Stir in flour until mixture is smooth. Cook 2 to 3 minutes. Add liquids, a little at a time, continuing to stir until mixture is thickened and smooth. Add vegetables and seasonings. Beat egg yolks. Stir a spoonful of the sauce into yolks, then add yolks to sauce. Stir to combine. Cook for 1 minute; remove from heat. Cool slightly. Beat egg whites until frothy; add cream of tartar, if desired, and continue beating until stiff but not dry. Fold whites into the vegetable–yolk mixture. Transfer to 5-cup soufflé dish. Bake uncovered 35 to 45 minutes or until puffy and browned. For a soft crust, bake soufflé set in pan of hot water. For a crisp crust, bake it on a baking sheet. Divide evenly. Makes 4 midday meal servings. Supplement as required.

Seasonings for Vegetables

Asparagus: 1 tablespoon diced pimento or ¼ teaspoon dried tarragon.

Broccoli or Cauliflower: ½ teaspoon dill weed, minced chives, or celery seed.

Carrots: 1 teaspoon dehydrated onion flakes, 1 tablespoon minced fresh parsley, and a pinch marjoram or thyme.

Mushrooms: 1 tablespoon minced fresh parsley and chervil or dash of dill weed.

Spinach: ¼ teaspoon basil, mace, marjoram, or nutmeg.

Summer Squash: Dash cinnamon, cloves, fennel, ginger, or rosemary.

Each serving is equivalent to: 2¼ servings Fat; 2¼ servings Something Extra (2¼ teaspoons flour); ¼ serving Milk (2 tablespoons evaporated skimmed milk); ¹/₆ serving Something Extra (2 tablespoons stock) or ⅛ serving Bonus (2 tablespoons tomato juice); ½ cup Vegetables; 1 Egg

Variations:

Tomatoes and Onion—In place of 2 cups cooked vegetables use 4 canned, medium tomatoes, finely chopped, and 8 ounces steamed chopped onion. Season to taste with thyme, salt, and pepper, or 1 garlic clove, finely minced. Add 2 ounces Limited Vegetable to equivalent listing.

Corn—In place of vegetables use 2 cups drained canned whole kernel corn and in place of ½ cup Chicken Stock and ½ cup evaporated skimmed milk use 1 cup skim milk.

Each serving is equivalent to: 2¼ servings Fat; 2¼ servings Something Extra (2¼ teaspoons flour); ¼ serving Milk (¼ cup skim milk); 1 serving Choice Group; 1 Egg

Eggs and Mushrooms à la Newburg

3 cups sliced mushrooms	1 teaspoon sherry extract
2 cups water	(optional)
1 teaspoon lemon juice	3 medium eggs, hard-cooked and
1 tablespoon flour, dissolved in 2	separated
tablespoons water	3 slices enriched white bread,
¼ teaspoon paprika	toasted and cut diagonally
Dash cayenne pepper	Salt and freshly ground pepper to
½ cup evaporated skimmed milk	taste

In saucepan combine mushrooms, water, and lemon juice. Simmer about 10 minutes or until mushrooms are tender. Remove mushrooms with a slotted spoon and set aside. Reduce mushroom liquid to about ¼ cup and stir in flour, paprika, and cayenne pepper. Add milk and extract if desired, and cook, stirring constantly, until mixture is smooth and thickened. Chop egg whites. Add egg whites and mushrooms to sauce. Put yolks through a sieve. Serve mushroom sauce on toast, topped with yolks. Season with salt and pepper. Divide evenly. Makes 3 morning or midday meal servings. Supplement as required.

Each serving is equivalent to: 1 cup Vegetables; 1 serving Something Extra (1 teaspoon flour); ⅓ serving Milk (2 tablespoons plus 2 teaspoons evaporated skimmed milk); 1 Egg; 1 serving Bread

Eggs "Benedict"

If eggs are prepared ahead, place them in hot water to reheat.

1 English muffin, split and toasted
1½ ounces cooked Canadian
 bacon slices
1 medium egg, poached
1 tablespoon imitation
 mayonnaise

1 caper or ½ teaspoon minced
 fresh parsley
1 teaspoon imitation (or diet)
 margarine (optional)

Cover one muffin half with Canadian bacon. Top with poached egg. Spread with mayonnaise. Place under preheated broiler for 1 minute to heat. Garnish with caper or parsley. Serve with remaining muffin half, spread with margarine, if desired. Makes 1 midday meal serving.

Each serving is equivalent to: 2 servings Bread (once-a-week selection); 1½ ounces "Beef" Group (cured); 1 Egg; 1½ servings Fat; ½ serving Fat (optional)

Variation:

Oysters "Benedict"—Omit bacon and cover muffin half with 2 ounces minced cooked oysters. In equivalent listing, substitute 2 ounces Fish for the 1½ ounces "Beef" Group.

Eggs Goldenrod

3 tablespoons margarine
2 tablespoons flour
1 teaspoon dehydrated onion
  flakes
¼ teaspoon salt
⅛ teaspoon Worchestershire
  sauce

Pepper and paprika to taste
1 cup skim milk
4 medium eggs, hard-cooked
4 slices enriched white bread,
  toasted

Melt margarine in top of double broiler over boiling water. Add flour and seasonings. Stir until smooth. Gradually stir in milk. Separate egg whites from yolks. Chop whites and add to sauce. On serving plate divide sauce evenly over hot toast. Force each yolk through a sieve over each serving. Makes 4 morning or midday meal servings. Supplement as required.

Each serving is equivalent to: 2¼ servings Fat; 1½ servings Something Extra (1½ teaspoons flour); ¼ serving Milk (¼ cup skim milk); 1 Egg; 1 serving Bread

Prune Pudding

1½ cups hot water or tea
8 dried medium prunes
2 slices enriched white bread,
  cubed

2 medium eggs
½ teaspoon grated lemon rind
½ teaspoon lemon juice

Combine water or tea and prunes in a small saucepan. Cook prunes, uncovered, until fruit is very soft. Remove and discard pits. Place fruit and liquid in blender container with bread, eggs, lemon rind, and juice. Process until smooth. Divide evenly into 2 individual ovenproof serving dishes and bake 30 minutes at 350°F. Serve warm. Makes 2 morning or midday meal servings. Supplement as required.

Each serving is equivalent to: 1 serving Fruit; 1 serving Bread; 1 Egg

CHEESE

You can do so much with an ounce or two of cheese! On our list are some that are mild and mellow, nippy and salty, sweet and nutlike, or sharp and pungent. Use your favorites in dips, open-faced sandwiches, au gratin, in salads, quiches, and soufflés. Yes, even in our own special version of cheesecake. Wonder of them all, you'll discover how to make our version of that most luscious of all French cheese dishes, Coeur à la Crème.

Keep a variety on hand for convenience. Storage of cheese is no trick at all when you know how. The enemies are evaporation and mold that wasn't planned at the cheesemakers. To keep hard or semisoft cheeses from drying out, always cover the cut side tightly; it will retain freshness for several weeks. You cannot expect such longevity for soft cheeses. Use them within a few days.

Hard cheeses can be kept even longer by freezing. Divide into serving amounts because, once unfrozen, the cheese should be used promptly. Wrap in small, airtight packages, or grate and store in covenient sizes in the freezer. Use for cooking, following your Menu Plan.

A foreign name doesn't necessarily mean imported. Many cheeses that originated abroad are now manufactured in the United States but still go by their foreign names.

Rules for Using Cheese

1. Amounts:
   Morning Meal: ⅓ cup or 2½ ounces soft cheese; or 1 ounce semisoft or hard cheese

Midday Meal: ⅔ cup or 5 ounces soft cheese; or 2 ounces semisoft or hard cheese

2. Do not use more than 4 ounces of semisoft or hard cheese weekly.

3. *Examples of Soft Cheeses*

Baker	Pot
Cottage (skim milk variety is preferable)	Ricotta, skim milk
	Schmierkäse

4. *Examples of Semisoft and Hard Cheeses*

American	Gouda
Asiago	Gruyère
Bel Paese	Limburger
Bleu	Monterey Jack
Brick	Mozzarella
Brie	Muenster
Caciocavalle	Parmesan
Camembert	Pecorino
Cheddar	Port de Salut
Cheshire	Primost (also called Mysost)
Chevret	Provolone
Colby	Romano
Edam	Roquefort
Emmenthaler	Sapsago
Feta	Stilton
Fontina	Swiss
Gorgonzola	Tilsit

Bean and Cheese Salad

2 teaspoons vegetable oil
2 teaspoons lemon juice
Hot sauce to taste
Salt to taste
1 cup fresh bean sprouts, blanched, if desired

3 ounces cooked dried white beans or chick peas
1 ounce Feta cheese, crumbled
½ teaspoon poppy seeds (optional)

In serving bowl combine first 4 ingredients. Add remaining ingredients, toss. Makes 1 midday meal serving.

Each serving is equivalent to: 2 servings Fat; 1 cup Vegetables; 3 ounces Legumes; 1 ounce Hard Cheese; ½ serving Something Extra (½ teaspoon poppy seeds) (optional)

Caesar Salad

1 garlic clove, crushed
2 cups romaine lettuce, torn into bite-size pieces
1 ounce grated Parmesan cheese
1 medium egg, coddled (see page 38)
2 teaspoons vegetable oil

2 teaspoons lemon juice
Dash Worcestershire sauce
Salt and freshly ground pepper to taste
1 slice enriched white bread, toasted and diced

Rub salad bowl with garlic. Place lettuce in bowl; sprinkle with cheese and top with egg. In small bowl combine oil, lemon juice, Worcestershire, salt and pepper; pour over salad. Add diced toast. Toss and serve immediately. Makes 1 midday meal serving.

Each serving is equivalent to: 2 cups Vegetables; 1 ounce Hard Cheese; 1 Egg; 2 servings Fat; 1 serving Bread

Chef's Salad

2 cups salad greens (iceberg, chicory, and romaine lettuce)
½ medium tomato, cut into 4 wedges
½ medium green pepper, seeded and sliced

1½ ounces ham or cooked smoked tongue, or 2 ounces cooked chicken, julienned
1 ounce hard cheese, julienned
¼ recipe Basic French Dressing (1 serving, see page 302)

Place salad greens in serving bowl. Arrange vegetables, meat, and cheese over greens. Serve chilled with French Dressing. Makes 1 midday meal serving.

Each serving is equivalent to: 2½ cups Vegetables; 1½ ounces "Beef" Group (cured) or 2 ounces Poultry; 1 ounce Hard Cheese; Basic French Dressing (see page 302)

Harvest Salad with Fruit French Dressing

4 medium endives, cut into ½-inch
  slices
2⅔ cups cottage cheese
2 medium apples, cored and
  sliced*
½ cup grapefruit sections, no
  sugar added

½ cup orange sections, no sugar
  added
Fruit French Dressing (see
  following recipe)

Arrange endive, evenly divided, on each of 4 salad plates. Top each
with ⅔ cup cottage cheese. Arrange fruit, evenly divided, around
cottage cheese. Serve each salad chilled with 1 serving Fruit French
Dressing. Makes 4 midday meal servings.

*Apple slices may be dipped in lemon juice to prevent discoloring.

Fruit French Dressing

½ cup orange juice
2 tablespoons vegetable oil
1 tablespoon lemon juice or cider
  vinegar

1 teaspoon chopped fresh mint
  (optional)
Salt and pepper to taste

Combine all ingredients in a small jar with tight-fitting cover. Shake
well. Divide evenly. Serve with Harvest Salad. Makes 4 servings.
Serve at mealtime only.

Each serving is equivalent to: ½ cup Vegetables; ⅔ cup Soft
Cheese; 1¼ servings Fruit; 1½ servings Fat

Tomato Salad with Creamy Cheese Dressing

4 medium tomatoes
4 lettuce leaves
2⅔ cups cottage cheese or 1⅓ cups
  cottage cheese and 4 ounces
  Bleu cheese, crumbled

1 garlic clove, minced
Salt and pepper to taste
1 teaspoon chives
Creamy Cheese Dressing (see
  following recipe)

Remove core from stem end of tomatoes. Make 2 criss-cross cuts through each tomato almost to the bottom, so that tomato opens. Set each tomato on a lettuce leaf. Process cottage cheese in blender container or food processor until smooth. Set aside 2 tablespoons for Creamy Cheese Dressing. Add Bleu cheese if used, garlic, salt, and pepper, and process until smooth. Stir in chives. Stuff each tomato with ¼ of the cheese mixture. Refrigerate. Serve with Creamy Cheese Dressing, evenly divided. Makes 4 midday meal servings.

Creamy Cheese Dressing

2 tablespoons imitation
  mayonnaise
2 tablespoons blended cottage
  cheese (see preceding recipe)
½ teaspoon salt

½ teaspoon paprika
2 tablespoons vegetable oil
1 tablespoon plus 1½ teaspoons
  cider vinegar

In a small bowl combine mayonnaise, cheese, salt, and paprika. Slowly add oil, beating constantly, until thick. Add vinegar and continue to beat until well blended. Keep refrigerated until ready to serve. Serve with Tomato Salad.

Each serving is equivalent to: ½ cup Vegetables; ⅔ cup Soft Cheese or ⅓ cup Soft Cheese and 1 ounce Hard Cheese; 2¼ servings Fat

Bleu Cheese Salad Ring

Serve with Tangy French Dressing (see page 337).

2 envelopes unflavored gelatin
¼ cup water
1⅓ cups cottage cheese
4 ounces Bleu or Roquefort cheese, crumbled
½ cup evaporated skimmed milk, whipped

½ cup imitation mayonnaise
1 teaspoon Worcestershire sauce
Dash crushed red pepper or hot sauce
Salt to taste

In small saucepan, sprinkle gelatin over water to soften. Heat, stirring to dissolve. In bowl, combine remaining ingredients. Stir in gelatin mixture. Pour into a 1-quart mold and chill until firm. Unmold on platter. Divide evenly. Makes 4 midday meal servings.

Each serving is equivalent to: 1 serving Something Extra (½ envelope gelatin); ⅓ cup Soft Cheese; 1 ounce Hard Cheese; ¼ serving Milk (2 tablespoons evaporated skimmed milk); 3 servings Fat

Fruit Cocktail Cottage Cheese Ring with Tangy Garden Dressing

2 cups canned fruit cocktail, no sugar added
1 envelope unflavored gelatin
1 cup cottage cheese
Artificial sweetener to equal 2 teaspoons sugar (optional)

Salad greens to garnish
Tangy Garden Dressing (see following recipe)

Drain juice from fruit cocktail into measuring cup; set fruit aside. Combine juice with enough water to make 1 cup. Pour into a small saucepan; sprinkle gelatin over liquid to soften. Stir over low heat until gelatin dissolves. Chill until syrupy. Process cottage cheese in blender container or food processor until smooth. Stir into gelatin mixture. Fold in fruit cocktail and sweetener, if desired. Pour mixture into a 6-cup mold. Chill until firm. Unmold. Garnish with salad greens. Serve with Tangy Garden Dressing. Divide evenly. Makes 4 midday meal servings. Supplement as required.

Tangy Garden Dressing

⅓ cup cottage cheese
1 cup plain unflavored yogurt
¼ medium green pepper, minced
1 tablespoon grated carrot
1 tablespoon water

1 teaspoon minced chives
1 teaspoon lemon juice
Salt, pepper, and garlic powder to
taste

Process cottage cheese in blender container or food processor until smooth. Combine with remaining ingredients. Serve with Fruit Cocktail Cottage Cheese Ring.

Each serving is equivalent to: 1 serving Fruit; ½ serving Something Extra (¼ envelope gelatin); ⅓ cup Soft Cheese; ½ serving Milk (¼ cup yogurt); 2¼ teaspoons Vegetables

Hard-and-Soft-Cheese Mold

2 envelopes unflavored gelatin
3 cups Beef Stock (see page 163)
1⅓ cups cottage cheese
¼ cup skim milk
4 ounces Bleu cheese, crumbled
8 ounces drained canned water
chestnuts, sliced

4 slices enriched white bread,
toasted and quartered
20 cherry tomatoes, halved
Parsley sprigs to garnish

In saucepan sprinkle gelatin over stock to soften. Heat stirring to dissolve. Pour a 1-inch layer of gelatin mixture into a round 1-quart mold and chill until firm. Reserve remaining gelatin. In blender container combine cottage cheese and milk. Process until smooth. Transfer to small bowl and combine with Bleu cheese. Spread over gelatin in mold. Pour a ¼-inch layer of reserved gelatin mixture over cheese. Chill until firm. Pour remaining gelatin mixture into mold. Refrigerate several hours until firm. Unmold onto platter and surround with water chestnuts, toast quarters, cherry tomatoes, and parsley. Use as first course for midday meal. Supplement as required. Divide evenly. Makes 4 midday meal servings.

Each serving is equivalent to: 2 servings Something Extra (½ envelope gelatin, ¾ cup stock); ⅓ cup Soft Cheese; ¹/₁₆ serving Milk (1 tablespoon skim milk); 1 ounce Hard Cheese; 2 ounces Limited Vegetable; 1 serving Bread; ¼ cup Vegetables

Two-Tone Salad

Tomato Aspic Layer

1 envelope unflavored gelatin	**¼ teaspoon celery seed**
1½ cups mixed vegetable juice	**¼ teaspoon seasoned salt**
2 teaspoons lemon juice	

Cottage Cheese Layer

2 envelopes unflavored gelatin	**¾ cup evaporated skimmed milk**
¼ cup water	**¾ teaspoon salt**
2 cups cottage cheese	**¼ teaspoon paprika**
1 medium cucumber, pared,	**Salad greens**
seeded, and chopped	**Lemon wedges to garnish**

Tomato Aspic Layer: In a medium saucepan sprinkle gelatin over vegetable juice to soften. Heat slowly, stirring until gelatin is dissolved. Add remaining ingredients; mix well. Pour into 6-cup mold and chill until almost firm.

Cottage Cheese Layer: In saucepan sprinkle gelatin over water to soften. Heat to dissolve; cool slightly. Combine in a bowl, with cottage cheese, cucumber, milk, salt, and paprika. Spoon evenly over tomato layer. Chill until firm. Unmold on salad greens and garnish with lemon wedges. Divide evenly. Makes 6 midday meal servings. Supplement as required.

Each serving is equivalent to: 1 serving Something Extra (½ envelope gelatin); ¼ serving Bonus (¼ cup mixed vegetable juice); ⅓ cup Soft Cheese; 1 tablespoon plus 1 teaspoon Vegetables; ¼ serving Milk (2 tablespoons evaporated skimmed milk)

Cheese Spread

Serve with a platter of crisp fresh vegetables.

1⅓ cups cottage cheese	2 tablespoons water
4 ounces very sharp Cheddar cheese, grated	Few drops hot sauce

Combine all ingredients in food processor or blender container; process until smooth. Add more water, a few drops at a time, if necessary. Spoon into a 2-cup serving container, cover and chill several hours. Divide evenly. Makes 4 midday meal servings.

Each serving is equivalent to: ⅓ cup Soft Cheese; 1 ounce Hard Cheese

Variation: Substitute Bleu, Gorgonzola, Limburger, or other hard cheese for the Cheddar.

Chive Creamy Cheese

1½ teaspoons unflavored gelatin	⅔ cup cottage cheese
¼ cup evaporated skimmed milk	2 teaspoons chives
2 teaspoons margarine	1 teaspoon chopped fresh parsley

In small saucepan, sprinkle gelatin over milk and let stand to soften. Place over low heat, stirring until gelatin dissolves. Remove from heat and stir in margarine. Process cottage cheese in blender container or food processor until smooth. Stir in chives and parsley. Add to gelatin mixture. Mix well. Spoon into a 1-cup mold and chill until firm. Divide evenly. Makes 2 morning or midday meal servings. Supplement as required.

Each serving is equivalent to: ½ serving Something Extra (¾ teaspoon gelatin); ¼ serving Milk (2 tablespoons evaporated skimmed milk); 1 serving Fat; ⅓ cup Soft Cheese

Variation: For a morning meal treat, divide Chive Creamy Cheese evenly into 4 portions and serve each portion with 1 ounce smoked salmon. Serve each on a bagel with ½ medium tomato, sliced, and capers. Garnish with lemon wedges.

Each serving is equivalent to: ¼ serving Something Extra (⅜ teaspoon gelatin); ⅛ serving Milk (1 tablespoon evaporated skimmed milk); ½ serving Fat; ¹/₆ cup Soft Cheese; 1 ounce smoked Fish; 2 servings Bread (once-a-week selection); ¼ cup Vegetables

Creamy Cheese Sauce

2 tablespoons margarine
2 tablespoons flour
1 cup skim milk

2 ounces grated Cheddar cheese
Dash Worcestershire sauce,
  nutmeg, or hot sauce (optional)

Melt margarine in top of double boiler over boiling water. Blend in flour. Add milk; cook, stirring constantly, until thickened. Stir in cheese. Season with Worcestershire, nutmeg, or hot sauce, if desired. Divide evenly. Makes 2 morning or midday meal servings. Supplement as required.

Each serving is equivalent to: 3 servings Fat; 3 servings Something Extra (1 tablespoon flour); ½ serving Milk (½ cup skim milk); 1 ounce Hard Cheese

Creamy Roquefort Dressing

In France, Roquefort is used as a dessert cheese. In this country it's the preferred cheese for salad dressing. Here's a great compromise; serve the dressing over slices of honeydew melon for dessert. This also makes an elegant first course for company. Multiply recipe to increase the number of servings as needed.

1 ounce Roquefort or Bleu cheese	**Salt and pepper to taste**
1 tablespoon water	**Dash dry mustard**
1 tablespoon mayonnaise	**Dash celery seed**
1 tablespoon lemon juice	

In a small bowl mash cheese with a fork; stir in water, mayonnaise, lemon juice, and seasonings. Serve on fruit or green salad. Makes 1 midday meal serving. Supplement as required.

Each serving is equivalent to: 1 ounce Hard Cheese; 3 servings Fat

Variation: Replace water and mayonnaise with 2 tablespoons plain unflavored yogurt and add 1 small minced garlic clove.

Each serving is equivalent to: 1 ounce Hard Cheese; ¼ serving Milk (2 tablespoons yogurt)

Quick-and-Easy Cheese Sauce

Serve over hot, baked apples, sliced fresh pears, or cooked vegetables.

4 ounces American cheese, diced	**Dash cayenne pepper**
¼ cup skim milk	**Salt and pepper to taste**
Dash Worcestershire sauce	

Combine all ingredients in top of double boiler over boiling water. Cook, stirring occasionally, until cheese is melted. Divide evenly. Makes 4 morning or midday meal servings. Supplement as required.

Each serving is equivalent to: 1 ounce Hard Cheese; $^1/_{16}$ serving Milk (1 tablespoon skim milk)

Variation: *Mushroom-Cheese Sauce*—Before serving, blend 2 cups sliced, cooked mushrooms and 1 teaspoon dehydrated onion flakes into Cheese Sauce in preceding recipe. Serve at midday meal over 4 cups hot, cooked zucchini, broccoli, or asparagus. Divide evenly. Makes 4 midday meal servings. Supplement as required. Add 1½ cups Vegetables to equivalent listing.

Cheese Soufflé

2 tablespoons margarine
2 tablespoons flour
¾ cup evaporated skimmed milk
½ cup skim milk
4 ounces grated Cheddar cheese

¼ teaspoon salt
⅛ teaspoon dry mustard
Dash hot sauce
4 medium eggs, separated

Preheat oven to 350°F. Melt margarine in top of double boiler over boiling water; stir in flour. Gradually add milk and cook over low heat, stirring constantly until sauce is thick and smooth. Add cheese; stir until cheese melts. Add seasonings. Beat egg yolks in a medium bowl. Stir a few tablespoons of hot cheese sauce into yolks, then stir egg yolks into sauce in pan and heat for one minute. Remove from heat. In separate bowl beat egg whites until stiff. Stir one third of egg whites into sauce. Gently fold in remaining egg whites. Pour into a nonstick 1-quart soufflé dish or one that has been treated with a release agent. Bake about 45 minutes or until the soufflé is set. Serve at once. Divide evenly. Makes 4 midday meal servings.

Each serving is equivalent to: 1½ servings Fat; 1½ servings Something Extra (1½ teaspoons flour); ½ serving Milk (2 tablespoons skim milk and 3 tablespoons evaporated skimmed milk); 1 ounce Hard Cheese; 1 Egg

Variations:

Two-Cheese Soufflé—For extra flavor, use half Cheddar cheese and half Parmesan or Romano. Add 1 tablespoon chopped fresh parsley or 1 teaspoon basil, sage, thyme, or other favorite herb.

Deviled Cheese Soufflé—Add 1 tablespoon plus 1 teaspoon catsup, 1 teaspoon Worcestershire sauce, and dash hot sauce to the cheese-yolk mixture with other seasonings. Add ½ serving Something Extra (1 teaspoon catsup) to equivalent listing.

Quick-and-Easy Cheese Soufflé

This is delicious served with tomato sauce.

3 slices enriched white bread,
  made into crumbs
¾ cup skim milk
3 ounces grated American cheese
¼ teaspoon salt

Dash hot sauce
Dash dry mustard
3 medium eggs, separated
3 tablespoons margarine

Preheat oven to 375°F. In saucepan combine bread crumbs and milk; cook over very low heat about 3 minutes. Stir in cheese and seasonings. Heat, stirring often, until cheese is melted. In a small bowl beat egg yolks and add to cheese mixture; heat gently 4 minutes longer. Remove from heat; stir in margarine until melted; beat egg whites until stiff but not dry. Fold into cheese-yolk mixture. Transfer to 1-quart nonstick soufflé dish or one that has been treated with a release agent. Set in pan holding 1 inch of water and bake for 30 minutes or until set. Serve at once. Divide evenly. Makes 3 midday meal servings.

Each serving is equivalent to: 1 serving Bread; ¼ serving Milk (¼ cup skim milk); 1 ounce Hard Cheese; 1 Egg; 3 servings Fat

Cheese Kabob

Cut 2 ounces of Muenster, Brick, or other hard cheese into cubes. Spear on toothpicks alternating with pineapple chunks made from ¼ medium fresh pineapple, or 20 small grapes. Makes 1 midday meal serving.

Each serving is equivalent to: 2 ounces Hard Cheese; 1 serving Fruit

Welsh Rarebit for One

You may omit the English muffin and serve rarebit on a sliced, medium tomato.

¼ cup tomato sauce, no sugar added

2 ounces Cheddar cheese, diced

Dash salt, hot sauce, and dry mustard

1 English muffin, split and toasted

In small saucepan combine all ingredients except muffin. Cook over low heat, stirring until cheese melts. Serve over warm muffin halves. Makes 1 midday meal serving.

Each serving is equivalent to: ½ serving Bonus (¼ cup tomato sauce); 2 ounces Hard Cheese; 2 servings Bread (once-a-week selection)

Cheddar Macaroni

½ cup skim milk

2 ounces grated Cheddar cheese

⅔ cup cooked enriched elbow macaroni, cauliflower, or broccoli, or 4 ounces cooked Brussels sprouts

1 medium tomato, sliced

Chopped fresh parsley or chives to garnish

Heat milk in a small saucepan. Add cheese; stir until cheese melts. Pour over macaroni or vegetables in a bowl. Serve with tomato slices and garnish with parsley or chives. Makes 1 midday meal serving.

Each serving is equivalent to: ½ serving Milk (½ cup skim milk); 2 ounces Hard Cheese; 1 serving Choice Group or ⅔ cup Vegetables or 4 ounces Limited Vegetable; ½ cup Vegetables

Cottage Cheese with Poppy Seed Noodles—Hungarian Style

2 cups cooked enriched broad
  noodles
1⅓ cups cottage cheese
½ cup plain unflavored yogurt

2 teaspoons poppy seeds
½ teaspoon paprika
½ teaspoon Worcestershire sauce
Salt and pepper to taste

Combine all ingredients in a medium saucepan. Heat slowly, stirring often, until cheese begins to melt. Divide evenly. Makes 4 midday meal servings. Supplement as required.

Each serving is equivalent to: 1 serving Choice Group; ⅓ cup Soft Cheese; ¼ serving Milk (2 tablespoons yogurt); ½ serving Something Extra (½ teaspoon poppy seeds)

Mexican Cheese, Corn, and Zucchini

4 ounces finely chopped onion
1 tablespoon plus 1 teaspoon
  margarine
4 cups sliced zucchini
2 cups canned whole kernel corn
2 cups skim milk

4 ounces grated Monterey Jack
  cheese
¼ cup chopped canned green chili
  pepper
Salt and pepper to taste

In top of double boiler, over boiling water, combine onion and margarine. Cook about 10 minutes or until onion is tender. Stir in remaining ingredients. Transfer vegetable-cheese mixture to a 2-quart casserole. Cover and bake at 375°F. for 30 minutes. Divide evenly. Makes 4 midday meal servings. Supplement as required.

Each serving is equivalent to: 1 ounce Limited Vegetable; 1 serving Fat; 1 cup plus 1 tablespoon Vegetables; 1 serving Choice Group; ½ serving Milk (½ cup skim milk); 1 ounce Hard Cheese

Spinach Quiche on Rice Crust

1½ cups cooked brown rice
3 medium eggs
3 ounces grated sharp Cheddar
    cheese, divided
Salt to taste

1 cup cooked chopped spinach
1 cup skim milk
3 ounces finely diced onion
Dash freshly ground pepper
Dash nutmeg

In bowl combine rice, 1 egg, 1½ ounces cheese, and salt. Press an even layer of mixture on the bottom and sides of a 9-inch pie or quiche pan. Bake at 425°F. for 25 minutes. Squeeze all liquid out of spinach. In bowl combine spinach with remaining ingredients. Pour into crust. Bake at 375°F. for 35 minutes. Divide evenly. Makes 3 midday meal servings.

Each serving is equivalent to: 1 serving Choice Group; 1 Egg; 1 ounce Hard Cheese; ⅓ cup Vegetables; ⅓ serving Milk (⅓ cup skim milk); 1 ounce Limited Vegetable

Vegetable Cheese Loaf for One

If lighting the oven for one seems a bit selfish, you can bake this with the family dinner and have it cold the following day. Any kind of vegetable can be used, either raw or cooked. You can change the texture completely by adding ½ cup of skim milk and pureeing everything in the blender. There is no end to the seasonings that can be included. This loaf is nice with a topping of Tomato Sauce, sliced tomato, or Ratatouille (see recipes, pages 307 and 291).

½ cup coarsely chopped spinach
    leaves
¼ cup coarsely chopped carrots
¼ cup coarsely chopped celery
1½ ounces peeled cooked potato,
    coarsely chopped
1½ ounces coarsely chopped
    drained canned beets
1 ounce coarsely chopped onion
1 medium egg

1 slice enriched white bread, made
    into crumbs
¼ cup drained canned whole
    kernel corn
1 ounce diced Cheddar or Colby
    cheese
1 tablespoon margarine, melted
Salt, pepper, and cinnamon to
    taste

Combine first 6 ingredients in a bowl and stir in egg, bread crumbs, corn, cheese, margarine, salt, pepper, and cinnamon. Mix well and transfer to a 3-cup nonstick loaf pan or casserole. Bake at 350°F. for about 45 minutes. Makes 1 midday meal serving.

Each serving is equivalent to: 1 cup Vegetables; 1 serving Choice Group; 2½ ounces Limited Vegetable; 1 Egg; 1 serving Bread; 1 ounce Hard Cheese; 3 servings Fat

Cheese Bologna Tidbits

2 ounces grated Cheddar or   **3 ounces bologna, sliced**
  crumbled Bleu cheese   **4 slices pimento**

Layer cheese evenly between the slices of bologna, beginning and ending with a bologna slice. Wrap in wax paper. Press firmly; chill. Cut into 4 wedges. Secure with toothpicks. Garnish with pimento. Divide evenly. Makes 2 midday meal servings.

Each serving is equivalent to: 1 ounce Hard Cheese; 1½ ounces Bologna; 1 tablespoon Vegetables

"Croque Monsieur"

Baked ham and cheese sandwich.

2 thin slices enriched white bread   **1½ ounces ham**
  (see page 79)   **1 ounce Swiss cheese**

Place ham and cheese between bread slices. Place in nonstick baking pan. Bake at 400°F. for 10 minutes. Serve at once. Makes 1 midday meal serving.

Each serving is equivalent to: 1 serving Bread; 1½ ounces "Beef" Group (cured); 1 ounce Hard Cheese

Variation: Substitute 2 ounces sliced cooked turkey for ham. Substitute 2 ounces Poultry for 1½ ounces "Beef" Group in equivalent listing.

Ham and Cheese Canapés

Chill Cheddar, Swiss, or American cheese before grating to make the job easier. A food processor will also grate cheese. Cut into cubes and process to desired degree of fineness.

6 ounces ham
1 ounce onion
2 teaspoons prepared brown
**   mustard**
Dash hot sauce

4 slices enriched white bread,
**   toasted**
4 ounces grated Cheddar cheese
½ teaspoon chopped fresh parsley

Put ham and onion through the grinder or food processor. Stir in mustard and hot sauce. Divide evenly into 4 portions and spread 1 portion on each slice of toast. Top each with 1 ounce cheese and sprinkle with parsley. Place on baking sheet; bake at 425°F. for 8 minutes or until cheese melts. Cut in quarters and serve. Makes 4 midday meal servings.

Each serving is equivalent to: 1½ ounces "Beef" Group (cured); ¼ ounce Limited Vegetable; 1 serving Bread; 1 ounce Hard Cheese

Fun Fondue

½ cup evaporated skimmed milk
2 ounces grated hard cheese
Dash each dry mustard, cayenne
**   pepper, and sherry extract**

1 cup crisp raw vegetables (carrot,
**   cucumber, celery, or fennel**
**   sticks)**

Heat milk in a small saucepan. Add cheese, seasonings, and extract; stir until cheese melts. Serve warm and use as a dip with vegetables. Makes 1 midday meal serving.

Each serving is equivalent to: 1 serving Milk (½ cup evaporated skimmed milk); 2 ounces Hard Cheese; 1 cup Vegetables

Green Beans au Gratin

Any vegetable may be done this way. Be sure to weigh or measure in accordance with the Weight Watchers Food Plan.

1½ cups cooked green beans	Salt and pepper to taste
½ cup mushrooms, sliced	¼ cup tomato sauce, no sugar
2 ounces grated Swiss cheese,	added
divided	1 slice enriched white bread, made
½ teaspoon dried herbs	into crumbs

In a 3-cup ovenproof casserole layer cooked green beans, mushrooms, 1½ ounces cheese, and herbs. Sprinkle with salt and pepper. Top with tomato sauce. Combine remaining cheese and crumbs; sprinkle over casserole. Bake at 350°F. for 25 minutes or until hot and bubbly. Makes 1 midday meal serving.

Each serving is equivalent to: 2 cups Vegetables; 2 ounces Hard Cheese; ½ serving Bonus (¼ cup tomato sauce); 1 serving Bread

Green Chilies Stuffed with Cheese

Serve with a green salad.

2 medium tomatoes, sliced	2 medium eggs, separated
Salt and pepper to taste	2 teaspoons flour
4 canned green chili peppers	½ teaspoon baking powder
2 ounces Monterey Jack or	
American cheese, cut into 4	
equal strips	

Preheat oven to 350°F. Season tomatoes with salt and pepper. Place in a shallow 1-quart casserole. Fill each pepper with a ½-ounce strip of cheese and layer over tomatoes. In bowl combine egg yolks, flour, and baking powder, and beat until thickened. In another bowl beat egg whites until stiff but not dry. Gradually fold beaten whites into yolk mixture and spread over layered peppers and tomatoes. Bake 30 minutes or until lightly golden and firm. Divide evenly. Makes 2 midday meal servings.

Each serving is equivalent to: 1 cup Vegetables; 1 ounce Hard Cheese; 1 Egg; 1 serving Something Extra (1 teaspoon flour)

Mexican Chilies and Cheese

6 ounces onion, chopped
4 roasted peppers, chopped (about
  1 cup)
4 medium tomatoes, chopped
¼ cup water

½ teaspoon salt
1⅓ cups pot or cottage
  cheese
8 tortillas, 6 inches each

Brown onion in nonstick saucepan. Add peppers, tomatoes, water, and salt. Bring to boil, reduce heat, and simmer 15 minutes. Stir in cheese and heat. Divide evenly and spoon over tortillas. Makes 4 midday meal servings, 2 tortillas each. Supplement as required.

Each serving is equivalent to: 1½ ounces Limited Vegetable; ¾ cup Vegetables; ⅓ cup Soft Cheese; 2 servings Bread (once-a-week selection)

Portuguese Tower

1 firm medium tomato
1 medium egg, lightly scrambled

1 ounce Cheddar cheese
Salt and pepper to taste

Cut a thin slice off the top of tomato. Scoop out pulp, leaving at least ¼ inch thickness on all sides. Fill cavity with egg and top with cheese. Bake at 350°F. until cheese melts. Chop tomato pulp; season with salt and pepper. Spoon over melted cheese. Makes 1 midday meal serving.

Each serving is equivalent to: ½ cup Vegetables; 1 Egg; 1 ounce Hard Cheese

Blueberry Cheesecake

¼ cup plus 2 tablespoons water
Artificial sweetener to equal ⅓ cup
 sugar
¼ cup lemon juice
1 envelope unflavored gelatin

1⅓ cups cottage cheese
½ teaspoon vanilla extract
½ cup chilled evaporated
 skimmed milk
1 cup blueberries, divided

In a small saucepan combine water, sweetener, and lemon juice. Sprinkle in gelatin; allow to soften. Stir over low heat until gelatin dissolves. Cool. Process cottage cheese in blender container or food processor until smooth. Add gelatin mixture and vanilla extract; process to combine. Transfer to a medium mixing bowl. Chill until set. In separate bowl whip evaporated skimmed milk until peaks form. Beat chilled gelatin mixture until smooth; fold in whipped milk. Pour into an 8-inch round cake pan. Process ½ cup blueberries in blender container or food processor until pureed. Combine with remaining blueberries and pour over gelatin mixture. Using a spoon or spatula, stir blueberries once or twice through gelatin mixture to give a marble effect. Chill until set. Divide evenly. Makes 4 midday meal servings. Supplement as required.

Each serving is equivalent to: ½ serving Something Extra (¼ envelope gelatin); ⅓ cup Soft Cheese; ¼ serving Milk (2 tablespoons evaporated Skimmed Milk); ½ serving Fruit

Cheesecake Pudding

½ cup canned pineapple chunks,
 no sugar added
1 medium egg
1 teaspoon lemon juice

⅛ teaspoon vanilla extract
⅓ cup skim milk ricotta cheese
1 teaspoon margarine
Cinnamon to taste

Combine pineapple chunks, egg, lemon juice, and vanilla in blender container. Process until smooth. Add cheese and process. Pour into a 2-cup ovenproof casserole. Dot with margarine; sprinkle with cinnamon and bake at 350°F. for 40 minutes. Serve chilled. Makes 1 midday meal serving.

Each serving is equivalent to: 1 serving Fruit; 1 Egg; ⅓ cup Soft Cheese; 1 serving Fat

Fruity Cottage Cheese

You can create many different flavors using any of the fruits on the Food Program. (See "Fruit Servings" on page 20).

⅔ cup cottage cheese
½ cup blueberries
Artificial sweetener to equal 2
   teaspoons sugar or to taste
   (optional)

Process cottage cheese in blender container or food processor until smooth. Transfer to a small serving dish. Mash berries in a small bowl or process in blender container or food processor until pureed. Add sweetener to berries, if desired. Gently fold into cheese to give a marble effect. Chill. Makes 1 midday meal serving.

Each serving is equivalent to: ⅔ cup Soft Cheese; 1 serving Fruit

Orange "Coeur à la Crème"

1 envelope unflavored gelatin
½ cup cold water
½ cup boiling water
1⅓ cups cottage cheese
Artificial sweetener to equal 4
   teaspoons sugar or to taste

½ teaspoon orange extract
½ teaspoon vanilla extract
¼ teaspoon coconut extract
1 small orange, peeled and
   sectioned

Sprinkle gelatin over cold water in blender container to soften. Add boiling water; process until gelatin is dissolved. Add remaining ingredients except orange; process until smooth. Pour into a small bowl; chill until consistency of unbeaten egg whites. Dice all but two orange sections, fold diced sections into gelatin mixture. Divide evenly into two 1½-cup molds; chill until set. Unmold and garnish each serving with one reserved orange section. Makes 2 midday meal servings.

Each serving is equivalent to: 1 serving Something Extra (½ envelope gelatin); ⅔ cup Soft Cheese; ½ serving Fruit

Strawberry-Cheese Yogurt Pie

1 cup ripe strawberries
8-inch Pie Crust (see page 84)
1½ teaspoons unflavored gelatin
½ cup water
1⅓ cups cottage cheese

1 cup plain unflavored yogurt
¼ cup frozen orange juice
   concentrate, thawed
1 teaspoon vanilla extract

Set aside 4 small strawberries for garnish; slice remaining berries and arrange in bottom of baked pie crust. In small saucepan soften gelatin in water. Heat, stirring until dissolved. Combine with remaining ingredients in blender container. Process until smooth. Pour into pie crust. Chill several hours, until firm. Garnish with reserved berries. Divide evenly. Makes 4 midday meal servings. Supplement as required.

Each serving is equivalent to: ¾ serving Fruit; 8-inch Pie Crust (see page 84); ¼ serving Something Extra (⅜ teaspoon gelatin); ⅓ cup Soft Cheese; ½ serving Milk (¼ cup yogurt)

BREAD AND CEREAL

You can't live by bread alone, but it's the basic ingredient for our croutons, crumb pie crusts, fruit cake, and bread custard. Gingerbread and Blueberry Muffins, Chocolate Raisin Cake with Apricot Sauce, and three different pie crusts are included. So, too, are matzo recipes for the Passover Holiday only, and a crunchy granola made with wheat germ and sesame seeds. You can even use your allotted bread to make seasoned crumbs for "oven-fried" fish and chicken. This chapter gives the how-to's.

Rules for Using Bread, Rolls, and Buns

1. Amounts
   Women: 2 servings daily
   Men: 4 servings daily
   Youth: 4 servings daily
2. One serving must be taken at the Morning Meal unless Cereal or Choice Group is selected.
3. Use packaged, presliced enriched or whole grain bread or packaged rolls or buns weighing approximately 1 ounce per serving; up to 75 calories per ounce.
4. The bread must be eaten at mealtimes only; never between meals.
5. Approved breads include cracked wheat, pumpernickel, rye, soy, sprouted rye, and raisin.
6. Thin-sliced bread is "legal," if 2 slices weigh approximately 1 ounce and do not exceed 75 calories.

7. Once a week you may omit 2 servings of bread and select one of the following. These items should weigh approximately 2 ounces each and contain about 150 calories.

   bagel, bialystock, or pita
   English muffin
   hamburger roll
   hard roll
   2 tortillas (6-inch diameter)
   or similar type bread

8. If the once-a-week bread item is selected at the Midday or Evening Meal, women must have cereal for breakfast.

9. For the week of Passover only, ½ board of matzo—regular, egg, or whole wheat—may be used in place of one serving of bread.

Thin-Sliced Bread

Use the following for making Melba Toast (see page 83) and Toast Cups (see page 83–84).

1. Packaged, presliced, thin-sliced bread. (See rule 6.)
2. A standard 1-ounce slice of bread, cut horizontally in half. A slicing gadget is available in many shops especially for this purpose.

Bread Crumbs

The following is the procedure for making bread crumbs. Cover blender container. Turn blender on high speed. Remove the clear plastic handle in the blender container cover. Tear each slice of bread into about 4 or 5 pieces. Drop each piece, one at a time, through the opening in the cover; place your hand over the opening to prevent crumbs from scattering. Continue this process until all bread is crumbled. If crumbs stop moving in blender container, empty container into a bowl and continue with remaining bread. Do not overprocess. For large crumbs, leave blender on for a few seconds; for fine crumbs, process longer.

Bread Crumbs au Gratin

Use as a topping for vegetables before baking.

1 slice enriched white bread, made into crumbs

1 ounce hard cheese, grated
1 teaspoon margarine

In small bowl combine all ingredients. Makes 1 midday meal serving. Supplement as required.

Each serving is equivalent to: 1 serving Bread; 1 ounce Hard Cheese; 1 serving Fat

"Buttery" Oven Toast

You get fine toast this way. Spread 1 slice enriched white bread with 1 teaspoon margarine. Place on baking sheet, margarine side up. Bake at 400°F., until browned. Makes 1 serving. Serve at mealtime only.

Each serving is equivalent to: 1 serving Bread; 1 serving Fat

Cheese Toast

Serve with tossed salad.

1 slice enriched white bread
1 teaspoon margarine, divided
1 ounce hard cheese
Prepared mustard to taste

½ teaspoon sesame, poppy, or caraway seeds, or curry powder to taste
Salt and pepper to taste

Spread bread with ½ teaspoon margarine. Top with cheese. Spread cheese with remaining margarine and mustard. Sprinkle with seeds or curry powder and salt and pepper. Bake at 375°F. until cheese melts. Cut into 8 pieces. Makes 1 midday meal serving. Supplement as required.

Each serving is equivalent to: 1 serving Bread; 1 serving Fat; 1 ounce Hard Cheese; ½ serving Something Extra (½ teaspoon seeds) (optional)

Croutons for Soup

1 slice enriched white bread   **Garlic salt to taste**

Cut bread into 8 pieces. Place on baking sheet. Bake at 300°F. to 350°F. until brown, turning several times, or broil 5 inches from source of heat. Check frequently to avoid burning and turn as necessary to brown all sides. When done, combine with garlic salt in plastic bag and shake. Divide evenly. Makes 2 servings. Serve at mealtime only.

Each serving is equivalent to: ½ serving Bread

Italian Bread Crumbs

1 teaspoon salt
¼ teaspoon paprika
¼ teaspoon basil
¼ teaspoon oregano

¼ teaspoon rosemary
Dash garlic powder (optional)
2 slices enriched white bread,
   made into crumbs

In plastic bag combine seasonings. Add bread crumbs and shake to combine. Divide evenly. Makes 4 servings. Serve at mealtime only.

Each serving is equivalent to: ½ serving Bread

Seasoned Crumbs

2 slices enriched white bread,
   made into crumbs
1 to 2 teaspoons fresh herbs

1 small garlic clove, mashed with 1
   teaspoon salt
2 teaspoons margarine, melted

In a bowl combine first 3 ingredients. Add margarine and mix well. Divide evenly. Makes 4 servings. Serve at mealtime only.

Each serving is equivalent to: ½ serving Bread; ½ serving Fat

Melba Toast

Use 2 thin slices enriched white bread (see page 79 for explanation). Cut bread into halves or quarters and place on baking sheet. Bake at 250°F. until crisp, turning as necessary. Makes 1 serving. Serve at mealtime only.

Each serving is equivalent to: 1 serving Bread

Curried Toast or Croutons

1 teaspoon margarine   **Dash salt and pepper**
⅛ teaspoon curry powder   **1 slice enriched white bread**

In a small bowl combine margarine, curry powder, salt, and pepper. Spread over bread slice. Place on baking sheet; bake at 375°F. 7 minutes or until bread is crisp and golden. Serve hot, or cut into cubes and store in airtight container. When ready to use, reheat in oven to crisp. Makes 1 serving. Serve at mealtime only.

Each serving is equivalent to: 1 serving Fat; 1 serving Bread

Toast Cups—I

Use as shells, for "creamed" fillings or salads.

6 thin slices enriched white bread
   (see page 79)

Trim crust from bread. Reserve crusts. Press one thin bread slice into each of 6 muffin cups (3-inch diameter). Bake 10 to 12 minutes at 350°F. or until golden brown. Make crumbs from crusts by processing them in blender container. Use crumbs, evenly divided, as topping for filled toast cups. Makes 3 servings, 2 toast cups each. Use at mealtime only.

Each serving is equivalent to: 1 serving Bread

Variation:
Miniature Toast Cups (for hors d'oeuvres)—Use the small muffin cups (1½-inch diameter). Cut thin bread slices into quarters before proceeding as above. Makes 3 servings, 8 toast cups each.

Toast Cups—II

6 thin slices enriched white bread (see page 79)
¼ cup water
½ teaspoon vanilla extract

Artificial sweetener to equal 2 teaspoons sugar

Press each thin slice of bread into a muffin cup (3-inch diameter). Combine remaining ingredients. Sprinkle bread with flavored water. Bake 12 to 14 minutes at 350°F. or until golden brown. Makes 3 servings, 2 toast cups each. Use at mealtime only.
   Each serving is equivalent to: 1 serving Bread

8-Inch Pie Crust

3 tablespoons water
¼ teaspoon vanilla extract

2 slices raisin or enriched white bread, made into crumbs

In a mixing bowl combine water and extract. Add bread crumbs and stir with fork until crumbs are evenly moistened. Press into 8-inch pie pan. Bake at 400°F. for 10 to 12 minutes. Cool. Divide evenly. Makes 2 or 4 servings. Use at mealtime only. Each serving is equivalent to: *2 servings*—1 serving Bread. *4 servings*—½ serving Bread

9-Inch Pie Crust

2 tablespoons skim milk
¼ teaspoon fruit-flavored extract
¼ teaspoon vanilla extract

3 slices raisin or enriched white bread, toasted and made into crumbs

In mixing bowl, combine skim milk and extracts. Add bread crumbs and stir with fork until crumbs are evenly moistened. Press into a 9-inch pie pan. Bake at 400°F. for 10 to 12 minutes. Cool. Divide evenly. Makes 3 or 6 servings. Use at mealtime only.

Each serving is equivalent to: *3 servings*—2 teaspoons skim milk; 1 serving Bread. *6 servings*—1 teaspoon skim milk; ½ serving Bread

Oil Pie Crust

8 slices raisin or enriched white bread, made into crumbs

¼ cup vegetable oil
1 teaspoon vanilla extract

In bowl, combine all ingredients. Mix well. Pat into a 9- or 10-inch pie pan. Bake at 400°F. for 10 minutes. Cool before filling. Divide evenly. Makes 8 or 16 servings. Use at mealtime only.

Each serving is equivalent to: *8 servings*—1 serving Bread; 1½ servings Fat. *16 servings*—½ serving Bread; ¾ serving Fat

Bread Stuffing

There are dozens of ways to use this stuffing. Think of it as a filling for precooked green pepper, tomato, squash, or eggplant. Bake it in a casserole to accompany your Thanksgiving day bird. Or tuck it under your cooked chicken or fish just before serving.

½ cup diced celery
1 cup Chicken Stock (see page 140)
2 slices day-old enriched white bread, diced

Salt and pepper to taste
¼ teaspoon thyme
¼ teaspoon savory

In saucepan cook celery in stock until celery is soft and stock is almost evaporated. Add bread and seasonings. Moisten with additional water, if stuffing is too dry. Heat and serve. Divide evenly. Makes 2 servings. Serve at mealtime only.

Each serving is equivalent to: ¼ cup Vegetables; ⅔ serving Something Extra (½ cup stock); 1 serving Bread

Instant "Pizza"

1 English muffin, split and toasted
¼ cup tomato sauce, no sugar
  added
¼ teaspoon oregano or Italian
  seasoning or to taste

2 slices Mozzarella, Cheddar,
  Muenster, or Swiss cheese, 1
  ounce each

Spread cut side of each muffin half with 2 tablespoons tomato sauce. Sprinkle each with ⅛ teaspoon oregano and top each with 1 ounce cheese. Place under broiler; broil just long enough to melt cheese. Makes 1 midday meal serving.

Each serving is equivalent to: 2 servings Bread (once-a-week selection); ½ serving Bonus (¼ cup tomato sauce); 2 ounces Hard Cheese

Variations:

1. Omit 1 ounce hard cheese. Arrange 1 ounce drained, canned tuna or sardines, flaked, on top of tomato sauce on each muffin half. Sprinkle with oregano. Grate 1 ounce hard cheese. Divide evenly over fish. Broil just until cheese melts. Makes 1 midday meal serving.

Each serving is equivalent to: 2 servings Bread (once-a-week selection); ½ serving Bonus (¼ cup tomato sauce); 2 ounces Fish; 1 ounce Hard Cheese

2. Omit 1 ounce hard cheese. Season tomato sauce with minced chives or dehydrated onion flakes to taste. Spread on muffin halves. Top each with 1 tablespoon cooked, chopped, or sliced mushrooms and ½ ounce grated hard cheese. Broil just until cheese melts. Makes 1 midday meal serving. Supplement as required.

Each serving is equivalent to: 2 servings Bread (once-a-week selection); ½ serving Bonus (¼ cup tomato sauce); 2 tablespoons Vegetables; 1 ounce Hard Cheese

3. Omit English muffin and use 2 thin slices enriched white bread, toasted (see page 79). Proceed as above, in basic recipe. Makes 1 midday meal serving.

Each serving is equivalent to: 1 serving Bread; ½ serving Bonus (¼ cup tomato sauce); 2 ounces Hard Cheese

Blueberry Muffins

1 slice raisin bread, made into crumbs	1 tablespoon water
⅓ cup nonfat dry milk	½ teaspoon vanilla extract
½ teaspoon baking soda	1 medium egg, separated
	½ cup blueberries

In a bowl, combine first 3 ingredients. Add water, vanilla, egg yolk, and blueberries. Stir to combine. In separate bowl beat egg white until stiff but not dry. Fold egg white into batter and pour into nonstick muffin tins. Bake at 350°F. for 20 minutes. Makes 1 morning or midday meal serving. Supplement as required.

Each serving is equivalent to: 1 serving Bread; 1 serving Milk (1 cup skim milk); 1 Egg; 1 serving Fruit

Gingerbread

2 slices raisin bread, made into crumbs	⅛ teaspoon nutmeg
2 tablespoons flour	1 cup skim milk
½ teaspoon cinnamon	2 medium eggs, beaten
⅛ teaspoon ginger	2 tablespoons unsalted margarine, melted

In bowl, combine first 5 ingredients. Stir in milk, eggs, and margarine. Pour into 2-cup baking pan or casserole which has been treated with a release agent. Bake at 350°F. for 40 minutes or until toothpick inserted in center comes out clean. Divide evenly. Makes 2 morning or midday meal servings. Supplement as required.

Each serving is equivalent to: 1 serving Bread; 3 servings Something Extra (1 tablespoon flour); ½ serving Milk (½ cup skim milk); 1 Egg; 3 servings Fat

Prune Bread Custard

2 slices enriched white bread, cut
   in cubes
1 cup skim milk
2 medium eggs, beaten
⅓ cup prune juice

1 teaspoon vanilla extract
Dash salt
4 dried medium prunes, pitted
   and diced
Cinnamon to taste

Place half the bread cubes in each of 2 individual casseroles. Combine milk, eggs, prune juice, vanilla, and salt in a medium bowl. Divide evenly and pour over bread. Top each casserole with ½ of the diced prunes. Sprinkle with cinnamon. Bake at 350°F. about 45 minutes or until pudding is brown and knife inserted near center comes out clean. Makes 2 morning or midday meal servings. Supplement as required.

    Each serving is equivalent to: 1 serving Bread; ½ serving Milk (½ cup skim milk); 1 Egg; 1 serving Fruit

Chocolate Meringue Pie

1 envelope unflavored gelatin
2 cups skim milk
Artificial sweetener to equal 8
   teaspoons sugar, divided
¼ teaspoon salt, divided
2 medium eggs, separated

1 tablespoon unsweetened cocoa,
   dissolved in 1 tablespoon water
½ teaspoon vanilla extract
8-inch Pie Crust (see page 84)
⅛ teaspoon cream of tartar

In saucepan sprinkle gelatin over milk to soften. Place over low heat and stir until gelatin dissolves. Remove from heat. Add sweetener to equal 4 teaspoons sugar and ⅛ teaspoon salt. In a bowl, beat egg yolks. Add a few teaspoons of hot milk mixture to beaten egg yolks, then stir yolks into milk. Blend in cocoa. Cook until mixture thickens slightly; remove from heat. Stir in vanilla. Pour into pie crust and refrigerate until firm. Beat egg whites with remaining sweetener and salt until frothy. Add cream of tartar and beat until mixture stands in stiff, glossy peaks. Spread over pie filling. Broil about 4 inches from heat for 30 seconds or until meringue is slightly browned. Serve at once or refrigerate and serve well chilled. Divide evenly. Makes 2 midday meal servings. Supplement as required.

Each serving is equivalent to: 2½ servings Something Extra (½ envelope gelatin and 1½ teaspoons cocoa); 1 serving Milk (1 cup skim milk); 1 Egg; 8-inch Pie Crust (see page 84)

Variation:
Mocha Meringue Pie—Replace skim milk with 2 cups strong coffee. Reduce cocoa to 1½ teaspoons, dissolved in 1½ teaspoons water. Add 1½ teaspoons maple extract with the vanilla. Follow recipe as above. In equivalent listing, eliminate Milk and reduce Something Extra to 1¾ servings (½ envelope gelatin and ¾ teaspoon cocoa).

Chocolate Raisin Cake with Apricot Sauce

4 medium eggs, separated
¼ cup water
Artificial sweetener to equal 10 teaspoons sugar
2 tablespoons plus 2 teaspoons unsweetened cocoa, dissolved in 3 tablespoons water

4 slices raisin bread, made into crumbs
Apricot Sauce (see following recipe)

Preheat oven to 350°F. Line an 8x8-inch baking pan with wax paper; set aside. In mixing bowl combine egg yolks, water, and sweetener. Beat for about 5 minutes or until thick. Add cocoa and beat to combine. Fold in bread crumbs. In a separate bowl beat egg whites until stiff peaks form. Carefully fold whites into yolk mixture. Pour mixture into prepared baking pan; bake for 30 minutes or until firm. Remove from pan and cool on a wire rack. To serve, divide cake into 4 equal portions and pour 1 serving Apricot Sauce over each portion. Makes 4 midday meal servings. Supplement as required.

Each serving is equivalent to: 1 Egg; 2 servings Something Extra (2 teaspoons cocoa); 1 serving Bread; Apricot Sauce (see following recipe)

Apricot Sauce

16 canned apricot halves with ½   Artificial sweetener to equal 2
cup juice, no sugar added   teaspoons sugar (optional)

Dice apricots and set aside. In a small saucepan combine juice and
sweetener; heat until liquid is reduced by ½. Stir in diced apricots.
Cool. Divide evenly. Makes 4 servings.
  Each serving is equivalent to: 1 serving Fruit

Fruitcake

1⅓ cups nonfat dry milk   Artificial sweetener to equal 8
1½ cups canned crushed   teaspoons sugar
  pineapple, no sugar added,   1 tablespoon lemon juice
  drain and reserve juice   1 teaspoon vanilla extract
½ cup orange juice   8 slices raisin bread, made into
2 cups cranberries, chopped   crumbs
2 medium apples, pared, cored,   ¼ teaspoon cinnamon
  and grated

Combine milk, pineapple juice, and orange juice in a large bowl. Beat
until frothy. Add remaining fruit, sweetener, lemon juice, and vanilla.
Combine bread crumbs and cinnamon. Add to fruit mixture and mix
well. Pour into an 8x8x3-inch nonstick pan and bake at 350°F. for 1
hour. Divide evenly. Makes 8 servings. Serve at mealtime only.
  Each serving is equivalent to: ½ serving Milk (½ cup skim milk); 1
serving Fruit; 1 serving Bread

Passover Recipes

For the Passover Holiday only, ½ board of egg, regular, or whole
wheat matzo may be used in place of 1 slice of bread.

Apple Matzo Kugel

2 matzo boards, broken into
  pieces
4 medium eggs, separated
3 medium apples, pared, cored,
  and grated
½ cup orange juice

1 teaspoon lemon juice
1 teaspoon grated lemon rind
Artificial sweetener to equal 4
  teaspoons sugar
½ teaspoon salt
¼ teaspoon cinnamon

In small bowl soak matzo in water until soft; drain in colander and squeeze dry. Transfer to medium bowl; add egg yolks, one at a time, mixing well after each addition. In a separate bowl combine grated apples, fruit juices, lemon rind, sweetener, and seasonings; add to matzo mixture and stir well. Beat egg whites, in a small bowl, until stiff but not dry; fold into matzo mixture. Place in a 1½-quart casserole and bake at 350°F. for about 1 hour or until top is browned. Divide evenly. Makes 4 midday meal servings. Supplement as required.

Each serving is equivalent to: 1 serving Bread; 1 Egg; 1 serving Fruit

Apple Orange Meichel

3 medium apples, pared, cored,
  and diced
½ cup orange juice
4 ounces cooked winter squash,
  mashed
Artificial sweetener to equal 6
  teaspoons sugar, divided

¼ teaspoon cinnamon
Dash ginger
1 matzo board, made into crumbs
⅛ teaspoon grated orange rind
1 tablespoon plus 1 teaspoon
  margarine, melted

Place apples and orange juice in a medium saucepan; cook over medium heat until tender. Add squash, artificial sweetener to equal 4 teaspoons sugar, cinnamon, and ginger; mix well. Divide evenly into 4 ovenproof custard cups. In a small bowl combine matzo crumbs, orange rind, and remaining sweetener. Add margarine and mix until well blended. Divide crumb mixture evenly over fruit mixture. Bake at 425°F. for 20 minutes. Serve hot or chilled. Makes 4 servings. Serve at mealtime only.

Each serving is equivalent to: 1 serving Fruit; 1 ounce Limited Vegetable; ½ serving Bread; 1 serving Fat

Banana Pudding

2 matzo boards, broken into
  2-inch pieces
4 medium eggs, beaten
1½ cups water
⅔ cup nonfat dry milk

Artificial sweetener to equal 4
  teaspoons sugar
½ teaspoon vanilla extract
⅛ teaspoon cinnamon
½ teaspoon salt
2 medium bananas, sliced

Pour hot water over matzo in a colander; drain. In a medium bowl combine eggs, water, milk, sweetener, vanilla, cinnamon and salt. Fold in matzo and banana. Pour into an 8x8x2-inch nonstick baking pan. Bake at 350°F. for 50 minutes or until knife inserted in center comes out clean. Serve warm or chilled. Divide evenly. Makes 4 midday meal servings. Supplement as required.

Each serving is equivalent to: 1 serving Bread; 1 Egg; ½ serving Milk (½ cup skim milk); 1 serving Fruit

Matzo Piecrust

2 matzo boards, made into fine
  crumbs

2 tablespoons plus 2 teaspoons
  margarine
2 tablespoons water

Preheat oven to 375°F. In medium bowl combine matzo crumbs and margarine. Using a fork or fingers, blend water into matzo. Press into sides and bottom of an 8-inch pie pan. Bake for 8 to 10 minutes or until golden brown. Divide evenly. Makes 4 servings. Use at mealtime only.

Each serving is equivalent to: 1 serving Bread; 2 servings Fat

Passover Provençal Quiche

4 medium eggs, beaten
2 tablespoons margarine, melted
2 matzo boards
2 medium tomatoes, peeled and
  sliced, divided

3 ounces onion, diced, divided
4 ounces American cheese, diced,
  divided
⅛ teaspoon garlic powder, divided
Salt and pepper to taste

Combine eggs and margarine in a bowl. *Break one matzo board into quarters and soak in hot water in shallow pan until soft. Using a spatula or pancake turner, lift matzo from water. Gently press out moisture and place in 8x8x2-inch nonstick baking pan. Pour ¼ egg mixture over matzo. Arrange half of the tomato, onion, and cheese over matzo. Season with half the garlic powder, salt, and pepper. Repeat procedure from asterisk(*). Pour remaining egg mixture over top. Bake at 375°F. for ½ hour or until a knife inserted in center comes out clean. Divide evenly. Makes 4 midday meal servings.

Each serving is equivalent to: 1 Egg; 1½ servings Fat; 1 serving Bread; ¼ cup Vegetables; ¾ ounce Limited Vegetable; 1 ounce Hard Cheese

Spinace con Matzo

2 cups cooked chopped spinach
1⅓ cups cottage cheese
1 cup cooked chopped mushrooms
4 medium eggs, beaten

4 ounces cooked chopped onions
1 matzo board, made into crumbs
¼ teaspoon onion powder
Salt and pepper to taste

In a large bowl combine all ingredients. Pour into a 1½-quart casserole; bake at 350°F. for 40 minutes or until firm. Divide evenly. Makes 4 midday meal servings.

Each serving is equivalent to: ¾ cup Vegetables; ⅓ cup Soft Cheese; 1 Egg; 1 ounce Limited Vegetable; ½ serving Bread

Sponge Cake

4 medium eggs, separated	1 teaspoon grated lemon rind
½ cup water	1 teaspoon vanilla extract
⅔ cup nonfat dry milk	2 matzo boards, made into fine
Artificial sweetener to equal 18	crumbs
teaspoons sugar, divided	

Preheat oven to 350°F. In a large bowl beat egg yolks until thick and lemon-colored. Slowly add water, continuing to beat. One at a time add milk, artificial sweetener to equal 12 teaspoons sugar, lemon rind, and vanilla, beating after each addition. Fold in matzo crumbs. In a medium bowl beat egg whites with remaining sweetener until stiff but not dry; fold into yolk mixture. Pour into a 10-inch nonstick tube pan. Bake for 35 minutes or until lightly browned. Remove from pan; cool. Divide evenly. Makes 4 midday meal servings. Supplement as required.

Each serving is equivalent to: 1 Egg; ½ serving Milk (½ cup skim milk); 1 serving Bread

Variation:
Mandelbrot—Prepare Sponge Cake adding ½ teaspoon almond extract with vanilla; slice into pieces about 1 inch thick. Arrange cut side down on a baking sheet; bake at 400°F. for about 10 minutes or until lightly toasted. Divide evenly.

Stuffed Fish Fillets

¼ cup chopped mushrooms	4 ounces American cheese, diced
1 medium tomato, peeled and	1 matzo board, made into crumbs
diced	4 fish fillets, 3 ounces each
1 ounce onion, finely chopped	Salt, pepper, and garlic powder to
3 tablespoons water	taste
2 tablespoons chopped fresh	Lemon slices and parsley sprigs to
parsley	garnish
1 garlic clove, minced or pressed	

In a nonstick skillet, combine mushrooms, tomato, onion, water, parsley and garlic. Cook over medium heat, stirring occasionally, until onion is tender. Remove from heat. Stir in cheese and matzo crumbs; set aside. Sprinkle fish with salt, pepper, and garlic powder. Place each fillet in a 1½-cup individual ovenproof casserole. Spoon equal amounts of stuffing mixture over each fillet. Bake at 350°F. for 20 minutes or until fish flakes easily at the touch of a fork. Garnish each serving with lemon slices and parsley sprigs. Makes 4 midday meal servings.

Each serving is equivalent to: 3 tablespoons Vegetables; ¼ ounce Limited Vegetable; 1 ounce Hard Cheese; ½ serving Bread; 2 ounces Fish

Rules for Using Cereal

1. Amounts
    Women, Men, and Youth: Ready-to-eat (not presweetened), 1 ounce
    Uncooked, 1 ounce
2. Select cereal at the Morning Meal only, up to 3 times weekly, if desired. When cereal is taken, bread may be taken at the Morning Meal or another meal. Cereal must be eaten with at least ½ serving milk.
3. Approved ready-to-eat cereals include corn flakes, toasted rice, wheat germ, bran flakes, bran morsels, and unprocessed bran. These may be used alone, or in any combination totaling 1 ounce.
4. Examples of uncooked cereals are oatmeal, farina, and toasted wheat.
5. The following Choice Group items may be taken as Cereal selections as well:
    cornmeal; enriched, 1 ounce dry
    cracked wheat (Bulgur), 1 ounce dry
    hominy grits, enriched, ¾ cup cooked

Cooked Cereal with Fruit

Cook 1 ounce uncooked cereal in ½ cup skim milk plus enough water to equal the amount of liquid indicated on package directions. Use a very low heat and stir constantly to avoid scorching. Add seasoning as desired—dash of salt, cinnamon. Just before cereal is done, stir in 4 pitted and diced, dried medium prunes. Heat and serve. Other fruit may be substituted (see "Fruit Servings," page 20). Makes 1 morning meal serving.

Each serving is equivalent to: 1 ounce Cereal; ½ serving Milk (½ cup skim milk); 1 serving Fruit

Green Mountain Deep-Dish Apple Pie

1 ounce corn flakes, crushed
2 tablespoons plus 2 teaspoons
 nonfat dry milk
Artificial sweetener to equal 2
 teaspoons sugar
¼ teaspoon vanilla extract
⅛ teaspoon cinnamon

Dash nutmeg
3 tablespoons water
1 teaspoon margarine, melted
1 medium apple, pared, cored,
 and sliced
½ cup water

In medium bowl combine first 8 ingredients in order given. Press half of the cereal mixture in the bottom of a 2-cup casserole. Set aside remaining mixture. In small saucepan combine apple and water. Cook until tender. Remove apple slices from saucepan with a slotted spoon and reserve 3 tablespoons liquid. Layer apples in baking dish. Top with remaining crumbs and sprinkle with reserved liquid. Bake at 325°F. for 20 minutes. Serve warm or chilled. Makes 1 morning meal serving.

Each serving is equivalent to: 1 ounce Cereal; ½ serving Milk (½ cup skim milk); 1 serving Fat; 1 serving Fruit

Sesame Granola with Wheat Germ

1⅓ cups nonfat dry milk
3 ounces uncooked oatmeal
1 ounce wheat germ
1 tablespoon plus 2 teaspoons flour
2 teaspoons sesame seeds
¼ teaspoon cinnamon
⅓ cup water

8 dried medium prunes, pitted
   and cut into small pieces
1 tablespoon plus 2 teaspoons
   vegetable oil
¼ teaspoon each vanilla and
   coconut extract (optional)

Combine nonfat dry milk, oatmeal, wheat germ, flour, sesame seeds, and cinnamon in a large bowl. In a small saucepan combine water and prunes. Bring to boil; cook about 3 minutes. Remove from heat; stir in oil and extracts, if desired. Combine with oatmeal mixture and spread in a 13x9-inch baking pan. Bake at 325°F. for 25 minutes, stirring occasionally. Allow to cool and store in a tightly closed container in refrigerator. Divide evenly. Makes 4 morning meal servings.

Each serving is equivalent to: 1 serving Milk (1 cup skim milk); 1 ounce Cereal; 1¾ servings Something Extra (1¼ teaspoons flour and ½ teaspoon sesame seeds); ½ serving Fruit; 1¼ servings Fat

CHOICE GROUP

Can you believe—recipes for Mushroom and Barley Soup, Kasha and Kasha Varnishkes, Rumanian Mamaliga, Mexican Tamale Pie, Southern Grits and Greens, Spoon Bread, Hot German Potato Salad, Risotto, and Wild Rice Casserole to go with your Thanksgiving turkey! Here they are—turn the page!

Rules for Using Choice Group

1. Omit 1 serving of bread and select 1 item from this list up to 3 times weekly, if desired:
   barley, ½ cup cooked
   beans
       lima, red, white, or soybeans (fresh, frozen, or canned fresh), ½ cup cooked
   black-eyed peas (cowpeas) (fresh, frozen, or canned fresh), ½ cup cooked
   buckwheat groats (kasha), 1 ounce dry
   corn
       ear, 1 medium
       whole kernel or cream style, ½ cup
   cornmeal, enriched, 1 ounce dry
   cracked wheat (Bulgur), 1 ounce dry
   hominy grits, enriched, ¾ cup cooked
   pasta, enriched
       macaroni or spaghetti, ⅔ cup cooked
       noodles, ½ cup cooked
   potato, white, fresh, or canned, raw or cooked, 3 ounces
   rice, enriched white or brown or wild, ½ cup cooked

2. Choice Group items may be split evenly, if they are consumed at the same meal.
3. Canned Choice Group items containing sugar are "illegal," except for canned corn.
4. Cornmeal, cracked wheat (Bulgur), and hominy grits may be taken as cereal selections as well as Choice Group items.

Barley and Vegetables

Use as a side dish.

¾ cup Beef Stock (see page 163)
½ cup diced carrot
½ cup diced white turnip
¼ cup diced celery

1 ounce minced onion
½ cup cooked barley
Salt and pepper to taste

Heat stock in a medium saucepan. Add vegetables and cook 15 minutes. Add barley; season with salt and pepper. Continue cooking until vegetables are tender and mixture becomes slightly thickened, stirring frequently. Serve hot. Makes 1 serving. Serve at mealtime only.

Each serving is equivalent to: 1 serving Something Extra (¾ cup stock); 1¼ cups Vegetables; 1 ounce Limited Vegetable; 1 serving Choice Group

Mushroom and Barley Soup

4 cups Beef Stock (see page 163)
4 cups mushrooms, thinly sliced
2 cups cooked barley, plus cooking liquid
1 cup shredded carrots
4 ounces diced onion

2 celery ribs, minced
1 tablespoon chopped fresh parsley
Dash nutmeg
Salt to taste

Combine all ingredients in large pot; cover and simmer slowly for 1½ hours, or until desired consistency. Divide evenly. Makes 4 servings. Serve at mealtime only.

Each serving is equivalent to: 1⅓ servings Something Extra (1 cup stock); 1½ cups Vegetables; 1 serving Choice Group; 1 ounce Limited Vegetable

Hoppin' John

Serve with pork or ham.

½ cup Ham or Chicken Stock (see page 140 or 163)
¼ cup cooked fresh black-eyed peas

¼ cup cooked enriched rice
Salt, pepper, and crushed red pepper to taste

Combine all ingredients in saucepan; cook until thoroughly heated. Makes 1 serving. Serve at mealtime only.

Each serving is equivalent to: ⅔ serving Something Extra (½ cup stock); 1 serving Choice Group

Boiled Corn

Drop 6 medium ears of husked corn into a large kettle of boiling salted water. Return water to boil, and cook corn about 5 minutes. Drain. Serve hot with 1 teaspoon margarine for each ear. Sprinkle with salt, if desired. Makes 6 servings, 1 ear of corn each. Serve at mealtime only.

Each serving is equivalent to: 1 serving Choice Group; 1 serving Fat

"Cream" of Corn Soup

1 tablespoon margarine	Dash pepper and paprika
2 ounces finely diced onion	1 cup skim milk
1 tablespoon flour	1 cup canned cream style corn
⅛ teaspoon salt	1 tablespoon chopped fresh chives

Melt margarine in top of double boiler over boiling water. Add onion and cook 4 minutes or until tender. Stir in flour, salt, pepper, and paprika. Gradually add milk, and cook, stirring constantly, until thickened. Add corn; cook 5 minutes, stirring frequently. Sprinkle with chives. Divide evenly. Makes 2 servings. Serve at mealtime only.

Each serving is equivalent to: 1½ servings Fat; 1 ounce Limited Vegetable; 1½ servings Something Extra (1½ teaspoons flour); ½ serving Milk (½ cup skim milk); 1 serving Choice Group

Mamaliga

Rumanians adore this robust mush. It may be used as a breakfast cereal or served as a meat accompaniment in place of bread.

4 ounces dry enriched yellow	1 teaspoon salt
cornmeal	3 cups boiling water
1 cup cold water	

In a medium bowl combine cornmeal, cold water, and salt. Gradually pour into boiling water in a medium saucepan, stirring constantly. Return to boil, stirring constantly. Reduce heat; cover. Cook for about 5 minutes, stirring occasionally. For a thicker dish, let stand 5 minutes before serving. Divide evenly. Makes 4 servings. Serve at mealtime only.

Each serving is equivalent to: 1 serving Choice Group or 1 ounce Cereal

Variations:
1. Make a well in each serving of Mamaliga and add 1 ounce crumbled Feta cheese and 1 teaspoon margarine to each portion. Add

garlic powder if desired. Makes 1 morning or midday meal serving. Supplement as required.

Each serving is equivalent to: 1 serving Choice Group; 1 ounce Hard Cheese; 1 serving Fat

2. Stir ⅓ cup cottage cheese into each serving of Mamaliga. Artificial sweetener and cinnamon may be added if desired. Makes 1 morning or midday meal serving. Supplement as required.

Each serving is equivalent to: 1 serving Choice Group; ⅓ cup Soft Cheese

3. Mamaliga may be spooned into a loaf pan. It will mold as it becomes cold. Slice and serve. To reheat Mamaliga, put one serving in individual casserole; top with one portion Ratatouille (see page 291), ½ cup vegetables, or ½ cup tomato sauce, no sugar added. Add 1 ounce hard cheese, if desired. Cover; bake at 375°F. for 20 to 30 minutes. Makes 1 midday meal serving. Supplement as required.

Each serving is equivalent to: 1 serving Choice Group; Ratatouille (see page 291) or ½ cup Vegetables or 1 serving Bonus (½ cup tomato sauce); 1 ounce Hard Cheese (optional)

Spoon Bread

A filling breakfast dish.

2 ounces dry enriched yellow cornmeal
¼ teaspoon salt
½ cup cold water
1 cup boiling water
⅓ cup nonfat dry milk
2 tablespoons flour

Artificial sweetener to equal 2 teaspoons sugar
1 teaspoon baking powder
2 medium eggs, beaten
2 tablespoons imitation (or diet) margarine, melted
¼ cup water

In medium saucepan stir cornmeal and salt into cold water. Add boiling water; cook 5 minutes. Remove from heat. In small bowl, combine remaining dry ingredients. Add eggs, margarine, and water, one at a time, mixing after each addition. Stir into cornmeal mixture. Pour into an 8x8-inch nonstick baking pan. Bake at 425°F. for 25 minutes or until firm. Divide evenly. Makes 2 morning or midday meal servings. Supplement as required.

Each serving is equivalent to: 1 serving Choice Group; ½ serving Milk (½ cup skim milk); 3 servings Something Extra (1 tablespoon flour); 1 Egg; 1½ servings Fat

Tamale Pie

The amount of chili powder you use depends on how spicy you like your food.

1 medium green pepper, seeded and diced	1 teaspoon chili powder or to taste
2 ounces onion, diced	¾ teaspoon salt, divided
1 garlic clove, minced	½ teaspoon oregano
12 ounces cooked ground beef, crumbled, or cooked chicken, julienned	⅛ teaspoon cumin
	Pepper to taste
1 cup tomato sauce, no sugar added	2 ounces dry enriched yellow cornmeal
	½ cup cold water
	1 cup boiling water

Cook green pepper, onion, and garlic in large nonstick skillet until browned. Add beef or chicken and tomato sauce; simmer 5 minutes. Stir in chili powder, ¼ teaspoon salt, oregano, cumin, and pepper. Set aside. In a small saucepan combine cornmeal, cold water, and remaining ½ teaspoon salt. Gradually add boiling water and cook stirring constantly for 5 minutes, or until mixture thickens. Spread half the cornmeal mixture in an 8x8-inch baking pan. Top with tomato sauce mixture and spread with remaining cornmeal. Bake at 350°F. for 30 minutes. Divide evenly. Makes 2 evening meal servings.

Each serving is equivalent to: ¼ cup Vegetables; 1 ounce Limited Vegetable; 6 ounces "Beef" Group or Poultry; 1 serving Bonus (½ cup tomato sauce); 1 serving Choice Group

Cold Kasha or Bulgur Salad

4 ounces dry buckwheat groats
  (kasha) or cracked wheat
  (Bulgur)
4 ounces drained canned water
  chestnuts, sliced
4 ounces cooked peas
1 cup sliced mushrooms
1 medium tomato, peeled, seeded,
  and chopped
½ medium cucumber, pared,
  seeded, and chopped
¼ cup chopped celery
2 ounces scallions, chopped
2 tablespoons chopped fresh
  parsley
1 tablespoon pimento, chopped
Garlic French Dressing (see
  page 302)
Lettuce

Cook buckwheat groats or cracked wheat in boiling salted water to
cover until tender. Drain. Place in bowl. Add remaining ingredients
except lettuce; mix well. Chill. Serve on bed of lettuce. Divide
evenly. Makes 4 servings. Serve at mealtime only.

Each serving is equivalent to: 1 serving Choice Group; 2½ ounces
Limited Vegetable; ½ cup Vegetables; Garlic French Dressing (see
page 302)

Groats and Corn

1 ounce dry buckwheat groats
  (kasha)
1½ cups Chicken Stock (see page
  140)
½ cup drained canned whole
  kernel corn
Salt and pepper to taste
2 teaspoons margarine

In a medium saucepan cook buckwheat groats in boiling Chicken
Stock about 25 minutes or until groats are tender and stock is
absorbed. Stir in corn, salt, and pepper, and heat. Remove from heat
and stir in margarine. Divide evenly. Makes 2 servings. Serve at
mealtime only.

Each serving is equivalent to: 1 serving Choice Group; 1 serving
Something Extra (¾ cup stock); 1 serving Fat

Kasha or Bulgur

2 cups water or chicken bouillon	4 ounces dry buckwheat groats
¼ teaspoon salt	(kasha) or cracked wheat
Dash pepper	(Bulgur)

In medium saucepan combine water or bouillon, salt, and pepper. Bring to boil. Slowly stir in groats or cracked wheat. Cover and cook, stirring occasionally, over low heat for 10 to 15 minutes or until liquid is absorbed and grains are tender. Divide evenly. Makes 4 servings. Serve at mealtime only.

Each serving is equivalent to: 1 serving Choice Group; ⅔ serving Something Extra (½ cup bouillon) (optional)

Variations:

Toasted Grains—Lightly brown the buckwheat groats or cracked wheat in a shallow baking pan when the oven is in use. Stir grains so they don't burn. This takes only a few minutes and adds a roasted nutty flavor to the grains. Proceed as in above recipe.

Belila—A favorite Arabic breakfast is cracked wheat cooked until very soft in boiling water with a dash of cinnamon. Just before serving, it is sweetened. (Use artificial sweetener to equal 3 teaspoons sugar for each serving.) Serve with skim milk or plain unflavored yogurt.

Pilaf

Use Beef Stock when serving Pilaf with meat, Chicken Stock when serving it with chicken.

1½ cups Beef or Chicken Stock	1 cup diced celery
(see pages 140, 163)	4 ounces dry buckwheat groats
1 cup diced mushrooms	(kasha) or cracked wheat
1 cup diced carrots	(Bulgur)

In a medium saucepan combine stock and vegetables. Cover and cook for 20 minutes or until vegetables are tender. Remove from heat.

Drain and measure liquid. Add enough water to measure 1½ cups
liquid. Return liquid to saucepan with vegetables. Bring to boil. Add
kasha or Bulgur; lower heat. Cover; cook 10 to 15 minutes or until all
liquid is absorbed. Divide evenly. Makes 4 servings. Serve at mealtime only.

Each serving is equivalent to: ½ serving Something Extra (¼ cup
plus 2 tablespoons stock); ¾ cup Vegetables; 1 serving Choice Group

Quick Kasha Varnishkes

¼ cup plus 2 tablespoons beef
  bouillon
½ ounce dry buckwheat groats
  (kasha)
¼ cup sliced mushrooms

1 ounce diced onion
⅓ cup cooked enriched bow-tie
  macaroni
1 teaspoon vegetable oil or
  margarine (optional)

In a small saucepan bring bouillon to a boil. Add kasha; reduce heat.
Cook until all liquid is absorbed. In a small saucepan brown mushrooms and onion. Add kasha mixture and macaroni. Reheat, adding
1 or 2 tablespoons water, if necessary. Remove from heat. Stir in oil or
margarine, if desired. Serve hot. Makes 1 serving. Serve at mealtime
only.

Each serving is equivalent to: ½ serving Something Extra (¼ cup
plus 2 tablespoons bouillon); 1 serving Choice Group; ¼ cup Vegetables; 1 ounce Limited Vegetable; 1 serving Fat (optional)

Hominy Grits Three Ways

1. That old Southern favorite, grits, like groats, is a word that
stems from the Old English word for sand. Hominy grits is made from
white or yellow corn, and you can buy regular or quick-cooking grits.
Prepare it according to package directions and, when thick and
creamy, measure ¾ cup per serving. Generally 3 to 4 tablespoons dry
will make the right amount for each serving.

2. *Grits and Greens:* Steam 1 cup washed collard, dandelion, kale,
kohlrabi, mustard, spinach, or turnip greens until soft. Season with
imitation bacon-flavored salt and serve with ¾ cup cooked enriched

hominy grits. Delicious as a side dish for pork. Makes 1 serving. Serve at mealtime only.

Each serving is equivalent to: 1 cup Vegetables; 1 serving Choice Group.

3. *Baked Grits and Cheese Casserole:* For each serving, transfer ¾ cup cooked enriched hominy grits to individual serving casserole, stir in ¼ cup evaporated skimmed milk, and top with 2 ounces grated Swiss, Cheddar, or Parmesan cheese. Bake at 350°F. for 30 to 35 minutes or until top is brown and bubbly. Makes 1 midday meal serving.

Each serving is equivalent to: 1 serving Choice Group; ½ serving Milk (¼ cup evaporated skimmed milk); 2 ounces Hard Cheese

Cooking Noodles

Noodles are egg pasta that are softer than macaroni, cook faster, and do not expand much during cooking. Prepare pasta according to package directions.

Variations on Basic Noodles:

1. Combine ½ cup hot cooked enriched noodles, ⅓ cup cottage cheese, 1 tablespoon margarine, 1 teaspoon toasted poppy seeds, and a dash each of Worcestershire sauce, salt, pepper, and paprika. Makes 1 midday meal serving. Supplement as required.

Each serving is equivalent to: 1 serving Choice Group; ⅓ cup Soft Cheese; 3 servings Fat; 1 serving Something Extra (1 teaspoon poppy seeds)

2. Combine ½ cup hot cooked enriched noodles with 2 ounces cooked diced onions and 2 tablespoons evaporated skimmed milk. Makes 1 serving. Serve at mealtime only.

Each serving is equivalent to: 1 serving Choice Group; 2 ounces Limited Vegetable; ¼ serving Milk (2 tablespoons evaporated skimmed milk)

3. Toss ½ cup hot cooked enriched noodles with 1½ ounces ham and 1 ounce grated hard cheese. Makes 1 midday meal serving.

Each serving is equivalent to: 1 serving Choice Group; 1½ ounces "Beef" Group (cured); 1 ounce Hard Cheese

4. Toss ½ cup hot cooked enriched noodles with ½ cup cooked chopped spinach, ¼ cup plain unflavored yogurt, and 1 teaspoon chives. Makes 1 serving. Serve at mealtime only.

Each serving is equivalent to: 1 serving Choice Group; ½ cup Vegetables; ½ serving Milk (¼ cup yogurt)

5. Combine ½ cup hot cooked enriched noodles with 1 cup cooked chopped broccoli, ⅓ cup cottage cheese, and 2 tablespoons minced fresh parsley. Makes 1 midday meal serving. Supplement as required.

Each serving is equivalent to: 1 serving Choice Group; 1 cup plus 2 tablespoons Vegetables; ⅓ cup Soft Cheese

6. Arrange ½ cup cooked enriched noodles in small baking pan. Dot with 2 teaspoons margarine. Bake at 350°F. until brown. Makes 1 serving. Serve at mealtime only.

Each serving is equivalent to: 1 serving Choice Group; 2 servings Fat

7. Leftover noodles need not go down the drain or down your hatch. Combine ¼ cup cooked enriched noodles with ½ serving of cooked kasha, barley, enriched rice (see "Rules for Using Choice Group, page 98) . . . or whatever Choice your refrigerator affords. Stir into ¾ cup Chicken Stock (see page 140) or water with dissolved bouillon cube. Season to taste, if desired; freeze in small containers. Reheat in small saucepan as a hearty first course for midday or evening meal. As part of the morning meal, serve hot with ½ cup skim milk or ¼ cup evaporated skimmed milk. Makes 1 serving. Serve at mealtime only.

Each serving is equivalent to: *Midday or Evening Meal*—1 serving Choice Group; 1 serving Something extra (¾ cup stock). *Morning Meal*—1 serving Choice Group; 1 serving Something Extra (¾ cup stock); ½ serving Milk (½ cup skim milk or ¼ cup evaporated skimmed milk)

Baked Macaroni, Cheese, and Cauliflower Casserole

2 cups cooked cauliflower florets
1⅓ cups cooked enriched elbow
   macaroni
½ cup canned mushroom stems
   and pieces

Salt and white pepper to taste
Creamy Cheese Sauce (see
   page 65)
Paprika to garnish

In a medium bowl combine all ingredients except paprika. Transfer to a 1-quart shallow casserole. Sprinkle with paprika. Cover; bake at 350°F. for 30 minutes. Uncover and bake 5 minutes longer or until top begins to brown. Divide evenly. Makes 2 midday meal servings. Supplement as required.

Each serving is equivalent to: 1¼ cups Vegetables; 1 serving Choice Group; Creamy Cheese Sauce (see page 65)

Cold Ditalini Salad

2⅔ cups cooked enriched ditalini
   or other small tube macaroni,
   chilled
¼ cup skim milk
4 ounces diced red onion
1 medium tomato, diced
1 medium green pepper, seeded
   and diced
1 medium dill pickle, diced,
   reserve 2 teaspoons brine

½ cup imitation mayonnaise
¾ cup plus 2 tablespoons plain
   unflavored yogurt
1 packet instant beef broth and
   seasoning mix
1 garlic clove, minced
¼ teaspoon salt
⅛ teaspoon white pepper
Chopped fresh dill or chives to
   garnish

Place ditalini in a large bowl and moisten with milk. Add diced vegetables and pickle. In a small bowl combine mayonnaise, yogurt, reserved pickle brine, broth mix, garlic, salt, and pepper. Pour over ditalini mixture and toss to combine. Cover and refrigerate until chilled. Sprinkle with dill or chives. Divide evenly. Makes 4 servings. Serve at mealtime only.

Each serving is equivalent to: 1 serving Choice Group; ½ serving

Milk (1 tablespoon skim milk and 3½ tablespoons yogurt); 1 ounce Limited Vegetable; ¼ cup plus 2 tablespoons Vegetables; 3 servings Fat; ¼ serving Something Extra (¼ packet broth mix)

Noodle, Cheese, and Prune Pudding

Cook the prunes with very little water so that when they are done, most of the liquid has evaporated, otherwise some of the sweet natural flavor of the fruit is lost in the liquid. We want it to stay in the fruit.

¾ cup skim milk
6 dried medium prunes, cooked,
    pitted, and diced
Artificial sweetener to equal 2
    tablespoons sugar

1 tablespoon flour
¼ teaspoon cinnamon
3 cups cooked enriched noodles
2 cups cottage cheese

In a medium bowl combine milk, prunes, sweetener, flour, and cinnamon. Set aside. Combine noodles and cottage cheese in a large bowl and transfer to a 10x6x1¾-inch baking dish. Pour prune mixture over noodles. Bake at 375°F. for about 1 hour or until hot and bubbly. Divide evenly. Makes 6 midday meal servings. Supplement as required.

Each serving is equivalent to: ⅛ serving Milk (2 tablespoons skim milk); ¼ serving Fruit; ½ serving Something Extra (½ teaspoon flour); 1 serving Choice Group; ⅓ cup Soft Cheese

Pasta Alfredo-Style

Cook the pasta firm (al dente), and drain well. If the pasta is going to be used immediately, it is not necessary to rinse.

2 tablespoons margarine
¼ cup plain unflavored yogurt
2 ounces Parmesan cheese, grated
2 ounces Cheddar cheese, diced

2⅔ cups cooked enriched linguine
    or spaghetti
Salt and freshly ground pepper to
    taste

Melt margarine in the top of a double boiler over hot water. Add the yogurt and cheese. Cook until cheese melts; add linguine or spaghetti. Mix well and season with salt and pepper. Serve hot. Divide evenly. Makes 4 midday meal servings. Supplement as required.

Each serving is equivalent to: 1½ servings Fat; ⅛ serving Milk (1 tablespoon yogurt); 1 ounce Hard Cheese; 1 serving Choice Group

Tips on Cooking Potatoes

Gently scrub potatoes under running water with a vegetable brush or cellulose sponge.

Here are some tips on cooking potatoes which will help to prevent the loss of nutritional value:

1. When boiling, use as little water as possible.
2. Steaming potatoes is an excellent way to conserve their nutrients.
3. Leave skin on potatoes during cooking.
4. If potatoes are pared before cooking, use a vegetable parer, removing as thin a layer of skin as possible, since many of the nutrients are found close to the skin.
5. Pared potatoes turn dark if not cooked right away. To keep them white, toss with a little lemon juice. Soaking in a bowl of cold water is not recommended as this usually results in a loss of vitamins.

Baked Potatoes

Pierce the skin of each 3-ounce potato in several places with the tines of a fork. This allows steam to escape and prevents the potato from bursting. Bake potatoes directly on oven rack or use a baking sheet. Oven temperature can range from 325°F. to 450°F. Potatoes are done when they feel soft. Baked potatoes can be wrapped in foil, frozen and reheated at 350°F. for 1 hour. Serve at mealtime only. One potato is equivalent to 1 serving Choice Group.

Boiled Potatoes

In a covered saucepan cook potatoes in about 1 inch of salted water until tender. Check occasionally and add more water if necessary. Whole potatoes will take 30 to 40 minutes, cut up, 20 to 25 minutes. Weigh and serve 3-ounce portions. Serve at mealtime only. Each portion is equivalent to 1 serving Choice Group.

Roast Potatoes

Prepare boiled potatoes and peel, or use drained canned potatoes. Pat dry and arrange in shallow nonstick baking pan; season with salt, pepper, and paprika, and bake at 425°F., turning occasionally until brown. Weigh and serve 3-ounce portions. Serve at mealtime only. Each portion is equivalent to 1 serving Choice Group.

Creamy Baked Potatoes

6 baked potatoes, 3 ounces each   **½ teaspoon salt or to taste**
¾ cup buttermilk   **Dash white pepper**
1 tablespoon chives   **Paprika to garnish**
1½ teaspoons margarine, melted

Cut baked potatoes in half lengthwise. From one half of each, scoop out pulp, leaving a thin shell that maintains its shape. From other half, scoop out all the pulp and discard skin. In bowl mash pulp and add remaining ingredients except paprika. Divide evenly and spoon into shells; sprinkle with paprika. Place on a baking sheet, bake at 350°F. for 25 minutes or until hot. Serve immediately. Makes 6 servings. Serve at mealtime only.

Each serving is equivalent to: 1 serving Choice Group; ¹/₆ serving Milk (2 tablespoons buttermilk); ¼ serving Fat

Creamy Curried Potato Soup

Here's a recipe that calls for using the liquid left from boiling potatoes. This recipe may be used only if the boiled potatoes are being consumed at the same meal. (See recipes for Boiled Potatoes, page 112, and Pureed Potatoes, page 115)

1 cup potato liquid	**½ teaspoon curry powder**
¼ medium banana, mashed	**2 tablespoons evaporated skimmed**
¼ cup minced celery and leaves	**milk**
1 packet instant chicken broth and	**Chopped chives and parsley to**
seasoning mix	**garnish**

In a small saucepan combine potato liquid, banana, celery, broth mix, and curry powder. Cover and cook 25 minutes or until celery is soft. Add more water if necessary. Process in blender container until pureed. Add milk and chill. Serve garnished with chives and parsley. Makes 1 serving. Serve at mealtime only.

Each serving is equivalent to: ½ serving Fruit; ¼ cup Vegetables; 1 serving Something Extra (1 packet broth mix); ¼ serving Milk (2 tablespoons evaporated skimmed milk)

Hot German Potato Salad

An old-time favorite.

1½ cups Ham Stock (see page 163)	**¼ cup cider vinegar**
½ cup water	**Artificial sweetener to equal 4**
1½ pounds pared potatoes, cut in	**teaspoons sugar**
¼ inch slices	**1½ teaspoons salt**
4 ounces onion, diced	**½ teaspoon celery seed**
1 celery rib, diced	**¼ teaspoon pepper**
1 tablespoon flour	

In medium saucepan, bring stock and water to boil. Add potatoes; cook until tender but still firm. Using a slotted spoon, remove potatoes from stock; set aside. Add onion and celery to stock. Cook until vegetables are tender and stock is reduced to approximately ½ cup. In measuring cup dissolve flour in vinegar; add sweetener and seasonings. Stir into stock in saucepan; cook until thickened. Pour over potatoes and toss gently. Serve at once. Divide evenly. Makes 8 servings. Serve at mealtime only.

Each serving is equivalent to: ⅝ serving Something Extra (3 tablespoons stock and ⅜ teaspoon flour); 1 serving Choice Group; ½ ounce Limited Vegetable; 1½ teaspoons Vegetables

Oven-Baked Potato Fans (in foil)

Make this when your oven is in use. For each serving, place a 3-ounce scrubbed potato on a board and with a sharp knife, slice down at ¼-inch intervals, almost through to the bottom. Place each potato on a square of heavy-duty aluminum foil. For each potato melt 1 teaspoon margarine in a small flameproof container. Remove from heat; add salt, pepper, chives, and paprika to taste. Brush one portion mixture into slices of each potato. Wrap tightly in foil. Bake at 400°F. about 45 minutes or until potato is tender. Open at the table and eat right out of the foil. Serve at mealtime only.

Each serving is equivalent to: 1 serving Choice Group; 1 serving Fat

Potato Kugel

6 ounces grated potato	1½ ounces grated onion
2 medium eggs	½ teaspoon salt
1 tablespoon plus 1 teaspoon margarine, melted	⅛ teaspoon baking powder
	Dash white pepper

Place potato in strainer and squeeze out excess moisture. In bowl beat eggs until thick. Stir in potatoes and remaining ingredients. Place in a shallow 1-pint casserole which has been treated with a release agent. Bake at 350°F. for 50 minutes or until golden. Divide evenly. Makes 2 midday meal servings. Supplement as required.

Each serving is equivalent to: 1 serving Choice Group; 1 Egg; 2 servings Fat; ¾ ounce Limited Vegetable

Potato Yogurt Salad

1 cup plain unflavored yogurt	1 medium cucumber, pared and
2 teaspoons prepared mustard	sliced
2 teaspoons prepared white	½ cup thinly sliced celery
horseradish	2 tablespoons dehydrated onion
1½ pounds peeled, cooked	flakes, reconstituted
potatoes, cubed	1 tablespoon chopped fresh chives

In a small bowl combine yogurt, mustard, and horseradish. Combine remaining ingredients in a large bowl. Pour yogurt mixture over salad and toss to combine. Refrigerate until chilled. Divide evenly. Makes 8 servings. Serve at mealtime only.

Each serving is equivalent to: ¼ serving Milk (2 tablespoons yogurt); 1 serving Choice Group; 2 tablespoons Vegetables

Pureed Potatoes

For a planned leftover, you can boil extra potatoes and put them through food mill or potato ricer, then freeze in 3-ounce patties and reheat on foil with oven meal.

1 pound 2 ounces pared potatoes	3 tablespoons margarine at room
1¼ teaspoons salt, divided	temperature
¾ cup skim milk	Dash nutmeg or to taste

Slice or quarter potatoes and place in saucepan. Add boiling water to cover and 1 teaspoon salt. Return to a boil, lower heat, and simmer 20 minutes or until potatoes are tender. Drain; reserve liquid, if desired, to use for Creamy Curried Potato Soup (see page 113) at same meal. Put potatoes through food mill or potato ricer. Heat milk in a medium saucepan. Slowly stir in potatoes. Continue stirring until heated throughout. Remove from heat; stir in margarine, remaining ¼ teaspoon salt, and nutmeg. Divide evenly. Makes 6 servings. Serve at mealtime only.

Each serving is equivalent to: 1 serving Choice Group; ⅛ serving Milk (2 tablespoons skim milk); 1½ servings Fat

Variation: Cook 3 cups shredded cabbage or cauliflower florets in boiling salted water to cover until very tender, about 20 minutes. Drain and combine with Pureed Potatoes. Season with additional salt and sprinkle with white pepper. A treat with ham or roast beef. Divide evenly. Makes 6 servings. Serve at mealtime only. Add ½ cup Vegetables to equivalent listing.

Basic Rice

Rice may be cooked on top of stove or in the oven; cooking times and amounts will vary according to the brand of rice; however, follow package directions. When cooked, be sure to measure ½-cup servings. Here's one cooking method.

3 cups water
1 cup uncooked enriched rice
1 teaspoon salt

In saucepan combine all ingredients. Bring to boil; reduce heat, cover and simmer 20 to 30 minutes. Remove from heat and let stand 15 to 20 minutes. Measure ½ cup cooked rice for each serving. Serve at mealtime only.

Each serving is equivalent to: 1 serving Choice Group

Reheating—Combine 1 cup cooked enriched rice with 2 tablespoons water in saucepan. Cover and cook over low heat for 4 minutes or until thoroughly heated. Divide evenly. Makes 2 servings. Serve at mealtime only.

Each serving is equivalent to: 1 serving Choice Group

Brown Rice—Use the same measurements as in basic recipe. Simmer, covered, 45 minutes or until all water is absorbed. Measure ½ cup cooked brown rice for each serving. Serve at mealtime only. To reheat, follow preceding method.

Each serving is equivalent to: 1 serving Choice Group

Curried Rice and Prune Salad

1 cup cooked enriched rice
1 teaspoon lemon juice
1 teaspoon vegetable oil
½ teaspoon curry powder
1 medium green pepper, seeded
 and diced fine
8 dried medium prunes, cooked,
 pitted, and diced

½ cup plain unflavored yogurt
2 tablespoons imitation
 mayonnaise
Salt to taste
Salad greens

Combine all ingredients, except greens, in bowl in order given. Mix well; press mixture gently into a 2-cup mold; chill. Unmold on plate. Surround with greens. Divide evenly. Makes 2 servings. Serve at mealtime only.

Each serving is equivalent to: 1 serving Choice Group; 2 servings Fat; ¼ cup Vegetables; 1 serving Fruit; ½ serving Milk (¼ cup yogurt)

Crunchy Tangerine Salad

1 cup cooked enriched rice
2 large tangerines, peeled and
 sectioned
2 ounces cooked peas

2 ounces drained, canned water
 chestnuts, diced
Tangy French Dressing
 (see page 337)
Salt to taste

Combine all ingredients in bowl in order given. Divide evenly. Makes 2 servings. Serve at mealtime only.

Each serving is equivalent to: 1 serving Choice Group; 1 serving Fruit; 2 ounces Limited Vegetable; Tangy French Dressing (see page 337)

Minted Rice

Serve with lamb.

2 cups cooked enriched rice
1 tablespoon chopped fresh
  parsley
2 teaspoons finely chopped fresh
  mint leaves or 1 teaspoon dried
  mint

Salt to taste
2 teaspoons margarine

In a medium saucepan combine rice, parsley, mint, and salt. Cook, stirring constantly, until heated through. Add a little water if necessary to prevent sticking. Remove from heat, stir in margarine. Divide evenly. Makes 4 servings. Serve at mealtime only.

Each serving is equivalent to: 1 serving Choice Group; ½ serving Fat

Mushroom Risotto

½ cup dried mushrooms
6 ounces onions, diced
½ teaspoon saffron

Salt and pepper to taste
3 cups cooked enriched rice

In bowl soak mushrooms in hot water to cover for 20 minutes. Drain and reserve liquid. Cut off and discard stems; chop mushroom caps. Brown onion in preheated nonstick skillet. Add chopped mushrooms and mushroom liquid, saffron, salt, and pepper. Heat to evaporate liquid. Stir in rice and reheat. Divide evenly. Makes 6 servings. Serve at mealtime only.

Each serving is equivalent to: 1 tablespoon plus 1 teaspoon Vegetables; 1 ounce Limited Vegetable; 1 serving Choice Group

Toasted Rice and Vermicelli

For a nutty flavor, start with ½ pound of uncooked enriched white rice (about 1 cup). Spread rice in a thin layer in a shallow baking pan. Bake at 350°F. to 425°F. whenever oven is on, for 10 to 20 minutes or until rice is brown. Store in airtight container and cook, following package directions, just as you would regular enriched white rice.

Break ½ pound uncooked enriched vermicelli or fine egg noodles (about 2½ cups) into ½-inch lengths. Follow above instructions for toasting. Check frequently, as this burns easily. When ready to cook, follow package directions for regular enriched vermicelli or egg noodles.

4 ounces onion, diced
1 garlic clove, minced
1⅓ cups cooked enriched
  vermicelli, made from toasted
  vermicelli (see above)
1 cup cooked enriched rice, made
  from toasted rice (see above)

¼ cup plus 2 tablespoons Chicken
  Stock (see page 140)
3 tablespoons chopped fresh
  parsley

In preheated saucepan brown the onion and garlic, stirring to prevent scorching. Add vermicelli, rice, Chicken Stock, and parsley. Simmer uncovered until mixture is almost dry, stirring occasionally. Divide evenly. Makes 4 servings. Serve at mealtime only.

Each serving is equivalent to: 1 ounce Limited Vegetable; 1 serving Choice Group; ⅛ serving Something Extra (1½ tablespoons stock)

Basic Wild Rice

4 cups water
1 teaspoon salt

1 cup uncooked wild rice

In saucepan bring water and salt to a boil. Stir in rice and return to boil. Reduce heat, cover and simmer about 40 minutes or until tender.

Do not overcook; drain any excess liquid. Measure ½ cup cooked rice for each serving. Serve at mealtime only.

Each serving is equivalent to: 1 serving Choice Group

Ham and Wild Rice Salad

A delicious midday meal using leftovers.

½ cup cooked wild rice or
  enriched white rice
½ teaspoon cider vinegar
Salt and pepper to taste
1 tablespoon mayonnaise
2 ounces cooked green peas

1½ ounces ham, diced
1 ounce Cheddar cheese, grated,
  or 1 medium egg, hard-cooked
  and chopped
1 tablespoon chopped dill pickle
1 teaspoon minced chives

In bowl combine rice, vinegar, salt, and pepper. Stir in mayonnaise. Add remaining ingredients; toss. Chill. Makes 1 midday meal serving.

Each serving is equivalent to: 1 serving Choice Group; 3 servings Fat; 2 ounces Limited Vegetable; 1½ ounces "Beef" Group (cured); 1 ounce Hard Cheese or 1 Egg; 1 tablespoon Vegetables

Traditional Wild Rice Stuffing

Serve with Cornish hens or chicken.

½ cup sliced mushrooms
½ medium green pepper, chopped
¼ cup chopped celery
2 ounces chopped onion

¾ cup chicken bouillon
4 cups cooked wild rice
1 teaspoon sage

In medium saucepan cook mushrooms, green pepper, celery, and onion in bouillon until soft. Add wild rice and sage; mix well. Transfer to 1½-quart baking dish and bake at 350°F. for ½ hour. Divide evenly. Makes 8 servings. Serve at mealtime only.

Each serving is equivalent to: 2 tablespoons Vegetables; ¼ ounce Limited Vegetable; ⅛ serving Something Extra (1½ tablespoons bouillon); 1 serving Choice Group

Wild Rice Casserole

Wild rice, the grain of a water reed, has a unique flavor. Use it by itself if you're feeling extravagant, or stretch it by mixing it with cooked brown rice, cooked Bulgur, or cooked egg noodles. For seasonings try dried chives, parsley, or marjoram.

2 cups cooked wild rice
2 cups sliced mushrooms
2 teaspoons flour
½ cup skim milk
1 teaspoon dehydrated onion
** flakes, reconstituted in 2**
** teaspoons water**

1 small bay leaf
¼ teaspoon thyme
Dash nutmeg
Salt and pepper to taste
½ cup Chicken Stock* (optional,
** see page 140)**

In a 1½-quart flameproof casserole combine wild rice and mushrooms. Sprinkle with flour and mix well. In small saucepan, scald milk with onion flakes and bay leaf. Remove and discard bay leaf; add milk to mushroom-rice mixture. Cook, stirring often, until rice mixture thickens slightly. Season with thyme, nutmeg, salt, and pepper. Bake at 350°F. for 15 to 20 minutes. To adjust consistency, add stock if desired. Serve hot. Divide evenly. Makes 4 servings. Serve at mealtime only.

Each serving is equivalent to: 1 serving Choice Group; ½ cup Vegetables; ½ serving Something Extra (½ teaspoon flour); ⅛ serving Milk (2 tablespoons skim milk)

*Note: If Chicken Stock is used, add an additional ⅙ serving Something Extra (2 tablespoons stock) to equivalent listing.

MILK

Milk shakes? Mousses? Puddings? The names sound sinful on the Weight Watchers Food Program—but they're all here, prepared our way, with lots of scintillating flavors. So don't pass them up!

You won't want to anyway, when you see how we've catered to your tastes, with recipes such as Peach Drink, Apple-Strawberry Chiffon, Brandylike Alexander. We even give you the how-to of making yogurt at home, with ribbons of fruit folded in for the perfect snack food.

Rules for Using Milk

1. Amounts
     Women and Men: 2 servings daily
     Youth: 3 to 4 servings daily
2. Select servings at any time:
     milk, skim, 1 cup (8 fluid ounces)
     milk, evaporated skimmed, ½ cup (4 fluid ounces)
     buttermilk, ¾ cup (6 fluid ounces)
     yogurt, plain, unflavored, ½ cup (4 fluid ounces)
3. The skim milk we allow is the instant nonfat dry milk, reconstituted according to label directions; or skim milk labeled either "skimmed milk" or "modified" or "fortified skim milk," with no whole milk solids added. Do not use milk labeled "a skimmed milk product" or "99% fat free."
4. You may use your milk at any time—at meals, as snacks, in coffee or tea, or in our popular milk shakes and whipped toppings—but you must consume the amount allotted to you in your Menu Plan.

transfer to blender container and process until smooth. Divide
evenly. Makes 2 servings.

Each serving is equivalent to: 1 serving Something Extra (1 teaspoon cocoa); 1 serving Milk (1 cup skim milk)

Chocolate Milk Shake

cup skim milk	½ teaspoon instant coffee
artificial sweetener to equal 2	½ teaspoon vanilla extract
teaspoons sugar	3 ice cubes
1½ teaspoons unsweetened cocoa	

Combine all ingredients except ice cubes in blender container; process until frothy. Add ice cubes one at a time, processing after each
addition. Serve in tall glass. Makes 1 serving.

Each serving is equivalent to: 1 serving Milk (1 cup skim milk); 1½
servings Something Extra (1½ teaspoons cocoa)

Variations:

Double-Strength Milk Shake—Use ⅔ cup nonfat dry milk and 1 cup
water to replace 1 cup skim milk. Continue as above. Extract may be
varied to taste. Add 1 serving Milk (1 cup skim milk) to equivalent
listing.

Super Milk Shake—Use ⅓ cup nonfat dry milk and 1 cup any flavor
dietetic soda in place of 1 cup skim milk. Extract and sweetener
may be omitted. Proceed as in basic recipe.

Fruit Shake—Omit cocoa and coffee from basic recipe. Add one of
the following: ½ medium banana, 1 cup strawberries, ½ cup blueberries, 1 medium peach, pitted, or any other desired fruit (see "Fruit
Servings," page 20). Process as in basic recipe above. Each serving is
equivalent to 1 serving Milk (1 cup skim milk); 1 serving Fruit

Orange Shake—Process, in blender container, the following: 1 cup
skim milk, ½ cup orange juice, 1 small orange, peeled and cut up, 2
tablespoons lemon juice, artificial sweetener to equal 2 teaspoons
sugar, and 4 ice cubes. Divide evenly. Makes 2 servings.

Each serving is equivalent to: ½ serving Milk (½ cup skim milk); 1
serving Fruit

5. Mix-and-match your milk, if you like. For example,
   use 1 serving skim milk (1 cup) and 1 serving evapor
   milk (½ cup) to complete the daily requirement.

Brandylike Alexander

½ cup water
⅓ cup nonfat dry milk
1½ teaspoons brandy or rum
  extract

Artificial sweetener to
  teaspoons sugar or t
4 to 5 ice cubes
Nutmeg to taste

Combine all ingredients except nutmeg in blender containe
until frothy. Divide evenly into two stemmed glasses. Top
dash of nutmeg. Makes 2 servings.
  Each serving is equivalent to: ½ serving Milk (½ cup sk

Cappuccino Chiller

2 cups double-strength coffee
2 cups skim milk

Cinnamon to taste
8 cinnamon sticks

Refrigerate coffee in a large container for 30 minutes. Add mil
Divide evenly into 8 tall glasses. Add ice if desired. Sprinkle ea
cinnamon and garnish each with a cinnamon stick. Makes 8 ser
  Each serving is equivalent to: ¼ serving Milk (¼ cup skim

Hot Chocolate

1½ cups water
2 teaspoons unsweetened cocoa
⅔ cup nonfat dry milk

Artificial sweetener to equal 8
  teaspoons sugar

Bring water to a boil in small saucepan; stir in cocoa until dissolv
Remove from heat. Stir in remaining ingredients, using a wire whi

Peach Drink

½ cup canned sliced peaches, no
   sugar added
⅓ cup evaporated skimmed milk

2 tablespoons orange-flavored
   dietetic soda

Combine all ingredients in blender container. Process until well blended, about 20 seconds. Serve in a tall glass, over ice. Makes 1 serving.

Each serving is equivalent to: 1 serving Fruit; ⅔ serving Milk (⅓ cup evaporated skimmed milk)

Tangy Strawberry Shake

¾ cup buttermilk
½ cup strawberries

Artificial sweetener to equal 2
   teaspoons sugar (optional)
¼ teaspoon lemon juice

Combine all ingredients in blender container. Process until smooth. Pour into a tall glass. Serve immediately. Makes 1 serving.

Each serving is equivalent to: 1 serving Milk (¾ cup buttermilk); ½ serving Fruit

Tiger Tiger

¾ cup skim milk
2 tablespoons frozen orange juice
   concentrate
1 tablespoon plus 1 teaspoon
   nonfat dry milk

1 teaspoon safflower oil
½ teaspoon vanilla extract
3 ice cubes (optional)

Combine all ingredients except ice cubes in blender container and process at low speed. If desired, add ice cubes, one at a time, and process until smooth. Divide evenly. Makes 2 servings. Serve at mealtime only.

Each serving is equivalent to: ½ serving Milk (½ cup skim milk); ½ serving Fruit; ½ serving Fat

Apple-Berry Cheese Mousse

2 envelopes unflavored gelatin
¼ cup cold water
¼ cup boiling water
1⅓ cups cottage cheese
¾ cup buttermilk
2 slices enriched white bread

2 medium apples, cored, pared, and quartered
Artificial sweetener to equal 4 to 6 teaspoons sugar
½ cup frozen blueberries, no sugar added

In blender container sprinkle gelatin over cold water to soften. Add boiling water; process until dissolved. Add remaining ingredients except berries, and process until smooth. Pour mixture into 9x9x2-inch baking dish. Top with berries. Place in refrigerator until firm. Divide evenly. Makes 2 midday meal servings.

Each serving is equivalent to: 2 servings Something Extra (1 envelope gelatin); ⅔ cup Soft Cheese; ½ serving Milk (¼ cup plus 2 tablespoons buttermilk); 1 serving Bread; 1½ servings Fruit

Apple-Strawberry Chiffon

1 envelope unflavored gelatin
¼ cup cold water
⅓ cup boiling water
⅔ cup nonfat dry milk
½ cup whole strawberries (reserve 2 strawberries)

Artificial sweetener to equal 8 teaspoons sugar
¼ teaspoon strawberry extract
8 to 10 ice cubes
½ medium apple, pared, cored, and diced

In blender container sprinkle gelatin over cold water to soften. Add boiling water; process until dissolved. Add milk, strawberries, sweetener, and extract. Process until smooth. Add ice cubes, two at a time, processing after each addition. Fold apple into mixture; divide evenly into 2 dessert glasses. Top each with a whole strawberry and chill. Makes 2 servings.

Each serving is equivalent to: 1 serving Something Extra (½ envelope gelatin); 1 serving Milk (1 cup skim milk); ½ serving Fruit

Blackberry Pudding

1 envelope unflavored gelatin
¼ cup cold water
¼ cup boiling water
1 cup fresh or frozen blackberries
or blueberries, no sugar added,
divided

½ cup buttermilk
Artificial sweetener to equal 8
teaspoons sugar
Few drops lemon or vanilla
extract

In blender container sprinkle gelatin over cold water to soften. Add boiling water and process until dissolved. Add ½ cup berries and remaining ingredients; process until smooth. Fold in remaining berries. Divide evenly into 2 dessert glasses. Chill. Makes 2 servings.

Each serving is equivalent to: 1 serving Something Extra (½ envelope gelatin); 1 serving Fruit; ⅓ serving Milk (¼ cup buttermilk)

Cinnamon Peach Creme

2 teaspoons unflavored gelatin
½ cup skim milk
Artificial sweetener to equal 6
teaspoons sugar

1 medium peach, pitted and diced
½ teaspoon brandy extract
¼ cup evaporated skimmed milk
Dash cinnamon

In saucepan sprinkle gelatin over milk to soften; add sweetener. Heat, stirring constantly, until gelatin has dissolved. DO NOT BOIL. Remove from heat; add peach and extract. Cool. Beat evaporated skimmed milk with rotary beater until stiff peaks form; fold immediately into peach mixture. Pour into small mold; sprinkle with cinnamon and chill for 1 hour. Makes 1 serving.

Each serving is equivalent to: 1⅓ servings Something Extra (2 teaspoons gelatin); 1 serving Milk (½ cup skim milk and ¼ cup evaporated skimmed milk); 1 serving Fruit

Flan l'Orange

1 cup evaporated skimmed milk
1 cup water
4 medium eggs
½ teaspoon orange rind

¼ teaspoon cinnamon
⅛ teaspoon nutmeg
Brown sugar substitute to equal
2 tablespoons brown sugar

Scald milk in a saucepan, remove from heat, allow to stand for a few minutes. Add remaining ingredients. Beat until mixture is frothy. Divide evenly into 4 individual ovenproof custard cups. Place in a shallow pan containing 1 inch water. Bake at 350°F. about 25 minutes or until a knife inserted comes out clean. Makes 4 morning or midday meal servings. Supplement as required.

Each serving is equivalent to: ½ serving Milk (¼ cup evaporated skimmed milk); 1 Egg

Frozen Dessert

1 envelope unflavored gelatin
¼ cup cold water
¼ cup boiling water
⅓ cup nonfat dry milk

Artificial sweetener to equal 6
    teaspoons sugar or to taste
½ teaspoon vanilla or other
    extract
6 to 8 ice cubes

In blender container sprinkle gelatin over water to soften. Add boiling water; process to dissolve gelatin. Add milk, sweetener, and extract. Process until smooth. Add ice cubes, one at a time, processing after each addition. Makes 1 serving.

Each serving is equivalent to: 2 servings Something Extra (1 envelope gelatin); 1 serving Milk (1 cup skim milk)

Frozen Peach Parfait

1 cup evaporated skimmed milk
½ cup water
2 medium eggs, beaten
½ teaspoon vanilla extract

Artificial sweetener to equal 8
    teaspoons sugar
2 medium peaches, peeled and
    pitted

In bowl combine milk and water; pour 1 cup of mixture into saucepan and scald. Remove from heat. Stir in beaten eggs. Return to low heat; cook, stirring constantly until thickened. Remove from heat and pour into blender container. Add remaining milk mixture, vanilla, artificial sweetener, and 1 peach. Process until smooth. Dice remaining peach; add to mixture. Pour into freezer trays and freeze until almost firm. Remove from freezer; transfer to bowl and beat. Serve immediately. Makes 2 midday meal servings. Supplement as required.

Each serving is equivalent to: 1 serving Milk (½ cup evaporated skimmed milk); 1 Egg; 1 serving Fruit

Hawaiian Mousse

2 envelopes unflavored gelatin
1½ cups water, divided
1½ cups evaporated skimmed milk
½ teaspoon rum extract
½ teaspoon coconut extract

¼ teaspoon vanilla extract
Artificial sweetener to equal 4 teaspoons sugar
1½ cups canned crushed pineapple, no sugar added

In a medium saucepan sprinkle gelatin over 1 cup water; heat, stirring until gelatin is dissolved. Pour gelatin mixture into blender container; add remaining water, milk, extracts, and sweetener. Process at low speed until smooth. Add pineapple, process at medium speed until smooth. Pour into a 1½-quart mold. Chill. Unmold. Divide evenly. Makes 6 servings.

Each serving is equivalent to: ⅔ serving Something Extra (⅓ envelope gelatin); ½ serving Milk (¼ cup evaporated skimmed milk); ½ serving Fruit.

Hot Lemon Custard

A delicious sauce over fruit.

2 medium eggs, well beaten
Artificial sweetener to equal 2 teaspoons sugar
¼ teaspoon lemon extract

⅓ cup nonfat dry milk
1 cup water
2 Baked Apples (see page 23)

In bowl combine eggs, sweetener, and extract; mix well. Combine milk and water in top of double boiler; heat over boiling water until milk forms tiny bubbles around the edges. Gradually stir milk into beaten eggs. Return to double boiler and heat until mixture thickens. Do not overcook. Divide evenly and serve each portion over one Baked Apple. Makes 2 midday meal servings. Supplement as required.

Each serving is equivalent to: 1 Egg; ½ serving Milk (½ cup skim milk); 1 serving Fruit

Pears with Chocolate Sauce

1 tablespoon plus 1 teaspoon
  unsweetened cocoa
2 tablespoons water
2 teaspoons cornstarch
¾ cup evaporated skimmed milk

Artificial sweetener to equal 4
  teaspoons sugar
12 canned pear halves with ¾ cup
  juice, no sugar added

Combine cocoa, water, and cornstarch in a small saucepan and stir until completely dissolved. Add milk and cook, stirring constantly until mixture comes to a boil. Remove from heat; add sweetener. Cover and chill. Place 2 pear halves and 2 tablespoons juice in each of 6 dessert dishes. Top each with equal amounts of sauce. Makes 6 servings.

Each serving is equivalent to: 1 serving Something Extra (⅔ teaspoon cocoa and ⅓ teaspoon cornstarch); ¼ serving Milk (2 tablespoons evaporated skimmed milk); 1 serving Fruit

Strawberry-Orange Soufflé

1 cup orange juice
½ cup water
1 envelope low-calorie
  strawberry-flavored gelatin (4
  servings)

Artificial sweetener to equal 16
  teaspoons sugar
1 cup evaporated skimmed milk
2 tablespoons lemon juice

Prepare 4 half-cup soufflé or custard dishes with foil collars, about 3 inches high. In medium saucepan combine orange juice and water.

Bring to a boil. Add gelatin and sweetener. Stir to dissolve gelatin. Remove from heat; chill to consistency of unbeaten egg whites. Pour evaporated skimmed milk into freezer tray. Freeze until soft ice crystals form around edges of tray. Transfer to bowl. Whip with rotary beater until foamy, about 1 minute. Add lemon juice and continue to whip until very stiff, about 1 minute longer. Fold into gelatin mixture. Divide evenly into prepared dishes. Chill until set. Carefully remove collars. Makes 4 servings, 1 soufflé each.

Each serving is equivalent to: ½ serving Fruit; ¼ envelope (1 serving) Specialty Food; ½ serving Milk (¼ cup evaporated skimmed milk)

Frozen Horseradish Cubes

1 cup chilled evaporated skimmed
   milk
½ cup prepared white horseradish

1 teaspoon dill weed
Salt and pepper to taste

In medium bowl, whip evaporated skimmed milk until peaks form. Fold in horseradish and seasonings. Pour into ice cube tray. Freeze until firm. Remove from tray and place in freezer container until ready to use. Dice and serve with cold fish. Divide evenly. Makes 8 servings.

Each serving is equivalent to: ¼ serving Milk (2 tablespoons evaporated skimmed milk)

Zucchini Soup

4 cups diced zucchini
4 ounces onion, diced
3 packets instant chicken broth
   and seasoning mix
½ bay leaf

2 cups water
1 cup evaporated skimmed milk
1 teaspoon Worcestershire sauce
Dash nutmeg
Salt and white pepper to taste

In a large saucepan combine zucchini, onion, broth mix and bay leaf. Cook for 10 minutes. Add water. Bring to boil. Lower heat. Simmer 10 minutes. Remove from heat. Discard bay leaf. Place in blender container; process until smooth. Return mixture to saucepan. Bring to a boil. Add milk, Worcestershire and nutmeg. Season to taste. Heat thoroughly but DO NOT BOIL. Divide evenly. Makes 4 servings.

Each serving is equivalent to: 1 cup Vegetables; 1 ounce Limited Vegetable; ¾ serving Something Extra (¾ packet broth mix); ½ serving Milk (¼ cup evaporated skimmed milk)

Homemade Yogurt

3¾ cups plus 2 tablespoons skim milk (or reconstituted nonfat dry milk)

1 tablespoon plain unflavored yogurt

In a large saucepan, heat milk to 110°–115°F. (or lukewarm) over direct heat. (For better control, use the top of a double boiler over boiling water.) Add yogurt and mix very well with a wire whisk. Divide evenly into yogurt-maker containers and process, following manufacturer's instructions. When thick and creamy, place in refrigerator until chilled. Divide evenly. Makes 4 servings.

Each serving is equivalent to: 1 serving Milk (¾ cup plus 3½ tablespoons skim milk and ¾ teaspoon yogurt)

Tips on controlling homemade yogurt: For a less tangy yogurt, refrigerate as soon as it is thick. Check every 2 hours. For tart yogurt, do not refrigerate as promptly.

Cucumber and Yogurt Salad

A cooling salad for a hot summer day. Serve with a barbecued kabob.

2 medium cucumbers, pared, seeded, and diced
1 cup plain unflavored yogurt

1 tablespoon chopped fresh mint
½ garlic clove, minced
¼ teaspoon salt

In bowl combine all ingredients. Divide evenly. Makes 4 servings.

Each serving is equivalent to: ¼ cup Vegetables; ½ serving Milk (¼ cup yogurt)

Labneh

An Israeli treat.

½ cup plain unflavored yogurt	**1 teaspoon dried mint**
1 teaspoon sesame oil	**Dash salt**

Place yogurt in serving dish. Sprinkle with remaining ingredients. Serve chilled as a dip with raw vegetables. Makes 1 serving. Serve at mealtime only.

Each serving is equivalent to: 1 serving Milk (½ cup yogurt); 1 serving Fat

Yogurt Combinations—Delicious Snacks

1. Reserve juice from 1 serving drained, canned fruit, no sugar added. Add fruit, crushed or pureed, to 1 cup plain unflavored yogurt. In saucepan cook reserved fruit juice until reduced to about 1 teaspoon and stir into yogurt mixture. Makes 1 serving.

Each serving is equivalent to: 1 serving Fruit; 2 servings Milk (1 cup yogurt)

2. In a bowl, mash 1 very ripe medium banana. Add 1 cup plain unflavored yogurt and spoon equal amounts of mixture into each of 2 dessert dishes. Chill in freezer. Before serving sprinkle with cinnamon or instant coffee if desired. Makes 2 servings.

Each serving is equivalent to: 1 serving Fruit; 1 serving Milk (½ cup yogurt)

3. In saucepan cook 4 dried medium prunes in a little water until very soft. Continue cooking until almost all liquid is evaporated. Pit prunes and puree. In bowl combine prunes with 1 cup plain unflavored yogurt. Divide evenly into 2 dessert dishes. Chill and serve. Makes 2 servings.

Each serving is equivalent to: ½ serving Fruit; 1 serving Milk (½ cup yogurt)

4. In bowl whip ¼ cup frozen orange juice concentrate with 1 cup plain unflavored yogurt. Transfer to freezer tray and freeze to soft

mush. Return to bowl and beat. Refreeze until consistency of sherbet. Divide evenly. Makes 2 servings.

Each serving is equivalent to: 1 serving Fruit; 1 serving Milk (½ cup yogurt)

Yogurt Milk Shake

½ cup skim milk
½ cup blueberries
¼ cup plain, unflavored yogurt
Artificial sweetener to equal 2
   teaspoons sugar

¼ teaspoon vanilla extract
3 ice cubes

Combine all ingredients, except ice, in blender container. Process until smooth. Add ice cubes. Process until frothy. Serve at once. Makes 1 serving.

Each serving is equivalent to: 1 serving Milk (½ cup skim milk and ¼ cup yogurt); 1 serving Fruit

Yogurt Pineapple Sherbet

1 cup plain unflavored yogurt
1 cup canned crushed pineapple,
   no sugar added

Artificial sweetener to equal 4
   teaspoons sugar
4 mint sprigs

Place yogurt in freezer tray; freeze until soft crystals form. Remove from freezer and transfer to bowl; beat well. Add fruit and sweetener; stir to combine. Return mixture to freezer tray; refreeze until soft crystals form. Remove from freezer and transfer to bowl; beat well and return to freezer. When chilled to firm consistency, divide evenly into 4 sherbet glasses. Garnish with mint. Makes 4 servings.

Each serving is equivalent to: ½ serving Milk (¼ cup yogurt); ½ serving Fruit

POULTRY, VEAL AND GAME

Some rewarding taste adventures await you here. Our test kitchen experts have created and adapted a number of unusual poultry, veal, and game dishes: Chicken Curry in Cantaloupe, Foil-Baked Chicken Rolls, Chicken Pilaf, Easy Chicken Mousse, Apple-Glazed Veal, Turkey Terrapin, and many others. We also show you how to make a marvelous stock. In short, some good things for you and your family appear in these pages.

Rules for Using Poultry, Veal, and Game

1. Amounts (net cooked weight):
   Women, Men, and Youth: 1 ounce at the Morning Meal
                                                     3 to 4 ounces at the Midday Meal
   Women and Youth: 4 to 6 ounces at the Evening Meal
   Men: 6 to 8 ounces at the Evening Meal
2. The range of 3 to 4 ounces of poultry, veal, and game at the Midday Meal, and 4 to 6 ounces for Women and Youth (6 to 8 ounces for Men) at the Evening Meal, provides flexibility. It is a way to individualize the Food Plan to meet your specific needs.
3. If smoked poultry or game is selected, use the *lower* end of the serving range.
4. Select chicken, turkey, other poultry (not duck or goose), veal, or wild game. Serve poultry with skin removed.

5. As a "rule of thumb," for each serving of poultry, veal, or game, allow 2 ounces for shrinkage in cooking and 2 ounces for bone. When splitting an item from the poultry, veal, and game category, for each half serving, allow 1 ounce for shrinkage in cooking and 1 ounce for bone. Weigh the serving after cooking, whenever possible.

6. *Cooking Procedures:*

Poultry and Game

May be boiled, poached, broiled, pan-broiled, roasted, or baked. Remove skin before eating.

If boiled with the skin, do not consume liquid. If boiled without the skin, liquid may be consumed. Refrigerate liquid; remove congealed fat. Six fluid ounces equal one serving of bouillon or broth.

If skin is removed, poultry (or game) may be browned in a non-stick skillet, or baked in a casserole with either raw or cooked ingredients. All ingredients may be consumed.

Veal

May be boiled, broiled, pan-broiled, roasted, or baked.

If boiled, liquid may be consumed. Refrigerate liquid; remove congealed fat. Six fluid ounces equal one serving of bouillon or broth.

If browned in a nonstick skillet: (a) transfer veal to another pan before adding raw or cooked ingredients; or, (b) wipe skillet clean before adding other ingredients.

If cooked in liquid (e.g., tomato juice or bouillon), veal must be removed from liquid with a slotted spatula. Whatever adheres to the veal may be consumed. Discard all other liquid.

Cooked veal may be used with added ingredients (e.g., casseroles, stews, etc.). Liquid and added ingredients may be consumed.

Raw ground veal may be combined with other ingredients such as fruit, eggs, cheese, bread, Choice Group items, milk, vegetables, and items from all categories in the Optional section only if boiled or baked (not broiled) on a rack.

Basic Roast Chicken

¾ cup chicken bouillon
1 tablespoon finely chopped celery
1 tablespoon dehydrated onion
  flakes

1 teaspoon dehydrated bell pepper
  flakes
Salt and pepper to taste
5- to 6-pound chicken

In small saucepan combine first 5 ingredients and simmer 15 minutes. Place chicken breast side up, on a rack in a shallow, uncovered roasting pan. Roast at 325°F., allowing about 20 minutes per pound. If meat thermometer is used, insert into center of the inner thigh muscle. Cook to an internal temperature of 180° to 185°F. Baste frequently with bouillon mixture. Remove skin and weigh portions. Makes about 8 evening meal servings.

Each serving is equivalent to: ⅛ serving Something Extra (1½ tablespoons bouillon); 6 ounces Poultry

Broiled Chicken

2½- to 3-pound chicken, cut in
  halves, quarters, or pieces

Salt and pepper to taste

Sprinkle chicken with salt and pepper. Place skin side down on broiler rack in pan. Broil 3 to 6 inches from source of heat. Broil 20 to 25 minutes, turn and broil 15 to 20 minutes or until fork-tender. Remove skin. Weigh portions and serve. Makes 4 evening meal servings.

Each serving is equivalent to: 6 ounces Poultry

Variations:

1. Combine ¼ cup Chicken Stock (see page 140), 2 tablespoons chopped fresh tarragon, and 2 teaspoons lemon juice. Pour over chicken and let stand 1 hour. Drain before broiling. Heat marinade and serve with chicken. Add $^1/_{12}$ serving Something Extra (1 tablespoon stock) to equivalent listing.

2. For each serving, spread 1 teaspoon low-calorie Italian or herb dressing over chicken before broiling. Add 1 teaspoon Specialty Food to equivalent listing.

3. Season chicken with garlic, lemon juice, salt, pepper, and paprika before broiling.

Pan-Broiled Chicken

Remove skin from cut-up chicken. If desired, bone and pound pieces flat so they brown evenly. Preheat nonstick skillet or pan sprayed with release agent. Add chicken and brown on all sides over moderate heat. Reduce heat and continue cooking, uncovered, turning the chicken frequently until cooked to desired degree of tenderness. Pan-broiled chicken is the basis for many different dishes.

Poached Chicken

Poaching is an excellent method for cooking skinned and boned chicken breasts and other skinned chicken parts. In a wide shallow saucepan, bring to a boil enough water to cover chicken. Reduce heat. Add chicken in one layer; cover and simmer until chicken is done, approximately 20 to 30 minutes, depending on size of chicken pieces. Remove chicken from liquid; serve or chill for later use. Poaching liquid may be chilled until fat congeals. Remove and discard fat. Liquid can be used in recipes calling for chicken stock.

¾ cup of liquid is equivalent to: 1 serving Something Extra

Poached Chicken in Sauce

Basic White Sauce (see page 296)	8 ounces skinned and boned
⅛ teaspoon nutmeg	poached chicken
⅛ teaspoon Worcestershire sauce	4 ounces Swiss or Cheddar cheese,
4 cups cooked broccoli florets	grated

Combine Basic White Sauce, nutmeg, and Worcestershire; set aside. In an ovenproof serving dish arrange broccoli and chicken. Pour sauce over chicken and top with cheese. Bake at 400°F. for approximately 15 minutes or until chicken and sauce are hot and cheese is melted and bubbly. Divide evenly. Makes 4 midday meal servings.

Each serving is equivalent to: Basic White Sauce (see page 296); 1 cup Vegetables; 2 ounces Poultry; 1 ounce Hard Cheese

Roast Chicken

5- to 6-pound chicken	2 tablespoons plus 2 teaspoons
Salt and pepper to taste	low-calorie salad dressing
¾ cup Chicken Stock (see page	¼ teaspoon paprika
140) or	

Wash and dry chicken. Remove skin. Sprinkle neck, body cavities, and surface with salt and pepper. Place chicken in shallow pan. Combine stock or salad dressing with paprika and brush 1 tablespoon over chicken. Roast at 375°F. approximately 30 minutes per pound. Baste every 20 minutes with paprika mixture. Chicken is done when drumstick meat feels soft when pressed between fingers and leg twists easily out of thigh joint. Carve and weigh portions. Makes about 8 evening meal servings.

Each serving is equivalent to: 6 ounces Poultry; ⅛ serving Something Extra (1½ tablespoons stock) or 1 teaspoon Specialty Food

Simmered or Stewed Chicken

5- to 6-pound stewing chicken,	2 celery ribs with leaves
skinned and cut in pieces	4 ounces onion, sliced
3 cups water	1 teaspoon salt
1 medium carrot, sliced	3 peppercorns

In large pot combine chicken, water, carrot, celery, onion, and salt. Bring to boil, then reduce heat and simmer about 15 minutes. Remove any foam that forms on surface. Cover and continue simmering about 1 hour; add peppercorns and continue simmering another hour or until meat is tender. Do not boil rapidly as this toughens the meat. Remove chicken from liquid and use immediately if desired or chill and use in recipes calling for cooked chicken. Weigh portions. Makes about 8 evening meal servings.

Each serving is equivalent to: 6 ounces Poultry

If desired, strain and refrigerate cooking liquid. Remove and discard congealed fat. Use liquid in recipes which call for chicken stock.

¾ cup liquid is equivalent to: 1 serving Something Extra

Note: If vegetables are consumed, add 2 tablespoons Vegetables and ½ ounce Limited Vegetable to equivalent listing.

Chicken Stock

2 chicken carcasses	3 parsley sprigs
2 quarts water	1 bay leaf
1 celery rib with leaves, sliced	¼ teaspoon thyme
6 peppercorns	Salt to taste

Combine all ingredients in large saucepan. Bring to boil; lower heat. Simmer for 1½ hours. Strain to remove solids. Refrigerate liquid; remove congealed fat. Divide into ¾-cup portions.

Each serving is equivalent to: 1 serving Something Extra (¾ cup stock)

Variations:

Thickened Stock—In a small saucepan dissolve 2 tablespoons flour in 2 tablespoons water; stir in 1½ cups Chicken Stock. Cook, stirring constantly, until thickened. Reduce heat and simmer 7 minutes. Use as a sauce for cooked poultry. Divide evenly. Makes 4 servings.

Each serving is equivalent to: 2 servings Something Extra (1½ teaspoons flour and ¼ cup plus 2 tablespoons stock)

Indian Style Stock—In a small saucepan combine 2 cups Chicken Stock, 1 cinnamon stick, and 2 crushed cardamom seeds. Simmer, covered, for 15 minutes. Strain to remove solids. Divide evenly. Makes 4 servings.

Each serving is equivalent to: ⅔ serving Something Extra (½ cup stock)

Double-Strength Chicken Stock—To each ¾ cup serving of hot Chicken Stock, add 1 packet instant chicken broth and seasoning mix.

Each serving is equivalent to: 2 servings Something Extra (¾ cup stock and 1 packet broth mix)

Extra-Strength Chicken Stock—For each serving, in saucepan simmer ¾ cup Chicken Stock until it is reduced by half.

Each serving is equivalent to: 1 serving Something Extra (¾ cup stock)

Garnishes—(1) Float slices of lemon or lime, or shreds of colorful rind, on ¾ cup hot stock.

(2) For chiffonade, add 2 tablespoons shredded lettuce to ¾ cup hot Chicken Stock before serving.

Each serving is equivalent to: 2 tablespoons Vegetables; 1 serving Something Extra (¾ cup stock)

Tomato-Chicken Stock—Combine ¾ cup Chicken Stock, 1 medium tomato, peeled, seeded, and diced, and herbs to taste in a small saucepan. Heat thoroughly. Try fresh or dried chives, dill, mint, parsley, rosemary, or tarragon.

Each serving is equivalent to: 1 serving Something Extra (¾ cup stock); ½ cup Vegetables

Chicken Stock with Seeds—Sprinkle ¾ cup hot Chicken Stock with 1 teaspoon caraway, poppy, or sesame seeds just before serving. Toast the sesame seeds if desired.

Each serving is equivalent to: 2 servings Something Extra (¾ cup stock and 1 teaspoon seeds)

Storing Stock
Refrigerate stock up to 2 days, or freeze in freezer containers in ¾-or 1½-cup containers. If freezing in glass jars, leave room for expansion.

Thrift Tips
Keep a small container in your freezer for trimmings from celery, mushrooms, and other vegetables. Use in preparation of stock.

Chicken in the Pot

For each serving combine ¾ cup Chicken Stock (see page 140), ¼ cup diced celery, and ¼ cup diced carrots in saucepan. Cover and simmer until vegetables are tender. Add 3 ounces cooked diced chicken; continue cooking for 5 minutes. If desired, add ½ cup cooked enriched rice or noodles. Makes 1 evening meal serving. Supplement as required.

Each serving is equivalent to: 1 serving Something Extra (¾ cup stock); ½ cup Vegetables; 3 ounces Poultry; 1 serving Choice Group (optional)

Chicken Soup with Vegetables

2 quarts water
1 pound skinned chicken pieces
1 cup sliced carrots
1 cup sliced celery
2 ounces diced onion

3 parsley sprigs
1 bay leaf
¼ teaspoon thyme
Salt and freshly ground pepper to
taste

Combine all ingredients except salt and pepper in a saucepan. Simmer for 1 hour. Season with salt and pepper. Discard parsley and bay leaf. Refrigerate soup; remove and discard congealed fat.* Measure 3 cups liquid. Remaining liquid can be frozen to be used at another time; ¾ cup is equivalent to 1 serving bouillon or broth. Combine measured liquid with solids in saucepan. Bring to a boil; lower heat. Simmer until chicken and vegetables are heated throughout. Divide evenly into large soup bowls. Makes 2 midday meal servings.

Each serving is equivalent to: 4 ounces Poultry; 1 cup Vegetables; 1 ounce Limited Vegetable; 2 servings Something Extra (1½ cups stock)

*If fat is difficult to remove, line a strainer with 4 layers of cheesecloth or a wet heavy paper towel. Place strainer over a bowl. Pour liquid with fat through cheesecloth or towel. Discard fat.

California Orange Chicken Salad

8 ounces cooked chicken, diced
1⅓ cups cottage cheese
2 small oranges, peeled and diced
4 ounces drained, canned water
    chestnuts, sliced
½ cup diced celery

2 tablespoons imitation
    mayonnaise
1 tablespoon grated fresh orange
    rind
½ teaspoon salt
⅛ teaspoon white pepper
4 large lettuce leaves

In bowl combine all ingredients except lettuce. Form lettuce into 4 cups; divide chicken mixture evenly into 4 lettuce cups. Makes 4 midday meal servings.

Each serving is equivalent to: 2 ounces Poultry; ⅓ cup Soft Cheese; ½ serving Fruit; 1 ounce Limited Vegetable; 2 tablespoons Vegetables; ¾ serving Fat

Variations:
1. Omit cottage cheese and use 4 ounces diced American or Cheddar cheese. Season with ⅛ teaspoon crushed red pepper or hot sauce. Serve with sliced red radishes or chili peppers. Substitute 1 ounce Hard Cheese for ⅓ cup Soft Cheese in equivalent listing.
2. Omit oranges and use 2 medium apples, pared, cored, diced, and sprinkled with lemon juice. Add 2 cups blanched chopped bean sprouts and 1 medium dill pickle, diced. Increase imitation mayonnaise to ¼ cup.

Each serving is equivalent to: 2 ounces Poultry; ⅓ cup Soft Cheese; ½ serving Fruit; 1 ounce Limited Vegetable; ¾ cup Vegetables; 1½ servings Fat

Chicken Curry in Cantaloupe

6 ounces poached chicken, diced
¼ recipe Curry Sauce (1 serving, see page 296)

1 ounce drained canned water chestnuts, diced

In bowl combine chicken, Curry Sauce, and water chestnuts; set aside. Using a melon baller, scoop out all of the pulp from cantaloupe, leaving rind intact. Fill rind with chicken mixture and garnish with melon balls. Serve chilled. Makes 1 evening meal serving.

Each serving is equivalent to: 6 ounces Poultry; Curry Sauce (see page 296); 1 ounce Limited Vegetable; 1 serving Fruit

Easy Chicken Mousse

1 envelope unflavored gelatin	Salt to taste
½ cup water	½ cup evaporated skimmed milk
¾ cup Double-Strength Chicken	1 pound cooked chicken, diced
Stock (see page 140)	½ cup diced celery
½ cup imitation mayonnaise	12 cooked medium asparagus
1 tablespoon lemon juice	spears, chilled
¼ teaspoon white pepper	½ cup pimento strips

In saucepan sprinkle gelatin over water to soften. Heat, stirring constantly until gelatin is dissolved. In bowl combine stock, mayonnaise, lemon juice, pepper, and salt; stir in gelatin mixture and milk; refrigerate until consistency of unbeaten egg whites, about 15 minutes. Fold in chicken and celery. Pour into a 6-cup ring mold. Chill until firm. Unmold on serving plate. Fill center with asparagus. Garnish with pimentos. Divide evenly. Makes 4 midday meal servings.

Each serving is equivalent to: 1 serving Something Extra (¼ envelope gelatin and 3 tablespoons Double-Strength Stock); 3 servings Fat; ¼ serving Milk (2 tablespoons evaporated skimmed milk); 4 ounces Poultry; ½ cup Vegetables

Chicken and Egg Loaf

12 ounces cooked chicken	2 teaspoons lemon juice
¾ cup sliced carrots	½ teaspoon salt
1 medium egg, hard-cooked	¼ teaspoon hot sauce
2 tablespoons pimento	⅛ teaspoon white pepper
3 slices enriched white bread,	1½ recipes Tomato Sauce (6
made into crumbs	servings, see page 307)
5 medium eggs, beaten	

Put chicken, carrots, hard-cooked egg, and pimento through food grinder or combine in food processor and process until well chopped.

Stir in the bread crumbs, beaten eggs, lemon juice, salt, hot sauce, and pepper. Transfer to nonstick loaf pan. Bake at 350°F. for about 30 minutes or until firm. Slice and serve with Tomato Sauce. Divide evenly. Makes 6 midday meal servings.

Each serving is equivalent to: 2 ounces Poultry; 2 tablespoons plus 1 teaspoon Vegetables; 1 Egg; ½ serving Bread; Tomato Sauce (see page 307)

Chicken and Sardine Acapulco

A Mexican dish inspired this recipe for combining leftovers.

1 ounce diced onion
1 small garlic clove, minced
1 medium tomato, chopped
¼ cup Chicken Stock (see page 140)
1 teaspoon chopped fresh parsley
2 ounces cooked chicken, diced

2 ounces drained, canned
  sardines, flaked
½ hot chili pepper, seeded and
  minced
Salt and pepper to taste
Shredded lettuce to garnish

Brown onion and garlic in nonstick skillet. Add tomato, stock, and parsley, and cook for 10 minutes. Add chicken, sardines, and chili pepper. Simmer uncovered about 3 minutes or until chicken is heated. Season with salt and pepper. Serve garnished with lettuce. Makes 1 midday meal serving.

Each serving is equivalent to: 1 ounce Limited Vegetable; ½ cup Vegetables; ⅓ serving Something Extra (¼ cup stock); 2 ounces Poultry; 2 ounces Fish

Chicken Pilaf

1½ cups Chicken Stock (see page 140)
½ cup cooked brown rice
8 canned plums, with ½ cup juice, no sugar added, pitted and diced

3 ounces pared potato, cut into ½-inch dice
Dash cinnamon
Dash cumin
12 ounces poached chicken, diced

In medium saucepan, combine all ingredients except chicken. Cover and simmer about 30 minutes or until potato is tender. Add chicken and heat. Divide evenly. Makes 2 evening meal servings.

Each serving is equivalent to: 1 serving Something Extra (¾ cup stock); 1 serving Choice Group; 2 servings Fruit; 6 ounces Poultry

Poached Chicken with Yogurt

Tart and refreshing on a summer day; prepare it in the cool of the morning.

½ cup plain, unflavored yogurt
1 tablespoon plus 2 teaspoons flour
¾ cup Chicken Stock (see page 140)
½ cup water
1 ounce diced scallions

1 tablespoon lemon juice
½ teaspoon salt
1 medium cucumber, pared and diced
12 ounces poached chicken breasts, cut into 1½-inch pieces

In a small bowl combine yogurt and flour. Set aside. In saucepan combine remaining ingredients except cucumber and chicken. Bring to a boil. Reduce heat. Stir in yogurt mixture. Simmer, stirring constantly until sauce is thickened. Add cucumbers. Heat thoroughly. Serve over chicken. Divide evenly. Makes 2 evening meal servings.

Each serving is equivalent to: ½ serving Milk (¼ cup yogurt); 3 servings Something Extra (2½ teaspoons flour and ¼ cup plus 2 tablespoons stock); ½ ounce Limited Vegetable; ¼ cup Vegetables; 6 ounces Poultry

Chicken Chinese Style

2 pounds skinned and boned
  chicken, cut into strips 3 inches
  long
1 cup diagonally sliced celery
1 cup sliced mushrooms
½ cup water

1 tablespoon minced fresh ginger
  root
1 packet instant chicken broth and
  seasoning mix
3 tablespoons soy sauce
1 tablespoon cornstarch, dissolved
  in 1 tablespoon water

Brown chicken in a preheated nonstick skillet. Add celery, mushrooms, water, ginger root, and broth mix. Cover and cook until chicken is tender, about 20 minutes. Add soy sauce and cornstarch and cook, stirring until thickened. Divide evenly. Makes 4 evening meal servings.

Each serving is equivalent to: 6 ounces Poultry; ½ cup Vegetables; 1 serving Something Extra (¼ packet broth mix and ¾ teaspoon cornstarch)

Variation: Before adding cornstarch, stir in 8 ounces Chinese pea pods or sliced drained canned water chestnuts. Heat for one minute. Add 2 ounces Limited Vegetable to equivalent listing.

Chicken Italian Style (Cacciatore)

2 pounds skinned and boned
  chicken breasts
1 medium green pepper, seeded
  and cut into strips
2 ounces sliced onion

1 garlic clove, minced
1½ cups tomato puree
1 teaspoon oregano
½ teaspoon salt

Brown chicken in a large preheated nonstick skillet. Add green peppers, onion, and garlic; cook 4 minutes. Add remaining ingredients; cover and simmer, stirring occasionally, for 40 minutes or until done. Divide evenly. Makes 4 evening meal servings.

Each serving is equivalent to: 6 ounces Poultry; 2 tablespoons Vegetables; ½ ounce Limited Vegetable; ¾ serving Bonus (¼ cup plus 2 tablespoons tomato puree)

Chicken Indian Style (Korma)

2 pounds skinned and boned
   chicken breasts
4 ounces chopped onion
1 garlic clove, minced
1 canned hot chili pepper,
   chopped

½ teaspoon paprika
¼ teaspoon cardamom
¼ teaspoon coriander
¼ teaspoon cumin
½ cup water
¼ cup tomato puree

Brown chicken in a large preheated nonstick skillet. Add remaining ingredients in order given. Cover and simmer, stirring occasionally, for 40 minutes or until chicken is tender. Divide evenly. Makes 4 evening meal servings.

Each serving is equivalent to: 6 ounces Poultry; 1 ounce Limited Vegetable; 1 tablespoon Vegetables; ⅛ serving Bonus (1 tablespoon tomato puree)

Foil-Baked Chicken Rolls

2 boned and skinned chicken
   breasts, 6 ounces each
Salt and freshly ground pepper to
   taste
2 teaspoons prepared mustard
2 teaspoons imitation (or diet)
   margarine

2 teaspoons chopped fresh chives
2 teaspoons chopped fresh parsley
1 teaspoon lemon juice
1 teaspoon lime juice
½ teaspoon garlic powder

Pound chicken breasts until they are about ¼ inch thick. Season with salt and pepper. Place each breast on a 12x12-inch piece of aluminum foil. Combine remaining ingredients in a small bowl. Divide evenly and spread over each chicken breast. Roll chicken breast, tucking ends in. Seal rolls in foil. Place in a baking pan. Bake at 375°F. for 30 minutes. Serve 1 foil packet per portion and open them at the table. Makes 2 midday meal servings.

Each serving is equivalent to: 4 ounces Poultry; ½ serving Fat

Oven-Barbecued Chicken with Vegetables

An all-in-one oven meal if you bake potatoes and apples in the oven with the chicken. Vary chicken seasonings. Garlic, oregano, or parsley adds a nice touch.

2 cups diced celery
2 cups diced carrots
4 ounces diced onion
1 broiling chicken, 2½ to 3
  pounds, skinned and cut into
  quarters

Salt, pepper, paprika, and
  poultry seasoning to taste
¼ cup catsup
2 tablespoons prepared mustard

In a 2-quart shallow casserole, combine celery, carrots, and onion. Season chicken pieces and place over vegetables. Combine catsup and mustard and pour evenly over chicken. Bake at 375°F. for 1 hour or until chicken is tender. Weigh portions of chicken and divide vegetables and sauce evenly. Makes 4 evening meal servings.

Each serving is equivalent to: 1 cup Vegetables; 1 ounce Limited Vegetable; 6 ounces Poultry; 1½ servings Something Extra (1 tablespoon catsup)

Oven-"Fried" Chicken

2 slices enriched white bread,
  made into crumbs
1 tablespoon flour
1 teaspoon dehydrated parsley
  flakes
½ teaspoon poultry seasoning
½ teaspoon salt
½ teaspoon paprika

¼ teaspoon garlic powder
⅛ teaspoon freshly ground pepper
1 pound skinned and boned
  chicken or turkey breasts, cut
  into serving pieces
2 tablespoons evaporated
  skimmed milk

In bowl combine bread crumbs, flour, and seasonings. Dip chicken in milk and then in bread crumb mixture to coat. Place in a nonstick baking pan. Sprinkle evenly with any remaining crumbs and milk. Bake at 400°F. for 15 to 20 minutes or until chicken is tender. Divide evenly. Makes 2 evening meal servings.

Each serving is equivalent to: 1 serving Bread; 1½ servings Something Extra (1½ teaspoons flour); 6 ounces Poultry; ⅛ serving Milk (1 tablespoon evaporated skimmed milk)

Variation:
Chicken Mozzarella—To serve 4 for midday meal, use 4 skinned and boned chicken breasts, each weighing 3 ounces. Prepare bread crumb mixture as above; follow directions for coating breasts. Bake as above. When chicken is tender, put a 1-ounce slice of Mozzarella cheese on each breast and bake until cheese melts. Serve each portion with ¼ cup tomato sauce, no sugar added, if desired.

Each serving is equivalent to: ½ serving Bread; ¾ serving Something Extra (¾ teaspoon flour); 2 ounces Poultry; $^{1}/_{16}$ serving Milk (1½ teaspoons evaporated skimmed milk); 1 ounce Hard Cheese; ½ serving Bonus (¼ cup tomato sauce) (optional)

Roast Cornish Hens with Spiced Cherry Sauce

1½ cups frozen pitted sweet
  cherries, no sugar added
3 Cornish hens, 1¼ pounds each
Salt, white pepper, garlic powder,
  and paprika to taste
¾ cup chicken bouillon
¾ cup black cherry-flavored
  dietetic soda

Artificial sweetener to equal 2
  teaspoons sugar
¼ cinnamon stick
¼ teaspoon lemon juice
1 clove
1 tablespoon cornstarch

Set cherries aside to thaw. Sprinkle hens with salt, pepper, garlic powder, and paprika. Place on a rack in roasting pan and roast at 350°F. for ½ hour or until done. Baste occasionally with bouillon. While hens are roasting, combine juice from cherries, soda, sweetener, cinnamon, lemon juice, and clove in a medium saucepan. Sprinkle cornstarch over liquid and stir to dissolve. Place over medium heat; cook, stirring constantly, until mixture thickens. Add cherries; stir until coated with sauce and thoroughly heated. To serve, cut hens in half and remove skin. Place each half on a dinner plate and top with ¹/₆ of the cherry sauce. Makes 6 evening meal servings.

Each serving is equivalent to: ½ serving Fruit; 6 ounces Poultry; ⅔ serving Something Extra (2 tablespoons bouillon and ½ teaspoon cornstarch)

Yogurt-Baked Chicken

2½ pounds skinned chicken pieces
1 garlic clove, cut
1 cup plain unflavored yogurt
4 ounces drained canned small
   onions

2 tablespoons minced fresh
   parsley
1 tablespoon water
¼ teaspoon sage
¼ teaspoon tarragon

Dry chicken pieces and rub with cut garlic clove. Place in shallow baking pan. Bake at 350°F. for 45 minutes or until tender. Combine remaining ingredients in a small bowl; spoon over chicken. Bake at 275°F. for 20 minutes or until sauce is hot and bubbly. Divide evenly. Makes 4 evening meal servings.

Each serving equivalent to: 6 ounces Poultry; ½ serving Milk (¼ cup yogurt); 1 ounce Limited Vegetable

Roast Turkey

Place turkey on a rack in a shallow roasting pan, breast side up. Roast at 325°F. Allow about 20 minutes per pound for a bird under 12 pounds, and about 15 minutes per pound if larger. If a meat thermometer is used, insert into the center of inner thigh muscle; when thermometer registers 180° to 185°F., turkey is done. Baste every half hour with mixture of dehydrated onion flakes, dehydrated bell pepper flakes, and chopped celery cooked in 1½ cups chicken bouillon. Remove skin and weigh portions.

Each serving is equivalent to: 4 to 6 ounces Poultry; ⅛ serving Something Extra (1½ tablespoons bouillon)

Turkey and Spaghetti Casserole

The perfect post-Thanksgiving dinner dish.

1½ cups tomato puree
1 cup diced celery
1 medium green pepper, seeded
  and diced
1 packet instant chicken broth and
  seasoning mix
1 garlic clove, minced
½ teaspoon basil

Artificial sweetener to equal ½
  teaspoon sugar or to taste
  (optional)
Mushroom White Sauce (see
  page 297)
2⅔ cups cooked enriched thin
  spaghetti
1½ pounds cooked turkey, cubed

In a medium saucepan combine tomato puree, celery, green pepper, broth mix, garlic, basil, and sweetener, if desired. Simmer for 15 to 20 minutes or until vegetables are tender. In a 2-quart shallow casserole, spread half of the Mushroom White Sauce. Add half the spaghetti, turkey, and tomato mixture. Repeat layers. Bake at 350°F. for 30 minutes or until piping hot. Divide evenly. Makes 4 evening meal servings.

Each serving is equivalent to: ¾ serving Bonus (¼ cup plus 2 tablespoons tomato puree); ¼ cup plus 2 tablespoons Vegetables; ¼ serving Something Extra (¼ packet broth mix); Mushroom White Sauce (see page 297); 1 serving Choice Group; 6 ounces Poultry

Turkey Casserole

4 ounces minced onion
2 medium green peppers, seeded
  and diced
1 cup sliced mushrooms
1 garlic clove, minced
¾ teaspoon paprika
½ teaspoon Worcestershire sauce

¼ teaspoon dry mustard
8 ounces cooked turkey, shredded
2⅔ cups cooked enriched elbow
  macaroni
4 ounces American or Cheddar
  cheese, grated
Paprika to garnish

In a nonstick skillet combine onion, green pepper, mushrooms, garlic, paprika, Worcestershire, and dry mustard; cook until vegetables are soft. Add turkey and cook 5 minutes longer. Place macaroni in a 2-quart casserole. Pour turkey mixture over macaroni; sprinkle with cheese and paprika. Bake at 400°F. for 25 minutes or until thoroughly heated. Divide evenly. Makes 4 midday meal servings.

Each serving is equivalent to: 1 ounce Limited Vegetable; ½ cup Vegetables; 2 ounces Poultry; 1 serving Choice Group; 1 ounce Hard Cheese

Turkey Terrapin

This dish was originally made with turtle (terrapin), which accounts for the name.

1 cup skim milk	4 ounces drained canned water
2 medium eggs, hard-cooked	chestnuts, sliced
2 tablespoons imitation (or diet)	½ cup sliced mushrooms
margarine, melted	1 tablespoon diced pimento
1 tablespoon flour	Salt and pepper to taste
⅛ teaspoon allspice	2 slices enriched white bread,
⅛ teaspoon nutmeg	toasted
4 ounces cooked turkey, diced	

Heat milk in top of a double boiler over boiling water. Cut eggs in half. Remove yolks. In small bowl mash egg yolks; add margarine, flour, allspice, and nutmeg; add to hot milk; cook until thickened and smooth. Chop egg whites and add to milk mixture with turkey, water chestnuts, mushrooms, pimento, salt, and pepper; cook until thoroughly heated. Divide evenly; serve each portion on 1 slice of toast. Makes 2 midday meal servings.

Each serving is equivalent to: ½ serving Milk (½ cup skim milk); 1 Egg; 1½ servings Fat; 1½ servings Something Extra (1½ teaspoons flour); 2 ounces Poultry; 2 ounces Limited Vegetable; ¼ cup plus 1½ teaspoons Vegetables; 1 serving Bread

Veal

Veal is actually young beef from a calf three to eight months old. It has a more delicate flavor and is lighter in color than beef. Veal has less fat than beef and may toughen more quickly, but the cooking principles in "How to Cook Meat" (see page 162), usually apply to veal as well.

Quick-and-Easy Vitello Tonnato

A summer salad.

5 ounces drained canned tuna
1 ounce drained canned anchovies
3 tablespoons imitation
  mayonnaise
2 teaspoons lemon juice

1 teaspoon capers
Dash celery seed
6 ounces sliced cooked veal
Freshly ground pepper to taste
Lemon slices to garnish

In bowl combine tuna, anchovies, mayonnaise, lemon juice, capers, and celery seed. Finely mash or process in food processor. Place veal in shallow container. Spread tuna mixture over veal and refrigerate several hours or overnight. Sprinkle with pepper. Garnish top with slices of lemon. Divide evenly. Makes 2 evening meal servings.

Each serving is equivalent to: 3 ounces Fish; 2¼ servings Fat; 3 ounces Veal

Variation: You can vary the amounts of fish and veal according to what you have, but do not exceed a combined total of 6 ounces cooked weight per serving. Adjust equivalents accordingly.

Apple-Glazed Veal

2-pound boned veal roast
½ cup beef bouillon
1 tablespoon soy sauce

¼ teaspoon salt
⅛ teaspoon pepper
Apple Topping (recipe follows)

Broil veal 3 inches from source of heat, turning to brown all sides. Transfer to baking pan. In measuring cup combine bouillon, soy sauce, salt, and pepper; pour over veal. Bake at 350°F. for 45 minutes. Add Apple Topping; cover and bake 30 minutes longer or until veal is tender. Baste several times with pan juices. Divide evenly. Makes 4 evening meal servings.

Apple Topping

2 medium apples, pared, cored, and sliced

2 tablespoons frozen orange juice concentrate
½ teaspoon cinnamon

Combine all ingredients in a small bowl and use as topping for veal. Makes 4 servings.

Each serving is equivalent to: 6 ounces Veal; ¹/₆ serving Something Extra (2 tablespoons bouillon); ¾ serving Fruit

Savory Rolled Roast of Veal

Serve this with any desired sauce. (See "Sauces and Salad Dressings.") Bake vegetables at the same time. Order a rump of veal for rolling, but don't have the butcher roll it. We're seasoning it first.

¼ cup chopped fresh Italian parsley
4 garlic cloves, pressed
1 tablespoon dehydrated onion flakes, reconstituted in 1 tablespoon water

3-pound boned rump of veal
Salt and pepper to taste
Garlic powder to taste

In a small bowl combine parsley, garlic, and onion flakes. Sprinkle inside of veal with salt and pepper. Spread with parsley mixture. Roll the veal and tie with string. Season outside of veal with salt, pepper, and garlic powder. Let stand 1 hour if possible. Insert meat thermometer; place veal on a rack in roasting pan and roast at 350°F. for about 2 hours or until thermometer registers 170°F. Divide evenly. Makes 6 evening meal servings.

Each serving is equivalent to: 6 ounces Veal

Variation: Spread veal evenly with a mixture of 1 tablespoon catsup and 1 tablespoon soy sauce 10 minutes before removing from oven. Add ¼ serving Something Extra (½ teaspoon catsup) to equivalent listing.

Buttermilk Veal Balls

1½ pounds ground veal
2 slices enriched white bread,
   made into crumbs
¼ cup buttermilk

¼ teaspoon garlic powder
⅛ teaspoon thyme
Dash salt and pepper

In a bowl combine all ingredients. Shape into balls 1½ inches in diameter. Place on a rack, and bake at 375°F. for 40 minutes or until browned. Divide evenly. Makes 4 midday meal servings.

Each serving is equivalent to: 4 ounces Veal; ½ serving Bread; $1/12$ serving Milk (1 tablespoon Buttermilk)

Sweet-and-Sour Veal Balls in Cabbage

2 pounds ground veal
½ teaspoon salt
¼ teaspoon garlic powder
⅛ teaspoon pepper
1 ounce grated onion

4 cups shredded cabbage (about 1
   pound)
3 ounces onion, sliced
2 tablespoons frozen orange juice
   concentrate
1 tablespoon lemon juice

In bowl combine veal, salt, garlic powder, pepper, and grated onion. Mix well and shape into balls 1 inch in diameter. Cook veal in preheated nonstick skillet, turning to brown all sides. Place the shredded cabbage and sliced onion in medium saucepan. Add orange juice concentrate, lemon juice, and enough water to cover. Bring to boil. Add veal balls, cover and simmer 20 minutes or until cabbage is soft. Divide evenly. Makes 4 evening meal servings.

Each serving is equivalent to: 6 ounces Veal; 1 ounce Limited Vegetable; 1 cup Vegetables; ¼ serving Fruit

Veal-Stuffed Manicotti

1 pound ground veal, shaped into
   4 patties
1 cup tomato sauce, no sugar
   added
2 teaspoons basil
1 teaspoon oregano
½ teaspoon garlic powder, divided
Salt and pepper to taste

1 cup cooked chopped spinach
½ cup chicken bouillon
1 tablespoon minced fresh parsley
Dash nutmeg
1⅓ cups cooked enriched
   manicotti shells
   (approximately 6)

Cook veal patties in preheated nonstick skillet until done. In a small bowl crumble one patty and add tomato sauce, basil, oregano, ¼ teaspoon garlic powder, salt, and pepper. Mix well. Set aside. Crumble remaining patties into medium bowl. Add remaining ingredients except manicotti shells; mix well. Divide mixture evenly and fill manicotti shells. Place in an 8x8-inch baking dish. Top with veal sauce mixture. Cover. Bake at 350°F. for 30 minutes. Divide evenly. Makes 2 evening meal servings.

Each serving is equivalent to: 6 ounces Veal; 1 serving Bonus (½ cup tomato sauce); ½ cup Vegetables; ⅓ serving Something Extra (¼ cup bouillon); 1 serving Choice Group

Hawaiian Veal

1 pound veal for stew, cut into
   1-inch cubes
1½ cups beef bouillon
1 tablespoon chopped fresh
   parsley
¼ teaspoon dill seed
Salt and pepper to taste

½ medium pineapple, pared,
   cored, and diced
1 cup sliced mushrooms
1 tablespoon cornstarch, dissolved
   in 1 tablespoon water
1 cup cooked enriched rice

Brown veal cubes in a preheated nonstick skillet. Transfer to a medium saucepan. Add bouillon, parsley, dill seed, salt, and pepper. Cover and simmer over low heat about 40 minutes or until veal is very tender. Add water if necessary to keep veal barely covered. Add pineapple and mushrooms; cover and simmer about 5 minutes or until mushrooms are cooked. Add cornstarch and cook, stirring constantly, until thickened. Serve over rice. Divide evenly. Makes 2 evening meal servings.

Each serving is equivalent to: 6 ounces Veal; 2½ servings Something Extra (¾ cup bouillon and 1½ teaspoons cornstarch); 1 serving Fruit; ½ cup Vegetables; 1 serving Choice Group

Italian Veal and Peppers

Any boned veal may be cut up and used for stewing if it is free of cartilage. Boned veal shoulder is excellent.

1 pound veal for stew, cut into
  1-inch cubes
1 cup tomato puree
½ cup water
4 ounces sliced onion
1 packet instant chicken broth and
  seasoning mix

1 garlic clove, minced
½ teaspoon basil
½ teaspoon oregano
Freshly ground pepper to taste
2 medium green peppers, seeded
  and cut into ½-inch strips

Brown veal in a preheated nonstick skillet. Remove veal and wipe pan clean. Replace veal and add remaining ingredients except green peppers. Cover and cook over low heat for 45 minutes. Add peppers and continue cooking 10 minutes longer or until veal and peppers are tender. Divide evenly. Makes 2 evening meal servings.

Each serving is equivalent to: 6 ounces Veal; 1 serving Bonus (½ cup tomato puree); 2 ounces Limited Vegetable; ½ serving Something Extra (½ packet broth mix); ½ cup Vegetables

Veal Paprika

Good served with boiled potatoes or enriched noodles

1½ pounds veal for stew, cut into
  ½-inch cubes
4 ounces chopped onion
1 cup tomato sauce, no sugar
  added

1 teaspoon paprika
¼ teaspoon salt
⅛ teaspoon garlic powder
⅛ teaspoon white pepper
¼ cup plain unflavored yogurt

Brown veal in a preheated nonstick skillet. Transfer to a medium saucepan. Add onion and cook, stirring occasionally until onion is browned. Add tomato sauce, paprika, salt, garlic powder, and white pepper. Cover and simmer for about 30 minutes or until veal is tender. Remove from heat; fold in yogurt. Divide evenly. Makes 4 midday meal servings.

Each serving is equivalent to: 4 ounces Veal; 1 ounce Limited Vegetable; ½ serving Bonus (¼ cup tomato sauce); ⅛ serving Milk (1 tablespoon yogurt)

Quick-and-Easy Veal Marengo

Cooked enriched rice or wide noodles is the usual accompaniment to this traditional dish.

1 tablespoon margarine
2 ounces diced onion
½ garlic clove, minced
1 tablespoon flour
¾ cup chicken bouillon
¼ cup tomato paste
12 ounces cooked veal, diced

1 cup sliced mushrooms
½ teaspoon sherry extract
  (optional)
¼ teaspoon thyme
¼ teaspoon tarragon
⅛ teaspoon grated orange rind
Dash pepper

Melt margarine in top of double boiler over boiling water. Add onion and garlic. Cook until onion is soft. Stir in flour and cook until blended; add bouillon and tomato paste. Cook, stirring constantly, until smooth and thickened. Stir in remaining ingredients; simmer 10 minutes. Divide evenly. Makes 2 evening meal servings.

Each serving is equivalent to: 1½ servings Fat; 1 ounce Limited Vegetables; 2 servings Something Extra (1½ teaspoons flour and ¼ cup plus 2 tablespoons bouillon); ½ serving Bonus (2 tablespoons tomato paste); 6 ounces Veal; ½ cup Vegetables

Hasenpfeffer (Rabbit Stew)

Chicken may also be prepared this way. Traditionally this is a very peppery dish. You might add more pepper than we've suggested if our Hasenpfeffer lacks the spice of Grandma's dish.

1½ cups cider vinegar
1½ cups water
4 ounces sliced onion
1 teaspoon salt
1 teaspoon ground cloves
3 bay leaves
¼ teaspoon cracked peppercorns
   or more to taste

⅛ teaspoon allspice
2½ pounds rabbit, cut in pieces
¾ cup chicken bouillon
¼ teaspoon browning sauce
2 teaspoons cornstarch, dissolved
   in 2 teaspoons water

In large bowl combine first 8 ingredients. Add rabbit; cover and refrigerate one to two days, turning occasionally. Remove rabbit; reserve marinade. Broil rabbit 4 inches from source of heat, turning once, for 12 minutes or until brown. Transfer rabbit and reserved marinade to a large saucepan; cover and simmer for one hour or until tender. Remove rabbit and keep warm. Add bouillon and browning sauce to marinade. Stir in cornstarch and cook, stirring constantly, until thickened. Strain sauce through double-layered cheesecloth. Discard solids. Serve sauce with rabbit. Divide evenly. Makes 4 evening meal servings.

Each serving is equivalent to: 6 ounces Game; ¾ serving Something Extra (3 tablespoons bouillon and ½ teaspoon cornstarch)

"BEEF" GROUP

Beef, ham, lamb, pork, tongue, bologna, frankfurters, knockwurst, beef sausages, and organ meats can provide hearty meals for you. Enjoy an excellent Old-Fashioned Pot Roast, Beef Chop Suey, Chili for Four, an easy Lamb and Barley Stew, Swiss-Style Pot-au-Feu, and even Homemade Sausage. Money-saving and delicious recipes for Meat Loaf and a Quick-and-Easy Cassoulet are all included.

Rules for Using "Beef" Group

1. Amounts (net cooked weight):
   Women, Men, and Youth: 1 ounce at the Morning Meal
   3 to 4 ounces at the Midday Meal
   Women and Youth: 4 to 6 ounces at the Evening Meal
   Men: 6 to 8 ounces at the Evening Meal
2. The range of 3 to 4 ounces of "Beef" Group at the Midday Meal and 4 to 6 ounces for Women and Youth (6 to 8 ounces for Men) at the Evening Meal provides flexibility. It is a way to individualize the Food Plan to meet your specific needs.
3. If smoked or cured meat is selected, use the lower end of the serving range.
4. Select up to 3 times weekly, if desired, from beef, ham, lamb, pork, and tongue.
5. Use lean meat. Remove visible fat before eating.
6. Select one of the following once a week, if desired, in place of a "Beef" Group item:
   bologna   beef sausages
   frankfurters   organ meats
   knockwurst

7. As a "rule of thumb," for each serving of a "Beef" Group item allow 2 ounces for shrinkage in cooking and 2 ounces for bone. When splitting an item from the "Beef" Group, for each half serving allow 1 ounce for shrinkage in cooking and 1 ounce for bone. Weigh the serving after cooking, whenever possible.

8. Bologna, frankfurters, knockwurst, beef sausages, Canadian bacon, and ham are precooked. Do not allow an additional 2 ounces for shrinkage.

9. Whether a selection from the "Beef" Group is taken by itself, or in combination with fish, poultry, meat, egg, cheese, or legumes, it must be considered a "Beef" Group meal.

10. *Cooking Procedures:*

May be boiled; or broiled, baked, or roasted on a rack.

If boiled, liquid may be consumed. Refrigerate liquid; remove congealed fat. Six fluid ounces equal one serving of bouillon or broth.

If broiled, baked, or roasted on a rack, natural juices flowing from the meat during cutting may be consumed.

Cooked "beef" may be used with added ingredients (e.g., casserole, stews, etc.). Liquid and added ingredients may be consumed.

Raw ground meat may be combined with other ingredients, such as fruit, eggs, cheese, bread, Choice Group items, milk, vegetables, and items from all categories in the Optional section only if boiled or baked (not broiled) on a rack.

How to Cook Meat

The most important thing to remember about cooking meat is that any cut can be delicious and tender if cooked properly. In most cases, the tenderness of the cut determines the preferred cooking method. Tender cuts are usually best when cooked by dry heat, such as roasting or broiling. Less tender cuts of meat are made tender by cooking with moist heat. Slow cooking in moisture softens the connective tissue, the part of the meat that cannot be made tender quickly.

Roasting—Good for tender cuts of beef, pork, and lamb.

Season with salt and pepper, if desired. Roasts may be seasoned either before, during, or after cooking, since salt only penetrates ¼ to ½ inch. Place meat on rack in open shallow roasting pan. Insert a meat thermometer, if available, in the center of largest muscle, not touching bone.

Do not add water, do not cover, and do not baste. It is not necessary to preheat the oven. Roast at 300°F. to 350°F. Small roasts should be cooked at 350°F., larger ones at lower temperatures. For browning, higher temperatures may be used. Roast to the desired degree of doneness. Then let roast stand 15 to 20 minutes after removing it from the oven for easier carving. Slice and weigh servings.

Broiling—Good for tender beef steaks, lamb chops, pork chops, ham steaks, and ground meats.

Place meat on rack in broiler pan and broil 2 to 5 inches from the heat, until top is brown. Season if desired. Turn and broil until done. Weigh and serve at once.

Cooking in Liquid (boiling)—Good for less tender cuts of meat.

Place meat in kettle and cover with water. When meat is covered entirely, it can be cooked evenly without turning. Season with salt, pepper, herbs, and spices if desired. Cover kettle and simmer until tender. Remove meat; slice and weigh servings. If desired, strain and refrigerate cooking liquid. Remove and discard congealed fat. Use liquid in recipes which call for beef stock.

¾ cup liquid is equivalent to: 1 serving Something Extra

Beef, Ham, Lamb, Veal Stock

Bones from beef, ham, lamb, or veal can be used to make stocks. To make these strongly flavored stocks, follow the directions for Chicken Stock (see page 140), but add 1 garlic clove and 1 tablespoon dehydrated onion flakes. For added flavor and color, brown bones on a rack, in a hot oven, before preparing the stock. Ham Stock is an excellent base for split-pea soup or any other soup made from legumes.

¾ cup stock is equivalent to: 1 serving Something Extra

Boiled Beef

3 pounds boned beef rump roast
2 quarts water
1 to 2 teaspoons salt
Bouquet garni (4 cloves, 2 sprigs
thyme, 1 bay leaf tied in
cheesecloth)
1 small head cabbage, cut in 6
wedges (4 cups)

1 pound 2 ounces pared potatoes,
diced
12 ounces small white onions
2 cups pared and diced white
turnips
2 cups sliced carrots
4 celery ribs with leaves, sliced

In Dutch oven or kettle combine beef, water, salt and bouquet garni;
cover and cook 2 to 3 hours or until beef is tender. Add more water if
necessary. Drain and refrigerate liquid. Discard bouquet garni. Cool
beef and refrigerate. Remove and discard congealed fat from liquid.
In a large kettle combine 4½ cups liquid, beef, and remaining ingredients. Cook about 45 minutes or until vegetables are tender. Remove
beef and vegetables from liquid; slice beef. Place on platter surrounded by vegetables. Divide beef and vegetables evenly. Divide
liquid evenly into soup bowls. Makes 6 evening meal servings.

Each serving is equivalent to: 6 ounces "Beef" Group; 1½ cups
Vegetables; 1 serving Choice Group; 2 ounces Limited Vegetable; 1
serving Something Extra (¾ cup broth)

Beef Soup

2 quarts water
12 ounces boneless chuck steak
1 cup sliced carrots
1 cup sliced celery
2 ounces diced onion

3 parsley sprigs
1 bay leaf
1 garlic clove, minced
Salt and freshly ground pepper to
taste

Combine all ingredients except salt and pepper in a saucepan. Simmer
for 1 hour. Season with salt and pepper. Transfer beef and liquid to
bowl. Discard all remaining solids. Refrigerate beef and liquid. Re-

move and discard congealed fat.* Measure 1½ cups liquid. Remaining liquid can be frozen to be used at another time; ¾ cup is equivalent to 1 serving bouillon or broth. Combine measured liquid with beef in saucepan. Bring to a boil; lower heat. Simmer until beef is heated throughout. Divide evenly into soup bowls. Makes 2 midday meal servings.

Each serving is equivalent to: 4 ounces "Beef" Group; 1 serving Something Extra (¾ cup broth)

*If fat is difficult to remove, line a strainer with 4 layers of cheesecloth or a wet heavy paper towel. Place strainer over a bowl. Pour liquid with fat through cheesecloth or paper towel. Discard fat.

Old-Fashioned Pot Roast

2 pounds bottom round of beef
12 ounces drained canned whole
   potatoes
1⅓ cups tomato juice
8 ounces onion, sliced
1 cup shredded carrots
1 medium green pepper, seeded
   and diced

2 celery ribs, diced
10 peppercorns, crushed
4 bay leaves
Artificial sweetener to equal 6
   teaspoons sugar (optional)
2 teaspoons salt
½ teaspoon paprika

Roast beef on a rack at 375°F. for 45 minutes or until done. Place in Dutch oven with remaining ingredients. Cover and simmer 1 to 1½ hours, or until meat is very tender. Remove beef and potatoes; slice beef. Transfer ½ cup remaining mixture from Dutch oven to blender container and process until smooth. Return to pot and mix thoroughly. Divide beef evenly and place each portion on an individual serving plate with 3 ounces potatoes. Divide sauce evenly and pour over each serving of beef and potatoes. Makes 4 evening meal servings.

Each serving is equivalent to: 6 ounces "Beef" Group; 1 serving Choice Group; ⅓ serving Bonus (⅓ cup tomato juice); 2 ounces Limited Vegetable; ½ cup Vegetables

Sauerbraten

4 pounds bottom round of beef	½ cup sliced carrot
1 tablespoon salt	1 celery rib, chopped
½ teaspoon freshly ground pepper	4 cloves
1 quart water	4 peppercorns
2 cups red wine vinegar	2 bay leaves
8 ounces onion, sliced	

Season beef with salt and pepper. Place in a large glass bowl. Add remaining ingredients. Cover and refrigerate 4 to 6 days, turning meat several times daily. Remove meat; reserve marinade. Roast meat on a rack at 375°F. for about 1 hour or until done. Place beef in a large saucepan and add marinade. Bring to boil; cover and simmer 1½ to 2½ hours or until beef is tender. Remove beef; strain liquid and discard solids. Boil marinade until reduced to about 2 cups. Slice beef and serve with marinade. Divide evenly. Makes 8 evening meal servings.

Each serving is equivalent to: 6 ounces "Beef" Group

Barbecued Steak

¼ cup dehydrated onion flakes	3 pounds boned steak, cut 1½
¼ cup Worcestershire sauce	inches thick
2 tablespoons lemon juice	1 tablespoon chopped fresh
1 garlic clove, minced	parsley
¾ teaspoon salt	2 tablespoons margarine
	(optional)

In bowl combine first 5 ingredients; let stand 10 minutes. Add beef. Cover and refrigerate 2 to 6 hours. Remove steak from marinade and broil on a rack, basting with remaining marinade. Cook until done to taste. Sprinkle with parsley. Dot with margarine, if desired. Divide evenly. Makes 6 evening meal servings.

Each serving is equivalent to: 6 ounces "Beef" Group; 1 serving Fat (optional)

Beef Chop Suey

Thinly sliced eye round or top sirloin could replace the flank steak in this and the recipes for Beef with Peppers and Tomatoes and Chinese Pepper Steak with Mushrooms.

2 pounds flank steak	**Salt to taste**
2 tablespoons soy sauce	**½ cup fresh or rinsed canned bean**
½ cup water	**sprouts**
4 ounces onion, sliced	**¼ cup canned sliced bamboo**
½ cup sliced fresh mushrooms	**shoots**
¼ cup sliced celery	**4 dried mushrooms, reconstituted**
¼ cup sliced carrots	**in warm water and sliced**
1 packet instant beef broth and	**1 tablespoon cornstarch, dissolved**
seasoning mix	**in 2 tablespoons water**
Artificial sweetener to equal 1	**1 medium tomato, cut into 8**
teaspoon sugar	**wedges**

Preheat broiler. Score steak and marinate in soy sauce for 10 minutes, turning once. Reserve marinade. Broil steak on a rack 6 minutes; turn, broil 4 minutes longer or until rare. Cool. Cut into strips. Set aside beef and juices from slicing. In a nonstick skillet over high heat, combine water, onion, fresh mushrooms, celery, carrots, and broth mix. Cook for about 2 minutes, stirring occasionally. Add reserved marinade, sweetener, and salt; mix well. When vegetables are tender-crisp, add steak slices and juices, bean sprouts, bamboo shoots, and dried mushrooms. Stir-cook 2 minutes. Add cornstarch; stir until mixture thickens. Add tomato wedges; mix well. Cook for 1 minute longer. Divide evenly. Makes 4 evening meal servings.

Each serving is equivalent to: 6 ounces "Beef" Group; 1 ounce Limited Vegetable; ½ cup plus 2 tablespoons Vegetables; 1 serving Something Extra (¼ packet broth mix and ¾ teaspoon cornstarch)

Beef with Peppers and Tomatoes

2 pounds flank steak
3 medium green peppers, seeded
  and sliced
4 ounces onion, sliced thin
2 garlic cloves, minced
1 packet instant beef broth and
  seasoning mix
1 teaspoon salt

½ teaspoon pepper
¼ cup soy sauce
¼ cup water
½ teaspoon sherry extract
2 teaspoons cornstarch
2 cups cut green beans
2 medium tomatoes, cut into
  wedges

Broil steak on a rack about 4 inches from source of heat about 15 minutes, or until rare, turning once. Cut into thin slices; set aside. In a nonstick skillet combine green peppers, onion, garlic, broth mix, salt, and pepper; cook for 5 minutes, stirring occasionally. In a small bowl combine soy sauce, water, and sherry extract. Add cornstarch; stir to dissolve. Stir into vegetable mixture; cook until thickened. Add steak and green beans. Cook until beans are tender-crisp. Add tomatoes and cook 3 minutes longer. Divide evenly. Makes 4 evening meal servings.

Each serving is equivalent to: 6 ounces "Beef" Group; 1 cup plus 2 tablespoons Vegetables; 1 ounce Limited Vegetable; ¾ serving Something Extra (¼ packet broth mix and ½ teaspoon cornstarch)

Chinese Pepper Steak with Mushrooms

2 pounds flank steak
6 medium green peppers, seeded
  and cut into long strips
2 cups sliced mushrooms
4 ounces sliced onion
1 garlic clove, minced

1½ teaspoons salt
½ teaspoon ginger
¼ teaspoon pepper
1½ cups beef bouillon
3 tablespoons soy sauce
2 tablespoons cornstarch

Broil steak on rack for 12 minutes or until rare, turning once to brown both sides. In a preheated nonstick skillet or wok, combine green peppers, mushrooms, onion, and garlic; cook for 3 minutes, stirring constantly. Add salt, ginger, and pepper. In a small bowl combine bouillon, soy sauce, and cornstarch; stir to dissolve cornstarch. Add to skillet. Bring to a boil, stirring constantly until sauce is thickened and clear. Remove from heat. Slice steak; place equal amounts of steak on each of 4 plates and top each portion with ¼ of the vegetable mixture. Makes 4 evening meal servings.

Each serving is equivalent to: 6 ounces "Beef" Group; 1¼ cups Vegetables; 1 ounce Limited Vegetable; 2 servings Something Extra (¼ cup plus 2 tablespoons bouillon and 1½ teaspoons cornstarch)

Polynesian Beef

1½ pounds boned beef chuck, cut into 1-inch cubes
1½ cups beef bouillon
1½ cups canned pineapple chunks, no sugar added, drained, reserve juice
3 ounces onion, grated
1 tablespoon soy sauce
1 tablespoon cider vinegar
1 garlic clove, pressed

½-inch slice fresh ginger root, mashed
¼ teaspoon salt
¼ teaspoon dry mustard
2 teaspoons cornstarch, dissolved in 2 tablespoons water
1½ cups cooked enriched rice
1 tablespoon chopped fresh parsley

Broil beef on rack, 5 to 8 minutes, turning to brown all sides. In bowl combine bouillon, pineapple juice, onion, soy sauce, vinegar, garlic, ginger, salt, and mustard. Add beef. Cover; refrigerate overnight. Transfer beef and marinade to saucepan and simmer about 30 minutes or until beef is tender. Stir in cornstarch and simmer until thickened. Add pineapple; cook 3 minutes. Divide evenly into 3 portions. Serve each portion over ½ cup hot rice. Sprinkle with parsley. Makes 3 evening meal servings.

Each serving is equivalent to: 6 ounces "Beef" Group; 1⅓ servings Something Extra (½ cup bouillon and ⅔ teaspoon cornstarch); 1 serving Fruit; 1 ounce Limited Vegetable; 1 serving Choice Group

Steak and Kidney Pie

1 pound, 2 ounces cooked beef kidneys (see Note)	1¾ cups water, divided
1 pound, 2 ounces cooked beef, cut into ¾-inch cubes	4 ounces onion, sliced
3 tablespoons plus 1 teaspoon flour	¼ cup chopped pimento
2 packets instant beef broth and seasoning mix	2 tablespoons Worcestershire sauce
1 teaspoon salt	¼ teaspoon thyme
⅛ teaspoon pepper	3 slices enriched white bread, made into crumbs
	Dash salt

In saucepan sprinkle kidneys and beef with flour, broth mix, salt and pepper. Add 1½ cups water, onion, pimento, Worcestershire, and thyme. Bring to a boil, reduce heat, and simmer, stirring often, until thickened. Place beef–kidney mixture in a 1½-quart casserole. Set aside. In bowl combine remaining ¼ cup water, crumbs, and salt, stirring with a fork until crumbs are evenly moistened. Place mixture between two large sheets of wax paper. Roll out in a shape to cover casserole. Remove from wax paper and place over steak–kidney mixture. Press crust to secure around ends of casserole. Bake at 325°F. for 45 minutes or until top is lightly browned. Divide evenly. Makes 6 evening meal servings.

Each serving is equivalent to: 3 ounces Kidneys; 3 ounces "Beef" Group; 2 servings Something Extra (1⅔ teaspoons flour and ⅓ packet broth mix); ⅔ ounce Limited Vegetable; 2 teaspoons Vegetable; ½ serving Bread

Note: Wash beef kidneys; remove excess fat and cartilage. Cut into ¾-inch slices. Place in covered saucepan with water to cover and simmer 1 hour or until tender. Drain and weigh.

Chili for Four

Tie a checked napkin on the handle of the pot full of chili and bring it to the table. Serve steaming hot with a crisp green salad to douse the fireworks.

1 pound ground beef
2½ cups water
2 medium green peppers, seeded and diced
4 ounces onion, chopped
½ cup diced celery
1 canned hot jalapeño pepper, diced
½ garlic clove, minced
3 canned medium tomatoes, chopped with liquid
1 cup tomato sauce, no sugar added

1 tablespoon chili powder
½ teaspoon black pepper
¼ to ½ teaspoon cayenne pepper or a few drops hot sauce or to taste
⅛ teaspoon cumin
2 cloves
1 bay leaf
Salt to taste
1 pound drained canned dried red kidney or pinto beans

In saucepan combine beef and water; simmer about 15 minutes or until beef loses its red color. Strain and refrigerate liquid and beef in separate containers. Chill liquid until fat congeals on top; remove fat and discard. Set aside ¾ cup liquid. Freeze remaining liquid for later use. In saucepan combine the next 5 ingredients. Cook 5 minutes. Add tomatoes, tomato sauce, seasonings, beans, reserved ¾ cup liquid, and beef. Simmer 30 minutes. Divide evenly. Makes 4 evening meal servings.

Each serving is equivalent to: 3 ounces "Beef" Group; ¾ cup Vegetables; 1 ounce Limited Vegetable; ½ serving Bonus (¼ cup tomato sauce); 4 ounces Legumes; ¼ serving Something Extra (3 tablespoons broth)

Lasagna

1 pound 2 ounces ground beef	2 cups tomato sauce, no sugar
4 ounces diced onion	added
¼ cup chopped fresh parsley,	¾ cup beef bouillon
divided	2 teaspoons oregano
¾ teaspoon garlic powder, divided	2 cups skim milk ricotta cheese
Salt and white pepper to taste	4 cups cooked enriched lasagna

In bowl combine beef, onion, 2 tablespoons parsley, ¼ teaspoon garlic powder, salt, and pepper. Shape into large patties and place on rack in baking pan. Bake at 400°F. for 20 minutes or until firm. Cool; crumble. In saucepan combine beef, tomato sauce, bouillon, oregano, ¼ teaspoon garlic powder, salt, and pepper. Simmer for 25 minutes, stirring occasionally. Set aside. In a separate bowl combine cheese, remaining 2 tablespoons parsley, ¼ teaspoon garlic powder, salt, and pepper. Spread a thin layer of meat sauce in the bottom of an 8x8-inch baking pan. Arrange alternate layers of lasagna, cheese, and meat sauce, ending with a layer of meat sauce. Bake at 350°F. for 40 minutes. Allow to stand 15 minutes before serving. Divide evenly. Makes 6 midday meal servings.

Each serving is equivalent to: 2 ounces "Beef" Group; ⅔ ounce Limited Vegetable; ⅔ serving Bonus (⅓ cup tomato sauce); ⅙ serving Something Extra (2 tablespoons bouillon); ⅓ cup Soft Cheese; 1 serving Choice Group

Meat Loaf

1 envelope unflavored gelatin	1 pound ground beef
¾ cup beef bouillon	Brown sugar substitute to equal 2
1 cup cooked, mashed carrots	teaspoons brown sugar
4 ounces grated onion, divided	(optional)
1 teaspoon salt, divided	½ teaspoon oregano
⅛ teaspoon dry mustard	Dash garlic powder
Dash white pepper	Freshly ground pepper to taste

In a small saucepan sprinkle gelatin over bouillon to soften. Place over low heat, and cook, stirring constantly, until gelatin is dissolved. Remove from heat; set aside. In a small bowl combine carrot, 2 ounces onion, ½ teaspoon salt, dry mustard, and white pepper. Set aside. In a large bowl combine ground beef, sweetener, if desired, oregano, garlic powder, pepper, remaining 2 ounces onion, ½ teaspoon salt, and ¼ cup bouillon mixture. On a sheet of wax paper, form beef mixture into a rectangle, about ½ inch thick. Spread with carrot mixture to within 1 inch of edges. Roll up from narrow end. Slide off of wax paper, seam side down, onto a rack in roasting pan. Brush remaining bouillon mixture over beef roll. Bake at 350°F. for 1 hour or until beef is done to taste. Divide evenly. Makes 2 evening meal servings.

Each serving is equivalent to: 1½ servings Something Extra (½ envelope gelatin and ¼ cup plus 2 tablespoons bouillon); ½ cup Vegetables; 2 ounces Limited Vegetable; 6 ounces "Beef" Group

Simmered Meatballs

6 ounces ground beef
2 medium eggs
2 slices enriched white bread,
    made into crumbs
½ garlic clove, minced (optional)

¼ teaspoon oregano (optional)
Salt and freshly ground pepper to
    taste
6 cups water

Combine all ingredients except water in a bowl. Form into 10 equal meatballs. Place in saucepan with water. Simmer 12 to 15 minutes or until meatballs are done to taste. Drain.* Divide meatballs evenly. Makes 2 midday meal servings.

Each serving is equivalent to: 2 ounces "Beef" Group; 1 Egg; 1 serving Bread

*Refrigerate liquid. Remove and discard congealed fat: ¾ cup liquid is equivalent to 1 serving bouillon or broth. If fat is difficult to remove, place a strainer lined with 4 layers of cheesecloth or a heavy wet paper towel over a bowl. Pour liquid through strainer. Discard fat.

Oriental Meat Balls with Rice

1 pound lean ground beef
¼ cup water
1 teaspoon garlic salt
½ teaspoon dry mustard
½ teaspoon ginger
1 cup cooked, sliced celery
½ cup orange juice

1 tablespoon soy sauce
1 tablespoon vinegar
Artificial sweetener to equal 2
    teaspoons sugar
1 cup cooked enriched rice
Chopped fresh parsley to garnish

Preheat broiler. Combine first 5 ingredients in mixing bowl; blend well. Form into 16 equal balls. Place on rack in broiler pan. Broil 3 to 4 inches from heat source, 5 to 7 minutes until brown; turn and brown other side. Place meatballs in saucepan. Combine celery, orange juice, soy sauce, vinegar, and sweetener in blender container. Process until smooth. Pour over meatballs. Heat and serve over rice. Garnish with chopped parsley. Divide evenly. Makes 2 evening meal servings.

Each serving is equivalent to: 6 ounces "Beef" Group; ½ cup Vegetables; ½ serving Fruit; 1 serving Choice Group

Hot-n-Spicy Meat Sauce

To serve over cooked pasta or cornmeal.

1½ pounds cooked ground beef,
    crumbled
3 cups water
2 canned medium tomatoes,
    pureed in food mill or blender
2 cups tomato puree
¼ cup dehydrated onion flakes
¼ cup finely chopped celery
3 tablespoons Worcestershire
    sauce
1 tablespoon minced fresh parsley

2 tablespoons brown sugar
    replacement
2 teaspoons garlic salt
2 teaspoons paprika
2 bay leaves
1 teaspoon chili powder, or to taste
½ teaspoon oregano
½ teaspoon salt
¼ teaspoon cinnamon
¼ teaspoon pepper
¼ teaspoon thyme
Chopped fresh parsley to garnish

Combine all ingredients, except garnish, in large saucepan. Simmer sauce, uncovered, for about two hours or until thick. Remove bay leaves. Garnish with parsley. Serve hot. Divide evenly. Makes 4 evening meal servings.

Each serving is equivalent to: 6 ounces "Beef" Group; ¼ cup plus 1 tablespoon Vegetables; 1 serving Bonus (½ cup tomato puree)

Lamb and Barley Stew

2 pounds boned lamb, cut into
    1-inch pieces
1 cup diced carrots
4 ounces sliced onion
2 canned medium tomatoes
4 packets instant chicken broth
    and seasoning mix
½ teaspoon paprika

¼ teaspoon garlic powder
1 bay leaf
Salt and pepper to taste
3 cups water
6 ounces pared potatoes, diced
2 cups cut green beans
1 cup cooked barley

Broil lamb on rack, turning to brown all sides; set aside. In a large saucepan combine carrots, onion, tomatoes, broth mix, paprika, garlic powder, bay leaf, salt, and pepper; cook 5 minutes, stirring frequently. Add lamb and water. Bring to a boil; lower heat. Simmer about 30 minutes or until lamb is tender. Add potatoes, green beans, and barley, and cook covered for about 1 hour or until potatoes are soft. Divide evenly. Makes 4 evening meal servings.

Each serving is equivalent to: 6 ounces "Beef" Group; 1 cup Vegetables; 1 ounce Limited Vegetable; 1 serving Something Extra (1 packet broth mix); 1 serving Choice Group

Moussaka (Greek-Style Lamb and Eggplant)

2 cups pared sliced eggplant, cut
    ½ inch thick
8 ounces diced onion
1 cup canned medium tomatoes,
    chopped
½ cup water
¼ cup tomato paste
2 tablespoons chopped fresh
    parsley

Dash cinnamon
Dash allspice
Salt and pepper to taste
12 ounces cooked ground lamb or
    beef, crumbled
½ recipe Basic White Sauce (2
    servings, see page 296)

Brown eggplant slices on both sides in nonstick skillet over high heat, pressing slices with back of spatula to release moisture. Set aside. In the same skillet, brown the onions slightly. Add tomatoes, water, tomato paste, parsley, cinnamon, allspice, salt, and pepper. Simmer for 5 minutes. Add crumbled meat and cook 10 minutes longer. In a nonstick casserole, place ½ the eggplant slices and ½ meat mixture; repeat layers. Spoon White Sauce on top. Bake at 375°F. for 35 minutes or until top begins to brown. Divide evenly. Makes 2 evening meal servings.

Each serving is equivalent to: 1½ cups plus 1 tablespoon Vegetables; 4 ounces Limited Vegetable; ½ serving Bonus (2 tablespoons tomato paste); 6 ounces "Beef" Group; Basic White Sauce (see page 296)

Quick-and-Easy Lamb Dinner

4 loin or rib lamb chops, about 1
    inch thick, 5 ounces each
1 tablespoon dehydrated onion
    flakes

1 teaspoon salt
½ teaspoon garlic powder
⅛ teaspoon pepper
2 medium tomatoes, cut in half

Broil chops on rack 3 to 4 inches from source of heat 6 to 7 minutes or until browned. In a small cup combine onion flakes, salt, garlic powder, and pepper. Turn chops and arrange tomato halves, cut side up, on broiler rack. Sprinkle onion flake mixture over chops and tomatoes. Broil 5 to 6 minutes or until chops are done. Divide evenly. Makes 2 evening meal servings.

Each serving equivalent to: 6 ounces "Beef" Group; ½ cup Vegetables

Savory Lamb Succotash

8 ounces cooked dried lima beans
6 ounces cooked lamb, diced
1½ cups chicken bouillon
3 canned medium tomatoes, chopped
3 ounces pared potato, diced
½ cup drained canned whole kernel corn
2 ounces diced onion
¾ teaspoon salt
¼ teaspoon thyme

Combine all ingredients in a medium saucepan. Cover and cook for about 1 hour or until sauce is very thick. Divide evenly. Makes 2 evening meal servings.

Each serving is equivalent to: 4 ounces Legumes; 3 ounces "Beef" Group; 1 serving Something Extra (¾ cup bouillon); ¾ cup Vegetables; 1 serving Choice Group; 1 ounce Limited Vegetable

Roast Pork

Season lean shoulder, leg, or loin of pork with salt, pepper, and desired spices or herbs. Insert meat thermometer into thickest part of roast, not touching bone. Place on rack in roasting pan. Roast at 350°F. between 30 and 40 minutes to the pound. Time will depend on the size and cut of meat. Pork is cooked when internal temperature registers 170° on meat thermometer. Slice and weigh portions.

Homemade "Sausage" with Hot Soup

1 pound 2 ounces cooked pork, cut
   into 2-inch pieces
1½ slices enriched white bread
¼ cup chopped fresh parsley
1½ ounces shallots or onion
1 teaspoon salt
1 garlic clove

¼ teaspoon pepper
¼ teaspoon sage
¼ teaspoon savory
¼ teaspoon marjoram
Dash nutmeg
6 cups Chicken or Beef Stock (see
   page 140 or 163)

Combine all ingredients except stock and put through food grinder or
grind in food processor. Blend well and form into a loaf on a piece of
cheesecloth. Wrap loaf in the cheesecloth and twist ends to seal.
Secure with string. Refrigerate overnight. Place in pot or fish poacher
with ends of cheesecloth at edge of pot. Add stock and poach about 50
minutes. Remove "sausage" from stock; refrigerate. Strain stock.
Slice "sausage" and serve evenly divided. Heat stock and divide
evenly into 3 soup bowls. Makes 3 evening meal servings.

Each serving is equivalent to: 6 ounces "Beef" Group; ½ serving
Bread; 1 tablespoon plus 1 teaspoon Vegetables; ½ ounce Limited
Vegetable; 2⅔ servings Something Extra (2 cups stock)

Paella

1½ teaspoons salt
1 teaspoon oregano
1 teaspoon lemon juice
¼ teaspoon freshly ground pepper
1 garlic clove, minced
1 pound skinned and boned
   chicken breast, cut into 1-inch
   pieces
6 ounces onion, chopped
1 medium green pepper, seeded
   and chopped
3 cups cooked enriched rice
9 ounces fresh or frozen small
   peas, thawed

9 ounces frozen artichoke hearts,
   thawed
1 cup boiling water
1 cup tomato sauce, no sugar
   added
¾ teaspoon capers
½ teaspoon ground coriander
½ teaspoon saffron
6 ounces cooked lobster
6 ounces cooked shrimp
6 ounces cooked pork, shredded
6 ounces drained, canned clams
Shredded pimentos to garnish

In small cup combine salt, oregano, lemon juice, pepper, and garlic · to make a paste. Brown chicken, onion, and green pepper in large, heavy, preheated saucepan or Dutch oven. Stir in seasoned paste. Add rice, peas, artichoke hearts, boiling water, tomato sauce, capers, coriander, and saffron; heat thoroughly. Stir in lobster, shrimp, pork, and clams. Heat; garnish with pimentos. Serve hot. Divide evenly. Makes 6 evening meal servings.

Each serving is equivalent to: 2 ounces Poultry; 4 ounces Limited Vegetable; 1 tablespoon plus 1 teaspoon Vegetables; 1 serving Choice Group; ⅓ serving Bonus (2 tablespoons plus 2 teaspoons tomato sauce); 3 ounces Fish; 1 ounce "Beef" Group

Note: This recipe must be counted as a "Beef" Group meal.

Swiss-Style Pot-au-Feu

Swiss skiing is great, and so is Swiss cooking. Whether you ski the Alps, the Green Mountains or any other slopes, here's the perfect hearty winter dish to enjoy. Broil the meat ahead, then put it into the slow cooker with the remaining ingredients before you leave for the slopes, or follow the method below when you get back from the mountain.

2 pounds boned pork shoulder, cut into 1-inch cubes
2 pounds boned veal shoulder, cut into 1-inch cubes
4 cups Chicken Stock (see page 140)
1½ pounds pared potatoes, cut into 1-inch cubes
3 cups sliced carrots, 2-inch slices

3 cups shredded cabbage
2 cups sliced pared white turnips, 2-inch slices
4 ounces diced onion
Bouquet garni: 2 cloves, 2 sprigs thyme, 1 bay leaf, tied in cheesecloth (optional)
¼ teaspoon pepper
Salt to taste

Broil pork and veal on rack until well browned on all sides. Transfer to heavy pot or Dutch oven. Add remaining ingredients. Bring to boil; reduce heat. Cover and simmer 1½ to 2 hours, or until meat is very tender. Remove cover for the last half hour if desired, to reduce liquid. Discard bouquet garni if used. Divide evenly. Makes 8 evening meal servings.

Each serving is equivalent to: 6 ounces "Beef" Group; ⅔ serving Something Extra (½ cup stock); 1 serving Choice Group; 1 cup Vegetables; ½ ounce Limited Vegetable

Baked Ham

To bake, place ham on rack in roasting pan. Insert meat thermometer into center, not touching bone. Bake at 325°F. about 18 to 24 minutes per pound or until thermometer registers 170°F. Slice and weigh portions.

Barbecue Ham on Rolls

2 ounces onion, finely diced
1 packet instant beef broth and
   seasoning mix
1 garlic clove, minced
8 ounces ham, cut into ¼-inch
   dice
½ cup tomato puree
3 tablespoons plus 1 teaspoon chili
   sauce

2 tablespoons cider vinegar
1 tablespoon prepared mustard
2 teaspoons lemon juice
½ teaspoon barbecue spice
Salt to taste
2 hamburger rolls, split

In nonstick skillet combine onion, broth mix, and garlic; cook 2 minutes. Add remaining ingredients except rolls and stir to combine. Simmer 10 minutes. Divide evenly. Serve each portion on 1 hamburger roll. Makes 2 evening meal servings.

Each serving is equivalent to: 1 ounce Limited Vegetable; 3 servings Something Extra (½ packet broth mix and 1 tablespoon plus 2 teaspoons chili sauce); 4 ounces "Beef" Group (cured); ½ serving Bonus (¼ cup tomato puree); 2 servings Bread (once-a-week selection)

Bologna Cornucopia Salad

6 ounces sliced bologna or boiled ham
6 ounces peeled cooked potatoes, diced
2 ounces cooked beets, diced

4 ounces cooked peas
¼ cup imitation mayonnaise
Dash prepared horseradish
2 medium dill pickles
Parsley sprigs to garnish

Roll each slice of meat into cone-shape cornucopias. In a bowl combine remaining ingredients except pickles and parsley; fill each cornucopia with an equal amount of mixture. Divide evenly into 2 portions. Serve each portion with 1 dill pickle and parsley to garnish. Makes 2 midday meal servings.

Each serving is equivalent to: 3 ounces "Beef" Group (cured); 1 serving Choice Group; 3 ounces Limited Vegetable; 3 servings Fat; ½ cup Vegetables

Barbecued Frankfurters

½ cup cold water
3 ounces chopped onion or 2 tablespoons dehydrated onion flakes
¼ cup plus 2 tablespoons catsup
3 tablespoons cider vinegar

¾ teaspoon dry mustard
¾ teaspoon paprika
Freshly ground pepper to taste
12 ounces frankfurters, cut in half lengthwise

In saucepan combine water, onion, catsup, vinegar, dry mustard, paprika, and pepper; bring to boil. Reduce heat; simmer 5 minutes. Arrange frankfurters side by side in shallow 9x9-inch baking dish. Cover with onion–catsup mixture and bake at 350°F. for 30 to 40 minutes. Divide evenly. Makes 3 evening meal servings.

Each serving is equivalent to: 1 ounce Limited Vegetable (optional); 3 servings Something Extra (2 tablespoons catsup); 4 ounces Frankfurters.

Quick-and-Easy Cassoulet

A modern-day version of a famous French stew that originally required long preparation. Done our way it's still delicious, and it's also economical and fast. Serve it with a tossed salad and fresh fruit for dessert.

1 pound drained canned dried kidney or white beans, plus ½ cup liquid
8 ounces frankfurters, cut into bite-size pieces

2 cups cooked sliced carrots
1 cup tomato sauce, no sugar added
2 teaspoons minced fresh parsley
1 small garlic clove, minced

Combine all ingredients in a large saucepan. Cover; bring to a boil. Lower heat and simmer about 15 minutes. Remove cover and continue cooking until thickened, stirring occasionally. Divide evenly. Makes 4 evening meal servings.

Each serving is equivalent to: 4 ounces Legumes; 2 ounces Frankfurters; ½ cup Vegetables; ½ serving Bonus (¼ cup tomato sauce)

Organ Meats

The variety meats referred to as "organ meats" on the Weight Watchers Food Program include hearts, kidneys, sweetbreads, and tripe. Tongue is also an organ meat but may be eaten more frequently than the above meats. (See "Rules for Using 'Beef' Group," page 161.)

Organ meats are usually good buys because they are a good source of nutrients and often in less demand than other cuts. Since organ meats are more perishable than other meats, they should be cooked and served as soon after purchase as possible.

Sweetbreads

Sweetbreads, the two lobes of the thymus gland, are a tender and delicately flavored meat. They should be used immediately after purchase or precooked and used within a day or two.

Soak sweetbreads 1 hour in cold water to cover. Drain. Then place in saucepan and cover with water. Add 1 teaspoon salt and 1 tablespoon lemon juice or vinegar for each quart of water used. Simmer, uncovered, 15 to 20 minutes. Drain and plunge sweetbreads in cold water to firm. When cool, trim to remove cartilage, tubes, membranes, and connective tissue. Weigh servings.

Suggestions for serving sweetbreads
For each serving:

1. Place 6 ounces cooked sweetbreads in shallow pan. Cover with 1 serving (¼ recipe) hot Basic White Sauce (see page 296) seasoned with lemon juice and parsley. Heat and serve in 2 Toast Cups-I (see page 83) with 4 ounces cooked peas. Makes 1 evening meal serving.

Each serving is equivalent to: 6 ounces Sweetbreads; Basic White Sauce (see page 296); Toast Cups-I (see page 83); 4 ounces Limited Vegetable

2. In shallow pan combine 3 ounces diced cooked sweetbreads and 2 ounces ham. Top with 1 serving (¼ recipe) Tomato Sauce (see page 307). Season with cayenne pepper and Worcestershire sauce. Heat and serve. Makes 1 evening meal serving.

Each serving is equivalent to: 3 ounces Sweetbreads; 2 ounces "Beef" Group (cured); Tomato Sauce (see page 307)

3. In nonstick pan scramble 1 medium egg with 2 ounces diced cooked sweetbreads. Serve topped with ¼ cup plain unflavored yogurt and ½ medium tomato, sliced. Makes 1 midday meal serving.

Each serving is equivalent to: 1 Egg; 2 ounces Sweetbreads; ½ serving Milk (¼ cup yogurt); ¼ cup Vegetables

Tripe

Tripe is usually partially cooked before it is sold. However, further preparation is necessary.

Put tripe in kettle and cover with water. Allow 1 teaspoon salt for each quart of water used. Simmer in covered kettle 1½ hours or until tender. Drain and dry between paper towels. Weigh servings.

Suggestions for serving tripe
1. Place 6 ounces cooked tripe in shallow baking pan and cover

with 1 serving (¼ recipe) Tomato Sauce (see page 307). Bake at 350°F. until bubbling. Makes 1 evening meal serving.

Each serving is equivalent to: 6 ounces Tripe; Tomato Sauce (see page 307)

2. Place 6 ounces cooked tripe in shallow pan, brush with 1 teaspoon margarine, and broil 1 minute. Makes 1 evening meal serving.

Each serving is equivalent to: 6 ounces Tripe; 1 serving Fat

3. Shred 6 ounces cooked tripe and combine in saucepan with ¾ cup Beef Stock (see page 163), ¼ cup each diced celery, carrot, and green pepper, 2 ounces diced onion, and 3 ounces diced pared potato. Cover and simmer until vegetables are tender. Add 2 tablespoons evaporated skimmed milk. Makes 1 evening meal serving.

Each serving is equivalent to: 6 ounces Tripe; 1 serving Something Extra (¾ cup stock); ¾ cup Vegetables; 2 ounces Limited Vegetable; 1 serving Choice Group; ¼ serving Milk (2 tablespoons evaporated skimmed milk)

Chicken Giblet Forestière

1½ pounds chicken giblets, sliced
8 ounces sliced onions
2 cups sliced mushrooms
2 packets instant chicken broth and seasoning mix
2 to 3 cups water, divided
¼ teaspoon poultry seasoning
¼ teaspoon browning sauce
Salt and freshly ground pepper to taste
1 tablespoon cornstarch, dissolved in 1 tablespoon water
2 cups cooked enriched rice

Place giblets in a medium saucepan. Cover with salted water. Bring to a boil; lower heat and cook for 15 minutes. Drain; set giblets aside. In a large saucepan combine onions, mushrooms, and broth mix. Cook over high heat, for about 2 to 3 minutes, stirring occasionally. Add 2 cups water, poultry seasoning, browning sauce, and giblets. Bring to boil; lower heat, cover, and cook for about one hour or until giblets are very tender. Add remaining water, if necessary (giblets should be barely covered). Season with salt and pepper. Stir in cornstarch; cook until thickened. Serve over rice. Divide evenly. Makes 4 midday meal servings.

Each serving is equivalent to: 4 ounces Giblets; 2 ounces Limited Vegetable; ½ cup Vegetables; 1¼ servings Something Extra (½ packet broth mix and ¾ teaspoon cornstarch); 1 serving Choice Group

Giblet Sandwich Spread

Cook 6 ounces giblets in boiling salted water until very tender. Drain; finely chop giblets. Place in a small bowl. Stir in 1 tablespoon imitation mayonnaise and salt and pepper to taste. Makes 1 midday meal serving.

Each serving is equivalent to: 4 ounces Giblets; 1½ servings Fat

Cooked Giblets and Giblet Broth

You may keep food bills down and create some mighty good dishes using what you'll find inside the cavities when buying chicken or turkey. Rinse giblets and dry with paper towels. Keep in covered containers in freezer and when you've accumulated enough prepare the following dish:

1 pound giblets	**1 teaspoon salt**
¼ cup chopped celery	**2 parsley sprigs**
¼ cup chopped carrot	**1 small bay leaf**
1 tablespoon dehydrated onion flakes	**4 peppercorns**

Combine ingredients in saucepan; cover with water and bring to a boil. Remove foam which has risen to surface. Reduce heat, cover, and simmer 1 hour or until giblets are tender. Drain; discard all solids except giblets. Refrigerate giblets and liquid in separate containers. Remove and discard congealed fat from liquid; measure 1½ cups. Place in saucepan with giblets and heat. Divide evenly. Makes 2 evening meal servings.

Each serving equivalent to: 6 ounces Giblets; 1 serving Something Extra (¾ cup broth)

Heart and Wheat Pilaf

Before cooking hearts, wash thoroughly; remove fat, arteries and veins. Weigh.

**3 pounds veal or beef heart, cut
into ½-inch slices
3 cups beef bouillon
6 ounces dry cracked wheat
(Bulgur)
6 ounces chopped onion**

**2 medium green peppers, seeded
and chopped
½ teaspoon cinnamon
½ teaspoon salt or to taste
¼ teaspoon pepper or to taste**

In saucepan simmer heart in water to cover, about 1 hour. Drain. Add remaining ingredients and cook about 1 hour or until heart is tender, adding water if necessary. Divide evenly. Makes 6 evening meal servings.

Each serving is equivalent to: 6 ounces Heart; ⅔ serving Something Extra (½ cup bouillon); 1 serving Choice Group; 1 ounce Limited Vegetable; 2 tablespoons plus 2 teaspoons Vegetables

Kidneys in Parsley "Butter"

A delicacy!

**1 pound trimmed veal or lamb
kidneys
2 teaspoons margarine
1 teaspoon lemon juice
Salt and freshly ground pepper to
taste**

**1 tablespoon chopped fresh
parsley
2 slices enriched white bread,
toasted**

Cut kidneys into slices ¼ inch thick. Melt margarine in top of double boiler over boiling water. Add kidneys, lemon juice, salt, and pepper. Cook 10 minutes or until tender. Stir in parsley and serve on toast. Divide evenly. Makes 2 evening meal servings.

Each serving is equivalent to: 6 ounces Kidneys; 1 serving Fat; 1 serving Bread

Boiled Fresh Beef Tongue

2½ to 3 pounds fresh beef or calf
   tongue
1 cup sliced carrots
2 celery ribs with leaves, sliced
4 sprigs fresh parsley

1 slice lemon
8 peppercorns
2 cloves
1 teaspoon salt for each quart
   water

Rinse tongue and place in a large pot with remaining ingredients except salt. Cover with boiling water; add salt. Bring to a boil; lower heat. Simmer until tongue is tender, about 2 to 3 hours. Add more water as needed. Drain. Cool by immersing tongue in cold water. When it is easy to handle, remove skin, roots, small bones, and gristle. Slice the tongue on a slight diagonal. Serve hot or cold. Weigh portions. Makes about 4 midday or evening meal servings.

Each serving is equivalent to: 4 or 6 ounces "Beef" Group

When using parboiled tongue—Follow directions above but cut cooking time in half.

When using smoked or pickled tongue—These tend to be salty. First blanch tongue for about 10 minutes. Immerse in cold water, drain, and proceed as above, omitting salt. When weighing portions, use the low end of the range (see "The Food Program," page 5).

Each serving is equivalent to: 3 or 4 ounces "Beef" Group (cured)

Tongue and Potato Salad

12 ounces peeled cooked potatoes,
   diced
8 ounces cooked peas
6 ounces cooked smoked beef
   tongue, diced
2 cups cooked cut green beans

¾ cup diced celery
¼ cup chopped dill pickle
¼ cup plain unflavored yogurt
2 tablespoons imitation
   mayonnaise
1 tablespoon lemon juice

In bowl combine first 6 ingredients. In separate bowl combine remaining ingredients; pour over potato mixture and toss to combine. Chill. Divide evenly. Makes 4 midday meal servings. Supplement as required.

Each serving is equivalent to: 1 serving Choice Group; 2 ounces Limited Vegetable; 1½ ounces "Beef" Group (cured); ¾ cup Vegetables; ⅛ serving Milk (1 tablespoon yogurt); ¾ serving Fat

Sweet-and-Sour Tongue with Water Chestnuts

1 slice raisin bread, torn into
  pieces
½ cup chicken bouillon
2 ounces diced onion
2 tablespoons cider vinegar
1 slice fresh ginger root

Artificial sweetener to equal 1
  teaspoon sugar (optional)
8 ounces Boiled Fresh Beef
  Tongue, sliced (see page 187)
4 ounces drained canned water
  chestnuts, sliced

In a small saucepan, combine first 6 ingredients. Cook, stirring occasionally, until bread falls apart and mixture thickens. Add tongue and water chestnuts. Cook until thoroughly heated. Divide evenly. Makes 2 midday meal servings.

Each serving is equivalent to: ½ serving Bread; ⅓ serving Something Extra (¼ cup bouillon); 3 ounces Limited Vegetable; 4 ounces "Beef" Group

LIVER

If you've only had broiled or baked liver, and pâtés at parties, we think you're in for a treat once you discover liver in all its versatile flavors and cooking styles. We've included enough recipes so you can go for months without repeating one!

Try marinating liver or cooking it Polynesian style. Flavor liver recipes with ginger, soy sauce, or our Basic White Sauce. There's really no end to the interesting variety you can get from a few kinds of liver. Try them all.

Rules for Using Liver

1. Amounts (net cooked weight):
   Women, Men, and Youth: 3 to 4 ounces at the Midday Meal
   Women and Youth: 4 to 6 ounces at the Evening Meal
   Men: 6 to 8 ounces at the Evening Meal
2. The range of 3 to 4 ounces of liver at the Midday Meal, and 4 to 6 ounces for Women and Youth (6 to 8 ounces for Men) at the Evening Meal, provides flexibility. It is a way to individualize the Food Plan to meet your specific needs.
3. Select liver only once a week.
4. As a "rule of thumb," for each serving of liver allow 2 ounces for shrinkage in cooking.
5. All liver is "legal." Do not split a liver meal. Do not take it as a breakfast selection.
6. *Cooking Procedures:* May be boiled, poached, broiled, pan-broiled, or baked. Cooked or uncooked liver may be used with added ingredients (e.g., casseroles, stews, etc.). Liquid and added ingredients may be consumed.

[189]

How to Cook Liver

For broiling, have liver sliced ½ to ¾ inch thick. Broil according to directions on page 162 ("How to Cook Meat") just long enough to brown lightly. Allow about 3 minutes on each side. To pan-broil, cook liver in a nonstick skillet, at moderate temperature, until done. Turn occasionally.

Beef Liver Orientale

4 ounces sliced scallions
½ cup chopped celery
1 garlic clove, minced
1½ pounds beef liver, cut into
   1-inch pieces

1 tablespoon flour
⅛ teaspoon ginger
⅛ teaspoon pepper
¾ cup water
3 tablespoons soy sauce

Cook scallions, celery, and garlic in nonstick pan for 3 minutes; remove from pan and set aside. Add liver to pan and cook over high heat, turning pieces to brown. Sprinkle with flour, ginger, and pepper. Stir in water and soy sauce, and cook for 3 minutes. Add vegetables and cook to heat vegetables. Divide evenly. Makes 4 midday meal servings.

Each serving is equivalent to: 1 ounce Limited Vegetable; 2 tablespoons Vegetables; 4 ounces Liver; ¾ serving Something Extra (¾ teaspoon flour)

Liver and Cucumber Soup

12 ounces beef liver, cut into
   bite-size pieces
1 medium cucumber, pared
1½ cups beef bouillon
1 small piece dried tangerine peel
   (optional)*

Salt and pepper to taste
1 cup cooked enriched rice
   (optional)

Blanch the liver in boiling water to cover for 3 minutes; drain and dry. Cut cucumber in half lengthwise; remove and discard seeds. Cut into ¼-inch slices. In saucepan combine liver, cucumber, bouillon, and tangerine peel, if desired. Bring to boil, lower heat, and simmer 20 minutes. Season with salt and pepper. Stir in rice if desired. Divide evenly. Makes 2 midday meal servings.

Each serving is equivalent to: 4 ounces Liver; ¼ cup Vegetables; 1 serving Something Extra (¾ cup bouillon); 1 serving Choice Group (optional)

*Available in Chinese grocery store.

Liver and Vegetables in One Pot

3 ounces pared potato, diced
2 ounces onion, diced
½ cup diced pared eggplant
½ cup sliced mushrooms
½ cup sliced zucchini
½ cup water
½ garlic clove, minced

1 teaspoon salt
Dash cayenne pepper
8 ounces beef liver, sliced ½ inch thick
2 ounces peas
1 tablespoon minced fresh parsley

Combine all ingredients except liver, peas, and parsley in saucepan; bring to a boil, reduce heat, and simmer covered about 15 minutes. Cut liver into strips 1 inch wide. In bowl cover liver with boiling water, let stand 3 minutes, drain and dry with paper towels. Add liver and peas to vegetables and cook about 5 minutes, or until liver strips are done. Sprinkle with parsley and serve. Makes 1 evening meal serving.

Each serving is equivalent to: 1 serving Choice Group; 4 ounces Limited Vegetable; 1½ cups Vegetables; 6 ounces Liver

Liver Chop Suey

½ cup dried mushrooms
1½ pounds beef liver, cut into ¼-inch slices
1 medium green pepper, cut into 1-inch dice
½ cup canned sliced bamboo shoots

1 garlic clove, minced
¾ cup chicken bouillon
1 tablespoon cornstarch
1 teaspoon soy sauce
4 ounces Chinese pea pods
1 medium tomato, cut into 8 wedges

In a small bowl cover mushrooms with boiling water and let soak for 20 minutes or until soft. Drain. Cut stems from mushrooms. Discard stems; slice and reserve caps. Cut sliced liver into ½-inch strips and place in medium bowl. Cover with boiling water. Drain and dry. Brown liver in preheated nonstick skillet or wok. Add green pepper, bamboo shoots, garlic, and mushrooms. Combine bouillon, cornstarch, and soy sauce. Mix well to dissolve cornstarch. Stir into liver-vegetable mixture. Cook, stirring often, until slightly thickened. Add pea pods and tomato. Cook 3 minutes. Divide evenly. Makes 4 midday meal servings.

Each serving is equivalent to: ½ cup Vegetables; 4 ounces Liver; 1 serving Something Extra (3 tablespoons bouillon and ¾ teaspoon cornstarch); 1 ounce Limited Vegetable

Variation: If Chinese pea pods are not available, 1 cup cooked green beans may be substituted. Add 1 ounce finely diced scallion before serving.

Each serving is equivalent to: ¾ cup Vegetables; 4 ounces Liver; 1 serving Something Extra; (3 tablespoons bouillon and ¾ tablespoon cornstarch); ¼ ounce Limited Vegetable

Liver Pudding

A Scandinavian dish.

12 ounces beef liver	4 dried medium prunes, pitted
2 ounces onion	and diced
1 cup cooked enriched rice, chilled	Salt and pepper to taste

In bowl pour boiling water over liver and let stand a few minutes. Drain and dry. Put liver and onion through food grinder or chop finely in food processor. Combine ground liver mixture, rice, prunes, salt, and pepper. Pour into a 3-cup nonstick baking pan. Bake at 350°F. about 45 minutes or until pudding is hot and bubbling. Divide evenly. Makes 2 midday meal servings.

Each serving is equivalent to: 4 ounces Liver; 1 ounce Limited Vegetable; 1 serving Choice Group; ½ serving Fruit

Broiled Liver and Onions

6 ounces sliced onion
½ cup chicken bouillon
¼ teaspoon Worcestershire sauce

Dash nutmeg
Salt and pepper to taste
1½ pounds calf or beef liver, sliced

In saucepan combine all ingredients except liver. Cook until onions are tender and most of the liquid is evaporated. Place liver on a rack; broil 4 inches from source of heat, turning once until done to taste. Serve onion mixture over liver. Divide evenly. Makes 4 midday meal servings.

Each serving is equivalent to: 1½ ounces Limited Vegetable; ⅙ serving Something Extra (2 tablespoons bouillon); 4 ounces Liver

Liver Casserole

1½ pounds calf or beef liver
2 cups thinly sliced carrots
12 ounces pared potatoes, thinly sliced
8 ounces onion, sliced
2 cups beef bouillon

4 canned medium tomatoes, chopped
1½ teaspoons basil
1 bay leaf
Salt and pepper to taste

Cut liver into strips; place in bowl and cover with boiling water; let stand 3 minutes. Drain and dry with paper towels. In saucepan add carrots to boiling water, cook 5 minutes; add potatoes, cook 5 minutes longer. Drain. Layer liver, carrots, potatoes, and onion in a 2½-quart casserole. Combine remaining ingredients and add to casserole. Bake at 350°F. for 1 hour or until vegetables are tender. Divide evenly. Makes 4 midday meal servings.

Each serving is equivalent to: 4 ounces Liver; 1 cup Vegetables; 1 serving Choice Group; 2 ounces Limited Vegetable; ⅔ serving Something Extra (½ cup bouillon)

Liver Mexican Style

2 pounds calf or beef liver
½ teaspoon garlic powder
Salt and pepper to taste
2 chili peppers, cut into strips
2 tablespoons plus 2 teaspoons
vegetable oil

2 tablespoons lemon juice
2 tablespoons chopped fresh
parsley
8 toasted tortillas (6 inches each)

Cut liver into strips; season with garlic powder, salt, and pepper. Brown in nonstick skillet over moderately high heat for 6 minutes or until done to taste. Transfer to serving bowl and toss immediately with chili peppers, oil, lemon juice, and parsley. Divide evenly onto toasted tortillas. Makes 4 evening meal servings.

Each serving is equivalent to: 6 ounces Liver; 2 tablespoons Vegetables; 2 servings Fat; 2 servings Bread (once-a-week selection)

Liver 'n Noodle Casserole

12 ounces calf or beef liver, cut
into ½-inch pieces
4 ounces sliced onion
½ medium green pepper, seeded
and diced
1 cup tomato sauce, no sugar
added

¼ teaspoon thyme
¼ teaspoon browning sauce
Salt and pepper to taste
1 cup cooked enriched wide
noodles
¾ cup cooked sliced carrots

Brown liver, onions, and green pepper in a preheated nonstick skillet. Add tomato sauce, thyme, browning sauce, salt, and pepper. Cook until peppers are tender. Stir in noodles and carrots and heat thoroughly. Divide evenly. Makes 2 midday meal servings.

Each serving is equivalent to: 4 ounces Liver; 2 ounces Limited Vegetable; ½ cup Vegetables; 1 serving Bonus (½ cup tomato sauce); 1 serving Choice Group

Baked Whole Calf Liver

2 pounds calf liver, unsliced
1 teaspoon salt
¼ teaspoon pepper
2 cups sliced mushrooms

4 ounces sliced onion
½ cup diced celery
¾ cup beef bouillon

Sprinkle liver with salt and pepper. Place in a 1-quart baking dish. Surround with mushrooms, onions, and celery. Add bouillon. Cover and bake at 350°F. for about 1½ hours or until liver is done to taste. Divide evenly. Makes 4 evening meal servings.

Each serving is equivalent to: 6 ounces Liver; ½ cup plus 2 tablespoons Vegetables; 1 ounce Limited Vegetable; ¼ serving Something Extra (3 tablespoons bouillon)

Calf Liver with Grapes

A ten-minute gourmet meal.

1 pound calf liver, cut into ½-inch
　slices
Salt and freshly ground pepper to
　taste

2 teaspoons lemon juice
40 small seedless green grapes
2 teaspoons margarine
2 teaspoons minced fresh parsley

Cut liver into 1-inch strips. In medium bowl pour boiling water over liver, drain and dry with paper towels. Season with salt and pepper. Brown liver in preheated nonstick skillet, remove from skillet and keep warm. Add lemon juice and grapes to skillet, mashing a few of the grapes to release their juices. Heat fruit; remove from heat and stir in margarine. Serve sauce over liver. Garnish with parsley. Divide evenly. Makes 2 evening meal servings.

Each serving is equivalent to: 6 ounces Liver; 1 serving Fruit; 1 serving Fat

"Creamed" Calf Liver

12 ounces calf liver, ¼-inch slices

½ recipe Basic White Sauce (2 servings, see page 296)
2 teaspoons chopped fresh parsley

Broil liver on a rack 4 inches from source of heat, turning once until done to taste. Cut into bite-size pieces and combine with remaining ingredients in top of double boiler over boiling water. Heat thoroughly. Divide evenly. Makes 2 midday meal servings.

Each serving is equivalent to: 4 ounces Liver; Basic White Sauce (see page 296)

Variation:
Liver Tetrazzini—Serve "Creamed" Calf Liver on a bed of 1⅓ cups cooked enriched spaghetti surrounded with 6 ounces canned drained artichoke hearts. Add 1 serving Choice Group and 3 ounces Limited Vegetable to equivalent listing.

Lemony Calf Liver

1½ pounds calf liver
Salt and freshly ground pepper to taste
2 tablespoons vegetable oil

1 tablespoon lemon juice
1 teaspoon finely chopped fresh parsley

Dry liver with a paper towel, season with salt and pepper. Place in a flameproof casserole and broil, 4 inches from source of heat, turning once, until done. Brush with oil and lemon juice. Place under broiler for 1 minute; sprinkle with parsley and serve. Divide evenly. Makes 4 midday meal servings.

Each serving is equivalent to: 4 ounces Liver; 1½ servings Fat

Mustard-Broiled Liver

1 pound calf liver, ½ inch-thick
   slices
Salt and pepper to taste
1 slice enriched white bread, made
   into crumbs
1 tablespoon minced fresh parsley

1 tablespoon Dijon mustard
1 teaspoon dehydrated onion
   flakes, reconstituted in 1
   teaspoon water
1 garlic clove, minced
1 tablespoon margarine

Sprinkle liver with salt and pepper; broil 3 inches from source of heat, turning once. In a bowl combine crumbs, parsley, mustard, onion flakes, and garlic. Place liver in flameproof shallow casserole. Top with crumb mixture. Dot with margarine. Place under broiler for 1 minute. Divide evenly. Makes 2 evening meal servings.

Each serving is equivalent to: 6 ounces Liver; ½ serving Bread; 1½ servings Fat

Poached Liver

1½ pounds unsliced calf liver
3 celery ribs, including leaves, cut
   into 2-inch pieces
10 parsley sprigs
1 tablespoon dehydrated onion
   flakes

6 black peppercorns, crushed
½ teaspoon salt
1 bay leaf

Place liver, celery, parsley, onion flakes, peppercorns, salt, and bay leaf in a 4-quart saucepan. Add enough water to barely cover meat. Bring to a boil; cover and reduce heat; simmer about 45 minutes or until liver is no longer pink in center when slashed. Remove from liquid and serve hot, or cool in liquid, cover, and refrigerate. Remove from liquid and serve cold. Divide evenly. Makes 4 midday meal servings.

Each serving is equivalent to: 4 ounces Liver

Brown Rice, Vermicelli, and Liver Pilaf

1½ pounds chicken livers, halved
¾ cup sliced mushrooms
4 ounces finely diced onion
½ medium green pepper, seeded
and finely diced
1⅓ cups cooked toasted enriched
vermicelli (see page 119)

1 cup cooked toasted brown rice
(see page 119)
1 cup tomato sauce, no sugar
added
½ cup chicken bouillon
Salt and pepper to taste

Place livers in broiler pan and broil 4 inches from source of heat 3 to 4 minutes, turning until all sides are browned. Transfer to saucepan and add vegetables. Cook 3 minutes. Add remaining ingredients and simmer 10 minutes. Divide evenly. Makes 4 midday meal servings.

Each serving is equivalent to: 4 ounces Liver; ¼ cup Vegetables; 1 ounce Limited Vegetable; 1 serving Choice Group; ½ serving Bonus (¼ cup tomato sauce); ⅙ serving Something Extra (2 tablespoons bouillon)

Chicken Liver and Celery Sandwich

4 ounces cooked chicken livers
½ cup chopped celery
¼ recipe Basic French Dressing (1
serving, see page 302)

1 slice rye bread
1 ounce red onion, sliced

In small bowl mash liver. Stir in celery and French Dressing. Cut bread horizontally to make two thin slices. Spread liver on one thin slice, top with onion and remaining slice bread. Makes 1 midday meal serving.

Each serving is equivalent to: 4 ounces Liver; ½ cup Vegetables; Basic French Dressing (see page 302); 1 serving Bread; 1 ounce Limited Vegetable

Chicken Livers in Orange Sauce

2 pounds chicken livers
Salt and pepper to taste
1 cup orange sections, no sugar added
1 cup orange juice
1 ounce chopped onion
1 teaspoon soy sauce

Cut each liver in half, sprinkle with salt and pepper, and place in broiler pan. Broil 3 inches from source of heat for about 1 minute on each side. Do not overcook; inside should be pink. In a 2-quart flameproof casserole, combine remaining ingredients. Bring to a boil; lower heat. Simmer 7 minutes or until mixture is reduced by about ⅓. Add broiled livers, cook just long enough to heat livers. Divide evenly. Makes 4 evening meal servings.

Each serving is equivalent to: 6 ounces Liver; 1 serving Fruit; ¼ ounce Limited Vegetable

Chicken Liver Rolls

4 ounces poached chicken livers
1 tablespoon mayonnaise
1 ounce grated onion
Salt and pepper to taste
4 lettuce leaves
½ medium tomato, sliced
½ medium cucumber, pared and sliced
4 white radishes, sliced
1 tablespoon sliced pimento

In small bowl, mash livers while still warm. Stir in mayonnaise, onion, salt, and pepper. Chill. Spoon ¼ of mixture onto each lettuce leaf. Roll, folding sides in; secure with toothpicks if necessary. Serve with tomato and cucumber. Garnish with radishes and pimentos. Makes 1 midday meal serving.

Each serving is equivalent to: 4 ounces Liver; 3 servings Fat; 1 ounce Limited Vegetable; 1½ cups Vegetables

Liver with Croutons

2 ounces onions, sliced
12 ounces chicken livers, halved
¼ cup chicken bouillon
3 tablespoons red wine vinegar
1 teaspoon capers
1 garlic clove, minced

¼ teaspoon salt
⅛ teaspoon pepper
1 cup cooked cauliflower florets
2 slices enriched white bread,
   toasted and cut into ½-inch
   cubes

In nonstick skillet, cook onions over medium heat until lightly browned. Add liver; cook 10 minutes. Add bouillon, vinegar, capers, garlic, salt and pepper. Simmer 10 minutes. Spoon chicken liver mixture onto serving platter. Surround with cauliflower florets and top with bread cubes. Divide evenly. Makes 2 midday meal servings.

Each serving is equivalent to: 1 ounce Limited Vegetable; 4 ounces Liver; ⅙ serving Something Extra (2 tablespoons bouillon); ½ cup Vegetables; 1 serving Bread

Polynesian Livers with Bean Sprouts

4 cups water
1 pound chicken livers
2 medium green peppers, seeded
   and cut into 1-inch pieces
1 cup bean sprouts
¾ cup chicken bouillon
2 ounces onion, diced
1 teaspoon salt
¼ teaspoon ginger

Pepper to taste
1 cup canned pineapple chunks,
   no sugar added
4 dried mushrooms, reconstituted
   in warm water and diced
2 tablespoons cider vinegar
1 tablespoon cornstarch, dissolved
   in 3 tablespoons water

Bring water to boil in large skillet; add livers and boil one minute. Drain and discard liquid. Add peppers, bean sprouts, bouillon, onion, salt, ginger, and pepper. Cover and cook 10 minutes. Add pineapple and mushrooms to skillet. Stir in vinegar and cornstarch; simmer, stirring constantly until mixture is thickened. Divide evenly. Makes 2 evening meal servings.

Each serving is equivalent to: 6 ounces Liver; 1 cup plus 2 tablespoons Vegetables; 2 servings Something Extra (¼ cup plus 2 tablespoons bouillon and 1½ teaspoons cornstarch); 1 ounce Limited Vegetable; 1 serving Fruit

Quick-and-Easy Chicken Livers and Mushrooms in One Dish

½ cup diced mushrooms
½ medium green pepper, seeded
  and diced
1 ounce diced onion
6 ounces chicken livers, quartered
2 teaspoons flour

½ teaspoon salt
⅛ teaspoon paprika
½ cup Chicken Stock (see page 140)
1 slice enriched white bread,
  toasted, or ½ cup cooked,
  enriched rice

In nonstick skillet brown mushrooms, green pepper, and onion. Add livers and sprinkle with flour, salt, and paprika. Cook over moderate heat, stirring frequently, until liver loses pink color. Add stock and bring to boil. Cook, stirring often, until thickened. Serve on toast or over rice. Makes 1 midday meal serving.

Each serving is equivalent to: ¾ cup Vegetables; 1 ounce Limited Vegetable; 4 ounces Liver; 2⅔ servings Something Extra (2 teaspoons flour and ½ cup stock); 1 serving Bread or 1 serving Choice Group

Variation: Add 3 ounces drained canned or frozen peas to preceding recipe. Add 3 ounces Limited Vegetable to equivalent listing.

Spiced Chinese Livers

1 pound chicken livers, halved	1 tablespoon lemon juice
1 ounce scallion, sliced	½ teaspoon sliced fresh ginger
3 tablespoons soy sauce	root
Artificial sweetener to equal 1	⅛ teaspoon anise seed
tablespoon sugar	1 teaspoon sesame oil

In saucepan, pour boiling water over livers, drain, dry, and return to pan. Add remaining ingredients except oil. Cover pan and cook 10 minutes or until livers are done. Transfer to bowl; stir in oil. Cover and chill for several hours or overnight. Remove livers from marinade; slice. Serve cold with marinade. Divide evenly. Makes 2 evening meal servings.

Each serving is equivalent to: 6 ounces Liver; ½ ounce Limited Vegetable; ½ serving Fat

FISH

Cast your fishing line in any ocean, lake, or stream around the world
. . . and anything you hook that's edible is also "legal." You can be
quite creative with fish, too. Use it in soups, stews, salads or pies, in
fish cakes and loaves, or even roll it around vegetables.

Rules for Using Fish

1. Amounts (net cooked weight):
   Women, Men, and Youth: 2 ounces at the Morning Meal
   3 to 4 ounces at the Midday Meal
   Women and Youth: 4 to 6 ounces at the Evening Meal
   Men: 6 to 8 ounces at the Evening Meal
2. The range of 3 to 4 ounces of fish at the Midday Meal, and 4 to 6
   ounces for Women and Youth (6 to 8 ounces for Men) at the
   Evening Meal, provides flexibility. It is a way to individualize the
   Food Plan to meet your specific needs.
3. If smoked fish is selected, use the *lower* end of the serving range.
4. Select any fish in the marketplace at least 3 to 5 times weekly. Vary
   selections. Use fresh, frozen, canned, or smoked fish. Do not use
   fish packed in olive oil. All canned fish must be well drained.
5. It is strongly recommended that 5 fish meals be eaten weekly.
   However, if fish is selected 3 or 4 times per week, chicken must be
   substituted for the 1 or 2 omitted fish meals.
6. As a "rule of thumb," for each serving of fish allow 2 ounces for
   shrinkage in cooking and 2 ounces for bone. When splitting an item
   from the fish category, for each half serving allow 1 ounce for

shrinkage in cooking and 1 ounce for bone. Weigh the serving after cooking, whenever possible.

7. As a "rule of thumb," count 5 small clams, oysters, scallops, or shrimp as equal to 1 ounce of fish.

8. When fish is selected at the Morning Meal or in combination with poultry, meat, egg, cheese, or legumes at the Midday Meal or Evening Meal, it may not be counted as a fish meal.

9. *Cooking Procedures:* May be boiled, poached, broiled, pan-broiled, or baked. Cooked or uncooked fish may be used with added ingredients (e.g., casseroles, stews, etc.). Liquid and added ingredients may be consumed.

Fish Tips

Fresh and Frozen Fish

Fresh and frozen fish are available in the following forms:

1. *Whole*—Fish as they come from the water. Before cooking, they must be scaled, eviscerated, and the head, tail, and fins removed.

2. *Dressed*—Whole fish with only scales and entrails removed. May be cooked as is or cut into fillets, steaks, or chunks. Small dressed fish are referred to as "pan dressed."

3. *Steaks*—Cross-section slices from large dressed fish. A cross section of the backbone is the only bone in a steak.

4. *Fillets*—Sides of the fish cut lengthwise away from the backbone.
   Single filllets: Cut from one side of a fish.
   Butterfly fillets: Two sides of the fish cut away from the backbone and held together by the uncut flesh of the belly.

5. *Chunks*—Cross section of large dressed fish cut 4 to 6 inches thick. May contain a cross section of the backbone.

Purchasing tips for fish

1. *Fresh Fish*—Flesh should be firm and elastic. Steaks and fillets should have a fresh-cut appearance. Odor should be fresh and mild. A fish just taken from the water has practically no odor. Eyes should be bright, clear, and transparent. They should not appear sunken. Gills should be red and free from slime. Skin should be shiny and bright in color.

2. *Frozen Fish*—Flesh should be solidly frozen, with no brown tinge or white cottony appearance. There should be little or no odor. Wrapping should be of moistureproof, vaporproof material, such as aluminum foil or freezer paper. There should be little or no air space between the fish and the wrapping, and the package should appear undamaged.

Shellfish

Shellfish are available in a wide variety of forms:
1. *Live in the Shell*—Clams, crabs, lobsters, mussels, and oysters must be kept alive until cooked.
2. *Cooked in the Shell*—Crabs, lobsters, and shrimp, chilled or frozen.
3. *Headless*—Lobster tails and shrimp ready to cook.
4. *Shucked or Fresh Meat*—Fresh or frozen clams, mussels, oysters, scallops, and shrimp.
5. *Cooked Meat*—Cooked clams, crabs, lobsters, mussels, oysters, and shrimp; meat picked from the shell. Available fresh, frozen, or canned.

Purchasing tips for shellfish:
   Clams and oysters in the shell should close tightly when tapped. If shell remains open, the shellfish is dead and not edible. Shucked oysters are plump, with a mild odor, creamy color, and a clear liquid. Cooked crabs and lobsters are bright red with no disagreeable odor. Fresh shrimp should be firm in texture with a mild odor. Scallops should have a mild, sweet odor and no excess liquid when purchased in packages.

Storage Tips for Fish and Shellfish

   Fresh fish and shellfish purchased in plastic wrap can be refrigerated in their original wrappings. If purchased in butcher wrap, they should be rewrapped in foil or plastic wrap before refrigeration. Refrigerate as soon as possible after purchasing. Do not hold longer than a day or two before cooking. Fresh shellfish should be stored at approximately 32°F. They are best if eaten on the day of purchase.
   Frozen fish and shellfish should be cooked immediately after

thawing. Never refreeze them. Do not keep uncooked frozen fish in the freezer longer than six months.

Cooked fish and seafood should be stored either in the refrigerator or freezer; in the refrigerator, for no longer than 3 or 4 days; in the freezer, no more than 3 months. Store in the refrigerator, in a covered container; in the freezer, in moistureproof, vaporproof wrapping materials intended for freezers, such as aluminum foil or freezer paper.

Cooking Fish

The following directions apply chiefly to fin fish, but the same methods may be adapted to shellfish.

Never overcook. Fish cooked at too high a temperature or for too long a time becomes tough, dry, and loses its delicate flavor. When cooked, fish should be opaque, flake easily, and fall away from the bones. Handle gently. Fish flesh is delicate. Frozen fillets and steaks do not have to be thawed before cooking if cooking time is increased to allow for thawing during the cooking process.

Baking—Baking is cooking with dry heat. This is one of the easiest methods of cooking fishery products. Fish should usually be baked in an uncovered baking dish at a moderate temperature, 350°F., for a relatively short period of time. This retains the moistness and flavor, prevents drying, and keeps fish tender and palatable.

Broiling—Broiling, like baking, is cooking with dry heat. In broiling, however, the heat is direct, intense, and comes from only one source. Place fish in a single layer in broiler pan. The surface of the fish should be 3 to 4 inches from the source of heat. Cooking time should range from 10 to 15 minutes. As a rule, fish fillets do not need to be turned because the heat of the pan cooks the underside adequately. Turn thicker pieces, such as pan-dressed fish halfway through the cooking time. Always serve broiled fish sizzling hot.

Poaching—Poaching is cooking in a simmering liquid. Use a shallow skillet wide enough to hold fish in a single layer. Barely cover with liquid, such as lightly salted water, fish stock, or water seasoned with spices and herbs. Simmer in covered pan until fish flakes easily, usually 5 to 10 minutes. The poaching liquid may be reduced and thickened to make a tasty sauce for the fish. Poached fish may be served as is, with a sauce, in a casserole, or chilled and flaked in cold dishes.

Steaming—Steaming is cooking by means of the steam generated from boiling water. Use a steam cooker, or a deep pan with a tight cover and steaming rack, to keep the fish from touching the water. Use plain water or water seasoned with various spices or herbs. Heat the water to a boil; then place the fish on the rack and cover the pan. Steam 5 to 10 minutes or until fish flakes easily when tested with a fork. Steamed fish may be served in the same manner as poached fish.

Court Bouillon for Poaching Fish

Enough for about 2 pounds of fish. If necessary, add more water to cover fish.

2 quarts water	**2 teaspoons salt**
1 cup diced celery	**4 sprigs fresh parsley**
1 cup sliced carrots	**3 peppercorns**
¼ lemon, sliced	**2 cloves**
1 tablespoon chives	**1 garlic clove, crushed**
1 tablespoon lemon juice	**1 bay leaf**

Combine all ingredients in saucepan. Bring to boil, simmer about 20 minutes. Drain and discard solids. Use court bouillon as poaching liquid for fish.

Fish Stock or Fumet

This broth can be the beginning of a hearty soup. It costs nothing if you ask for the trimmings when you buy a dressed fish. Stock the trimmings in your freezer until you have enough to use, then just add vegetables and cook as below. You can ad lib seasonings: thyme and marjoram one time, a sprig of basil and oregano the next. The cooked, strained broth can be frozen too.

2 pounds fish bones and heads, gills removed	1 tablespoon lemon juice
1 quart water	2 garlic cloves, crushed
½ cup sliced carrots	2 sprigs fresh parsley
½ cup chopped celery with leaves	1 bay leaf
2 ounces sliced onion	5 peppercorns
	Salt to taste

Rinse the fish bones and heads thoroughly under running water. Combine with remaining ingredients in large saucepan. Simmer 30 to 40 minutes, skimming off foam. Strain, pressing out juices. Adjust seasonings, if desired. Use in recipes calling for fish stock.

Bastes for Fish

Lean fish should be basted before it is baked or broiled. Other fish may be basted for additional flavor, if desired. Here are some suggestions:

1. A mixture of vegetable oil or melted margarine and lemon juice can be used for fish if it is to be baked. Use individual casseroles. Allow 1 serving of Fat for each serving of fish. Pan juices must be consumed.
2. Fish to be broiled can be basted with low-calorie garlic, herb, Italian or French Dressing (see "Specialty Foods," page 315). *Do not baste* with a mixture of vegetable oil or melted margarine and lemon juice.
3. *After* fish is broiled, it *may* be basted with a mixture of melted margarine or vegetable oil and lemon juice, provided the broiling pan has sides that will contain the pan juices. The broiled fish, topped with this baste, may be put under the broiler for no more than 1 minute (see "Cooking Procedures," page 206). Serve fish with pan juices. Allow 1 serving of Fat for each serving of fish.
4. Slices of tomato put on fish before baking or broiling will keep it moist.
5. Two tablespoons of evaporated skimmed milk thinned with 1 tablespoon Fish Fumet (see page 207) or water can be used as a

baste for each serving of fish to be either baked or broiled. All pan juices must be consumed. Each serving of this baste is equivalent to ¼ serving Milk (2 tablespoons evaporated skimmed milk).

Fish—a First Course

Anchovy Roll—Wrap 1 ounce flat anchovies around ¼ cup small radishes; secure with toothpicks. Garnish with capers speared on ends of toothpicks. Makes 1 serving. Serve at mealtime only. Supplement as required.

Each serving is equivalent to: 1 ounce Fish; ¼ cup Vegetables

Mashed Tuna—Combine 2 ounces drained tuna, flaked, and 1 tablespoon imitation mayonnaise. Stuff into 1 whole roasted pepper and sprinkle with 1 teaspoon vinegar. Serve on lettuce leaves. Makes 1 serving. Serve at mealtime only. Supplement as required.

Each serving is equivalent to: 2 ounces Fish; 1½ servings Fat; ½ cup Vegetables

Sardine Canapés—In bowl mash 2 ounces drained canned sardines with 2 teaspoons chopped pimento, 1 teaspoon catsup, 1 teaspoon dehydrated onion flakes, dash Worcestershire sauce, salt and pepper to taste. Stir in 1 tablespoon imitation mayonnaise or 1 tablespoon plain unflavored yogurt. Spread sardine mixture on 1 serving Melba Toast (see page 83) and cut as desired. Makes 1 serving. Serve at mealtime only. Supplement as required.

Each serving is equivalent to: 2 ounces Fish; 2 teaspoons Vegetables; ½ serving Something Extra (1 teaspoon catsup); 1½ servings Fat or ⅛ serving Milk (1 tablespoon yogurt); Melba Toast (see page 83)

Seafood Cocktail—Chill 3 ounces cooked crab, shrimp, or lobster meat. Serve on ½ cup shredded lettuce with 1 serving (¼ recipe) Cocktail Sauce (see page 305). Makes 1 evening meal serving. Supplement as required.

Each serving is equivalent to: 3 ounces Fish; ½ cup Vegetables; Cocktail Sauce (see page 305)

Smoked Salmon Canapés—Arrange ½ ounce onion, thinly sliced, ¼ medium tomato, sliced, and 1½ ounces smoked salmon on 1 slice pumpernickel bread. Cut into quarters. Makes 1 midday meal serving. Supplement as required.

Each serving is equivalent to: ½ ounce Limited Vegetable; 2 tablespoons Vegetables; 1½ ounces Smoked Fish; 1 serving Bread

Baked Fish

For easy clean-up, line pan with aluminum foil.

1 pound fish fillets   **½ cup clam juice**
Salt, pepper, and paprika to taste

Place fish in nonstick pan and season. Add clam juice; bake at 350°F.
about 20 minutes or until fish flakes readily. Divide evenly and serve.
Makes 2 evening meal servings.

Each serving is equivalent to: 6 ounces Fish; ¼ serving Bonus (¼
cup clam juice)

Baked Mullet with Grapes

2 pounds dressed mullet   **¾ cup chicken bouillon**
¼ teaspoon thyme   **2 tablespoons lemon juice**
Salt and pepper to taste   **40 small seedless grapes**
4 ounces sliced onion   **1 tablespoon chopped fresh**
1 bay leaf   **parsley**

Place fish in a shallow ovenproof dish. Sprinkle with thyme, salt, and
pepper. Top with onion and bay leaf and add bouillon and lemon juice
to dish. Cover and bake at 400°F. for 15 minutes. Add grapes and
continue baking for 10 minutes or until fish flakes at the touch of a
fork. Sprinkle with parsley. Divide evenly. Makes 4 midday meal
servings.

Each serving is equivalent to: 4 ounces Fish; 1 ounce Limited
Vegetable; ¼ serving Something Extra (3 tablespoons bouillon); ½
serving Fruit

Baked Fish Creole

Serve this delicious dish with cooked hominy grits, a traditional accompaniment to Fish Creole.

Arrange 1 pound fish fillets in shallow baking dish. Prepare ½ recipe Creole Sauce (2 servings, see page 304). Pour over fish. Bake, uncovered, at 350°F. for 30 to 35 minutes or until fish flakes easily at the touch of a fork. Divide evenly. Makes 2 evening meal servings.

Each serving is equivalent to: 6 ounces Fish; Creole Sauce (see page 304)

Bouillabaisse for One

Freeze the odd amounts of different types of fish and when you've accumulated 8 ounces, here's your evening meal.

2 ounces diced onion or leeks	Dash paprika
1 garlic clove, minced	Salt and pepper to taste
1 parsley sprig	2 cups water
1 small bay leaf	1 medium tomato, diced
Dash saffron	3 ounces pared potato, diced
Dash thyme	8 ounces boned fish

In small saucepan cook onion and garlic 2 minutes. Add parsley and seasonings; cook 1 minute longer. Add remaining ingredients, except fish. Cover; simmer 5 minutes. Add fish, simmer about 7 minutes or until fish flakes easily at touch of a fork. Serve in soup bowl. Makes 1 evening meal serving.

Each serving is equivalent to: 2 ounces Limited Vegetable; ½ cup Vegetables; 1 serving Choice Group; 6 ounces Fish

Variation: Omit potato. Place 1 slice French Bread (approximately 2 ounces) in soup bowl. Pour Bouillabaisse over bread. Eliminate 1 serving Choice Group and add 2 servings Bread (once-a-week selection) to equivalent listing.

Fish Baked on Bed of Vegetables

1 medium green pepper, seeded
   and sliced
1 medium tomato, sliced
4 ounces onion, sliced
1 pound fish fillets

¼ teaspoon salt
⅛ teaspoon pepper
¼ cup water
1 tablespoon margarine
⅛ teaspoon paprika

Place ½ of vegetables in baking dish. Season fish with salt and pepper and arrange on top of vegetables. Cover with remaining vegetables. Add water, dot with margarine, and sprinkle with paprika. Bake at 350°F. 20 to 25 minutes or until fish is cooked. Divide evenly. Makes 2 evening meal servings.

Each serving is equivalent to: ½ cup Vegetables; 2 ounces Limited Vegetable; 6 ounces Fish; 1½ servings Fat

Fish Pie

12 ounces peeled cooked potatoes
½ cup skim milk
1 tablespoon plus 1 teaspoon
   margarine
2 medium eggs, hard-cooked
8 ounces cooked fish, flaked
4 ounces diced onion, boiled

2 medium eggs
¼ cup tomato puree
1 tablespoon chopped fresh
   parsley
1 teaspoon Worcestershire sauce
Salt and pepper to taste

In medium bowl mash potatoes with milk and margarine until blended. Set aside. Chop hard-cooked eggs and place in separate bowl; add fish, onion, 1 egg, tomato puree, parsley, Worcestershire, salt, pepper, and ½ cup potato mixture; mix well. Spoon into 8x8x2-inch baking dish. Spread with remaining potato mixture. Beat remaining egg and pour over potato. Bake at 400°F. for 20 to 30 minutes or until top is golden brown. Divide evenly. Makes 4 midday meal servings.

Each serving is equivalent to: 1 serving Choice Group; ⅛ serving Milk (2 tablespoons skim milk); 1 serving Fat; 1 Egg; 2 ounces Fish; 1 ounce Limited Vegetable; ⅛ serving Bonus (1 tablespoon tomato puree)

Fish Stew in Green Sauce

1 pound fish fillets, cut up
¼ cup lime juice
1 teaspoon salt, divided
2 medium green peppers, seeded
  and finely chopped
2 medium green tomatoes, peeled
  and chopped
4 ounces onion or shallots, finely
  chopped

4 ounces peas
1 teaspoon chopped fresh parsley
1 teaspoon red wine vinegar
1 garlic clove, chopped
¼ teaspoon pepper
2 teaspoons vegetable oil
  (optional)

Place fish in a medium bowl. Add enough water to cover. Add lime juice and ½ teaspoon salt. In another bowl combine remaining ingredients except oil. Spread half the mixture in a shallow saucepan. Drain fish; place over vegetable mixture. Top with remaining vegetable mixture. Cover and simmer on low heat about 15 minutes or until liquid is almost evaporated. Remove from heat. Drizzle with oil, if desired, and serve hot. Divide evenly. Makes 2 evening meal servings.

Each serving is equivalent to: 6 ounces Fish; 1 cup Vegetables; 4 ounces Limited Vegetable; 1 serving Fat (optional)

Halibut Ring

4 medium eggs, separated
12 ounces halibut fillets, ground
¼ cup evaporated skimmed milk
½ teaspoon salt

¼ teaspoon pepper
2 cups cooked whole green beans
1 cup tomato sauce, no sugar
  added, heated

Preheat oven to 375°F. In large bowl beat egg yolks slightly. Add fish, milk, salt, and pepper; mix thoroughly. In separate bowl, beat egg whites until stiff and fold into fish mixture. Pour into a 1-quart nonstick tubepan; set in pan containing 1 inch of water; bake 30 to 40 minutes. Unmold onto serving platter. Garnish with green beans and serve with tomato sauce. Divide evenly. Makes 4 midday meal servings.

Each serving is equivalent to: 1 Egg; 2 ounces Fish; ⅛ serving Milk

(1 tablespoon evaporated skimmed milk); ½ cup Vegetables; ½ serving Bonus (¼ cup tomato sauce)

Variation: Grind 2 ounces onion with the fish. Make 2 slices enriched white bread into crumbs; soak crumbs in ¼ cup skim milk and stir into fish mixture before folding in egg white. Add ½ ounce Limited Vegetable, ½ serving Bread, and ¹/₁₆ serving Milk (1 tablespoon skim milk) to equivalent listing.

Lemon-Broiled Trout

1 pan-dressed trout, 10 ounces
¼ cup lemon juice, divided
1 teaspoon margarine

2 teaspoons chopped fresh parsley
Lemon wedges to garnish

Cut trout in half lengthwise. Place skin side up on foil-lined broiling pan. Sprinkle with 2 tablespoons lemon juice. Broil 4 inches from source of heat for 3 minutes. Turn trout over and sprinkle with remaining lemon juice; broil 3 to 5 minutes till fish flakes easily at the touch of a fork. Dot trout with margarine and broil 1 minute longer. Garnish with parsley and lemon wedges. Makes 1 evening meal serving.

Each serving is equivalent to: 6 ounces Fish; 1 serving Fat

Mackerel in Mustard Sauce

1 dressed mackerel, 2½ pounds
¼ cup lemon juice, divided
1½ teaspoons salt, divided
1 tablespoon plus 2 teaspoons
  Dijon mustard

2 teaspoons minced fresh parsley
2 garlic cloves, minced
Freshly ground pepper to taste

In bowl cover fish with water. Add 2 tablespoons lemon juice and 1 teaspoon salt; let stand 15 minutes. Drain and dry fish. In a small bowl, combine remaining ingredients. Spread over fish. Loosely wrap fish in foil or parchment paper; place on baking sheet. Bake at 350°F. for about 30 minutes or until fish flakes easily at the touch of a fork. Divide evenly. Makes 4 evening meal servings.

Each serving is equivalent to: 6 ounces Fish

Smoked Salmon and Potato Pudding

1 pound, 2 ounces peeled cooked potatoes, sliced	3 medium eggs, slightly beaten
6 ounces diced onion	½ teaspoon salt
9 ounces smoked salmon, diced	½ teaspoon pepper
2 cups skim milk	3 medium eggs, hard-cooked and sliced

Line bottom of 1½-quart casserole with half of the potatoes. Add a layer of half the onion and half the smoked salmon. Repeat layers. In a bowl combine milk, beaten eggs, salt, and pepper. Pour into casserole. Bake at 375°F. for 1¼ hours or until eggs are set. Arrange slices of hard-cooked eggs on top. Divide evenly. Makes 6 midday meal servings.

Each serving is equivalent to: 1 serving Choice Group; 1 ounce Limited Vegetable; 1½ ounces Smoked Fish; ⅓ serving Milk (⅓ cup skim milk); 1 Egg

Steamed Fish Chinese Style

This is a simple and good way to prepare almost every kind of fish: butterfish, flounder, red snapper, sea bass, shad, sole, striped bass, yellow pike, or whiting.

8 ounces fish fillets or 10 ounces fish steak	2 teaspoons soy sauce
½ ounce sliced scallions	½ teaspoon shredded fresh ginger root

Wash fish and pat dry with paper towels. Place fish on a heat-resistant plate. Top with scallions, soy sauce, and ginger root. For easy removal, tie the plate in a piece of cheesecloth. Pour boiling water into a steamer below the level of the steaming rack. Put the plate holding the fish on the rack. You can raise the level of the rack, if necessary, to prevent fish from touching water, by setting it on two coffee cups. Place cover over fish and steamer, bring water to boiling point, and steam fish 5 to 10 minutes for thin fillets and up to 10 to 15 minutes for thick steaks. Serve fish hot on the plate in which it was steamed, or flake and chill for use in salads. Makes 1 evening meal serving. You can do this for 1 serving or for many, depending on the size of your steamer. It must be large enough to accommodate the fish in a single layer.

Each serving is equivalent to: 6 ounces Fish; ½ ounce Limited Vegetable

Baked Shrimp Thermidor

¼ cup unsalted margarine
1 cup sliced mushrooms
¼ cup flour
1 teaspoon salt
½ teaspoon dry mustard
Dash cayenne pepper
1 cup skim milk

8 ounces cooked shrimp, cut in
    half lengthwise
2 slices enriched white bread,
    made into crumbs
2 ounces grated Parmesan cheese
2 ounces Cheddar cheese, finely
    diced
½ teaspoon paprika

Melt margarine in top of double boiler over boiling water; add mushrooms. Cook for 5 minutes. Blend in flour, salt, mustard, and cayenne. Slowly add milk, stirring constantly; cook until thick. Add shrimp; stir to combine. Transfer mixture to a 1½-quart casserole. In a medium bowl combine bread crumbs, Parmesan cheese, Cheddar cheese, and paprika. Sprinkle over shrimp mixture. Bake at 400°F. for 20 minutes or until top is brown and bubbly. Divide evenly. Makes 4 midday meal servings.

Each serving is equivalent to: 3 servings Fat; ¼ cup Vegetables; 3 servings Something Extra (1 tablespoon flour); ¼ serving Milk (¼ cup skim milk); 2 ounces Fish; ½ serving Bread; 1 ounce Hard Cheese

Baltimore Crab Cakes

1 pound cooked crab meat, flaked
4 slices enriched white bread,
  made into crumbs
¼ cup minced fresh parsley
¼ cup mayonnaise

2 tablespoons prepared mustard
¼ teaspoon salt
⅛ teaspoon pepper
Few drops hot sauce

Combine all ingredients in a large bowl. Divide mixture evenly into 8 portions and shape into patties. Place on a baking sheet. Bake at 350°F. for 15 minutes; turn patties over and bake 10 minutes longer or until crispy. Makes 4 midday meal servings, 2 patties each.

Each serving is equivalent to: 4 ounces Fish; 1 serving Bread; 1 tablespoon Vegetables; 3 servings Fat

Baked Scampi

Shrimp is the most popular of all shellfish sold in America, and this may be the most popular method of preparing it. Allow about 1½ pounds unpeeled shrimp to make 1 pound peeled. Weigh after peeling and deveining.

1½ pounds jumbo peeled and
  deveined shrimp
2 tablespoons lemon juice
¼ cup unsalted margarine, melted
¼ cup finely chopped fresh
  parsley, divided

2 garlic cloves, minced
2 slices enriched white bread,
  made into crumbs
1 teaspoon paprika
4 lemon wedges

Butterfly the shrimp by cutting lengthwise along the back, being careful not to cut all the way through; spread and flatten to form the butterfly shape. Place 6 ounces shrimp in each of 4 individual baking dishes. Sprinkle each with 1½ teaspoons lemon juice. In a small bowl, combine margarine, 3 tablespoons parsley, and garlic; dot each portion of shrimp with ¼ of margarine mixture. In another bowl, combine bread crumbs, remaining parsley, and paprika. Sprinkle ¼ of bread crumb mixture over each shrimp serving. Bake at 400°F. for approximately

15 minutes or until shrimp are pink and crumbs golden brown. Garnish each serving with 1 lemon wedge. Makes 4 midday meal servings.

Each serving is equivalent to: 4 ounces Fish; 3 servings Fat; ½ serving Bread

Clam, Crab, or Mussel Chowder

4 ounces diced onion
½ cup diced celery
2¼ cups chicken or beef bouillon
6 ounces pared potatoes, diced

8 ounces cooked or drained
canned seafood (see Note)
¼ cup evaporated skimmed milk

Cook onion and celery in a covered medium saucepan stirring occasionally until transparent. Add bouillon and bring to a boil. Add potatoes; cover and simmer 15 to 20 minutes or until vegetables are almost tender. Stir in seafood and milk; heat but do not boil. Divide evenly into bowls. Makes 2 midday meal servings.

Each serving is equivalent to: 2 ounces Limited Vegetable; ¼ cup Vegetables; 1½ servings Something Extra (1 cup plus 2 tablespoons bouillon); 1 serving Choice Group; 4 ounces Fish; ¼ serving Milk (2 tablespoons evaporated skimmed milk)

Note: Select one of the following.
Clams—Use 8 ounces drained, canned, minced clams. If desired, reduce bouillon to 1½ cups and add ½ cup clam juice. Eliminate ½ serving Something Extra (¼ cup plus 2 tablespoons bouillon) from equivalent listing and add ¼ serving Bonus (¼ cup clam juice) if clam juice is used.
Crab—Use 8 ounces drained canned crab meat, flaked. If desired, add 4 ounces cooked peas with the fish. Add 2 ounces Limited Vegetable to equivalent listing, if peas are used.
Mussels—Steam mussels until shells open. Cool. Remove from shells and discard the rubberlike band that surrounds each mussel. Weigh 8 ounces. If desired, add ½ medium green pepper, diced, with potato. For seasoning, add Worcestershire sauce to taste. Add 2 tablespoons Vegetables to equivalent listing if green pepper is used.

Clam or Smoked Fish Dip

Here's a dip for vegetables or spread for pumpernickel bread.

1⅓ cups cottage cheese
8 ounces drained canned minced
   clams or 6 ounces smoked fish,
   minced

2 to 4 tablespoons water
¼ teaspoon dill weed
¼ teaspoon Worcestershire sauce
Dash white pepper

Puree cottage cheese in food mill, blender container, or food processor. Stir in remaining ingredients, adjusting the amount of water until desired consistency. Divide evenly. Makes 4 midday meal servings.

Each serving is equivalent to: ⅓ cup Soft Cheese; 2 ounces Fish or 1½ ounces Smoked Fish

How to Prepare Packaged Frozen Lobster Tails

To broil: Thaw lobster tails. Cut under-shell around edges and remove. Grasp tail in both hands and bend backwards toward shell side to crack and prevent curling; or insert skewer to keep tail flat. Arrange shell side up on rack of broiler pan. Place 5 inches from source of heat; broil 5 minutes. Turn flesh side up; sprinkle with lemon juice and broil according to timetable below. To serve, loosen meat by inserting fork between meat and shell. Weigh portions. Serve with measured amount of melted margarine and lemon wedges.

To boil: Place lobster tails, either thawed or frozen, into a large kettle of boiling salted water to cover. (Use 1 teaspoon salt for each quart of water.) When water returns to the boiling point, lower heat and begin counting the time, following timetable below. To remove meat easily, drain lobster tails and rinse with cold water. Cut through under-shell with kitchen scissors. Insert fingers between shell and meat, and pull firmly. Weigh portions. Serve hot with measured amount of melted margarine and lemon wedges; or chill and serve on a bed of shredded lettuce with Cocktail Sauce (see page 305).

Timetable for Preparing Lobster Tails (in minutes)

Weight	3 oz.	4 oz.	5 oz.	6 oz.	7 oz.	8 oz.	9 oz.
Broiling:							
Shell Side	5	5	5	5	5	5	5
Flesh Side	6	6	6	6	7	7	7
***Boiling:**							
Thawed	4	5	6	7	8	9	10
Frozen	6	7	8	9	10	11	12

*As a general rule, thawed lobster tails should be boiled one minute longer than their individual weight in ounces. Add two minutes to all boiling times, if tails are cooked frozen.

The above table is based on weights of *individual* tails. When two or more tails of the same weight are cooked at the same time, use time indicated for a single tail.

Lobster Rarebit

In the top of a double boiler over boiling water prepare Enriched White Sauce (see page 297). Stir in 8 ounces cooked diced lobster, 4 ounces diced sharp Cheddar cheese, 1 tablespoon plus 1 teaspoon catsup, and a few drops Worcestershire sauce. Heat to melt cheese. Divide evenly into 4 portions. Serve each portion over 1 slice enriched white bread, toasted. Sprinkle with chopped parsley. Makes 4 midday meal servings.

Each serving is equivalent to: Enriched White Sauce (see page 297); 2 ounces Fish; 1 ounce Hard Cheese; ½ serving Something Extra (1 teaspoon catsup); 1 serving Bread

Manhattan Clam Chowder

1 cup clam juice
½ cup water
½ cup finely diced celery
1 canned medium tomato, chopped
3 ounces pared potato, diced
1 ounce onion, diced

1 packet instant chicken broth and seasoning mix
½ bay leaf
¼ teaspoon garlic powder
¼ teaspoon thyme
4 ounces drained canned minced clams

Combine all ingredients, except clams, in a medium saucepan. Bring to boil; lower heat and simmer 15 minutes or until potato and celery are tender. Add clams and heat thoroughly. Remove bay leaf before serving. Makes 1 midday meal serving.

Each serving is equivalent to: 1 serving Bonus (1 cup clam juice); 1 cup Vegetables; 1 serving Choice Group; 1 ounce Limited Vegetable; 1 serving Something Extra (1 packet broth mix); 4 ounces Fish

Mussels Vinaigrette

12 ounces drained canned mussels　　**2 ounces sliced red onion**
Basic French Dressing　　　　　　　**2 cups shredded lettuce**
**　(see page 302)**

Combine all ingredients except lettuce in bowl and refrigerate 1 hour. Serve on lettuce. Divide evenly. Makes 4 evening meal servings. Supplement as required.

Each serving is equivalent to: 3 ounces Fish; Basic French Dressing (see page 302); ½ ounce Limited Vegetable; ½ cup Vegetables

Oysters Creole Maryland

Serve over hot rice.

1 pound drained, canned oysters　　**Creole Sauce (see page 304)**
**　or 1½ pounds shucked fresh**
**　oysters**

In saucepan combine oysters and Creole Sauce. Simmer 5 minutes or until thoroughly heated. If using fresh oysters, cook until edges of oysters curl. Divide evenly. Makes 4 midday meal servings.

Each serving is equivalent to: 4 ounces Fish; Creole Sauce (see page 304)

Oyster Stew

2 tablespoons plus 2 teaspoons
  margarine
2 tablespoons plus 2 teaspoons
  flour
1 teaspoon salt

1 teaspoon Worcestershire sauce
Dash hot sauce
1 cup skim milk
1½ pounds shucked oysters

Melt margarine in top of double boiler, over boiling water. Stir in flour, salt, Worcestershire, and hot sauce. Slowly add milk, stirring constantly, and cook until thickened. Add oysters and cook 4 minutes or until edges of oysters curl. Divide evenly. Makes 4 midday meal servings.

Each serving is equivalent to: 2 servings Fat; 2 servings Something Extra (2 teaspoons flour); ¼ serving Milk (¼ cup skim milk); 4 ounces Fish

Peppery Shrimp

Try as a first course.

1½ pounds peeled and deveined
  shrimp
1½ cups Double-Strength Chicken
  Stock (see page 140)
½ cup red wine vinegar
4 ounces sliced onion

2 teaspoons dry mustard
1 teaspoon hot sauce
½ teaspoon thyme
Lemon slices to garnish
Parsley sprigs to garnish

In saucepan combine all ingredients except lemon and parsley. Bring to boil; reduce heat and simmer about 4 minutes or until shrimp turn pink. Remove from heat. Allow to cool. Chill shrimp in liquid. Drain and discard liquid. Garnish shrimp and onions with lemon slices and parsley sprigs. Divide evenly. Makes 8 midday or evening meal servings. Supplement as required.

Each serving is equivalent to: 2 ounces Fish; ½ serving Something Extra (3 tablespoons Double-Strength stock); ½ ounce Limited Vegetable

Portuguese Mussel Soup

3 cups water
6 ounces pared potato, sliced
4 ounces onion, sliced
3 packets instant chicken broth
    and seasoning mix
1 garlic clove, minced

Dash thyme
1½ pounds cleaned shucked
    mussels
1 cup cooked enriched rice
1 teaspoon minced fresh parsley

In a large saucepan combine water, potato, onion, broth mix, garlic, and thyme. Bring to a boil; lower heat and cover. Cook for 15 minutes or until potato is tender. Add mussels and rice; cook 5 minutes or until mussels are tender. Sprinkle with parsley. Divide evenly. Makes 4 midday meal servings.

Each serving is equivalent to: 1 serving Choice Group; 1 ounce Limited Vegetable; ¾ serving Something Extra (¾ packet broth mix); 4 ounces Fish

Riverboat Shrimp

½ cup chicken bouillon
4 ounces onion, chopped
1 medium green pepper, seeded
    and chopped
4 medium tomatoes, chopped
1 teaspoon oregano

1 teaspoon salt
½ teaspoon rosemary
½ teaspoon pepper
Dash hot sauce
1½ pounds cooked shrimp
2 cups cooked enriched rice

In a medium saucepan, combine chicken bouillon, onion, and green pepper. Simmer until tender, about 5 minutes. Add tomatoes and seasonings; simmer gently for 10 minutes. Add shrimp and heat thoroughly. Divide evenly into 4 portions and serve each over ½ cup hot rice. Makes 4 evening meal servings.

Each serving is equivalent to: $^1/_6$ serving Something Extra (2 tablespoons bouillon); 1 ounce Limited Vegetable; ½ cup plus 2 tablespoons Vegetables; 6 ounces Fish; 1 serving Choice Group

Scallops

There are two kinds of scallops. Bay scallops are tiny, creamy, pink or tan, and especially delicate. Sea scallops are larger, firmer, and whiter than bay scallops.

Poached Scallops

In skillet combine scallops, bay leaf, and a few sprigs of fresh parsley. Cover with water and poach 3 to 5 minutes (see directions for poaching fish, page 207). Weigh portions and serve.

Broiled Scallops

If scallops are very large cut them into equal-size pieces. Dip them in lemon juice or chicken bouillon and broil until firm (see directions for broiling fish, page 206). Weigh portions and serve.

Baked Scallops

3 ounces scallops, diced
½ recipe Creamy Cheese Sauce (1
    serving, see page 65)
Dash Worcestershire sauce

½ slice enriched white bread,
    made into crumbs

Combine all ingredients except bread crumbs in bowl and spoon into large shell or individual casserole. Top with bread crumbs. Bake at 425°F. about 15 to 20 minutes or until top is browned. Makes 1 midday meal serving.

    Each serving is equivalent to: 2 ounces Fish; Creamy Cheese Sauce (see page 65); ½ serving Bread

Seafood Chef's Salad

⅔ cup cooked enriched macaroni
  twists
2 ounces cooked seafood, cut into
  bite-size pieces
¼ cup diced celery
¼ medium green pepper, seeded
  and diced
½ ounce minced scallion

2 tablespoons imitation
  mayonnaise
1 tablespoon chili sauce
Salt and pepper to taste
Lettuce leaves
1 medium egg, hard-cooked and
  quartered

In bowl combine macaroni, seafood, celery, green pepper, and scallion. In separate bowl combine mayonnaise and chili sauce; pour over salad; toss to combine. Season with salt and pepper; chill. Serve on lettuce leaves surrounded with egg quarters. Makes 1 midday meal serving.

Each serving is equivalent to: 1 serving Choice Group; 2 ounces Fish; ¼ cup plus 2 tablespoons Vegetables; ½ ounce Limited Vegetable; 3 servings Fat; 1½ servings Something Extra (1 tablespoon chili sauce); 1 Egg

Seafood Salad

½ medium red apple, cored and
  diced
1 tablespoon lemon juice
4 ounces cooked seafood, cut into
  bite-size pieces
½ medium dill pickle, chopped

¼ medium cucumber, pared and
  diced
2 tablespoons imitation
  mayonnaise
1 tablespoon chopped pimento
Lettuce leaves

Place apple in a medium bowl; sprinkle with lemon juice and toss. Add remaining ingredients except lettuce. Chill. Serve on a bed of lettuce leaves. Makes 1 midday meal serving.

Each serving is equivalent to: ½ serving Fruit; 4 ounces Fish; ½ cup Vegetables; 3 servings Fat

Shrimp Cantonese with Rice

2 cups diagonally sliced celery
4 ounces sliced onions
1 pound cooked shrimp, cut in half
    lengthwise
3 cups chopped spinach leaves
4 ounces Chinese pea pods
4 ounces drained canned water
    chestnuts, sliced
½ cup canned sliced bamboo
    shoots

1½ cups Chicken Stock (see page
    140
¼ cup soy sauce
2 tablespoons cornstarch,
    dissolved in 2 tablespoons water
¼ teaspoon pepper
2 cups cooked enriched rice

In a large nonstick skillet, brown celery and onions. Add shrimp, spinach, pea pods, water chestnuts, and bamboo shoots. Cover and cook 1 minute. In small bowl combine stock, soy sauce, cornstarch, and pepper. Stir into shrimp-vegetable mixture. Cook, stirring until sauce is thickened, about 2 minutes. Serve over hot rice. Divide evenly. Makes 4 midday meal servings.

Each serving is equivalent to: 1¼ cups plus 2 tablespoons Vegetables; 3 ounces Limited Vegetable; 4 ounces Fish; 2 servings Something Extra (¼ cup plus 2 tablespoons stock and 1½ teaspoons cornstarch); 1 serving Choice Group

Variation:
Shrimp and Pork Cantonese—Follow basic recipe but use 8 ounces cooked shrimp and 8 ounces shredded cooked pork. Change equivalent listing from 4 ounces Fish to 2 ounces Fish and 2 ounces "Beef" Group.

Stuffed Clams Oreganato

1½ pounds shucked fresh clams,
    reserve shells
2 slices enriched white bread,
    made into crumbs
2 ounces minced onion
½ canned medium tomato,
    chopped

¼ cup finely chopped mushrooms
2 tablespoons chopped fresh
    parsley
2 tablespoons vegetable oil
1 teaspoon oregano
1 garlic clove, minced
Salt to taste

Chop clams, place in bowl, and combine with remaining ingredients. Spoon an equal amount of mixture into each shell, packing tightly. Place on a baking sheet and bake at 400°F. for 20 minutes. Divide evenly. Makes 4 midday meal servings.

Each serving is equivalent to: 4 ounces Fish; ½ serving Bread; ½ ounce Limited Vegetable; 2 tablespoons Vegetables; 1½ servings Fat

Red Clam Sauce

Serve this tempting sauce over cooked enriched spaghetti.

1 medium green pepper, seeded and chopped
2 ounces onion, finely chopped
1 garlic clove, minced
½ cup clam juice
4 canned medium tomatoes, crushed

½ teaspoon oregano
¼ teaspoon salt
⅛ teaspoon pepper
8 ounces drained canned minced clams
2 tablespoons chopped fresh parsley

In saucepan combine green pepper, onion, and garlic. Cook 3 minutes. Add clam juice, tomatoes, oregano, salt, and pepper. Bring to boil, reduce heat, and simmer 5 minutes. Add clams and parsley. Cook 3 minutes longer. Divide evenly. Makes 4 midday or evening meal servings. Supplement as required.

Each serving is equivalent to: ½ cup plus 2 tablespoons Vegetables; ½ ounce Limited Vegetable; ⅛ serving Bonus (2 tablespoons clam juice); 2 ounces Fish

White Clam Sauce (for Pasta)

1 cup clam juice
½ cup chicken bouillon
2 tablespoons chopped fresh parsley
1 garlic clove, minced

1 bay leaf
¼ teaspoon salt
⅛ teaspoon white pepper
8 ounces drained canned minced clams

Combine all ingredients except clams in a small saucepan. Bring to a boil; lower heat and simmer 5 minutes. Add clams; heat thoroughly.

Remove bay leaf. Divide evenly. Makes 4 midday or evening meal servings. Supplement as required.

Each serving is equivalent to: ¼ serving Bonus (¼ cup clam juice); ¹/₆ serving Something Extra (2 tablespoons bouillon); 2 ounces Fish

Anchovies, Capers, and Endive Salad

2 Belgian endive
1 ounce drained, canned anchovy
    fillets, chopped
¼ recipe Basic French Dressing (1
    serving, see page 302)

¼ teaspoon Dijon mustard
1 garlic clove, minced
½ teaspoon drained capers

Trim base of endive and cut in half lengthwise. Place in a shallow saucepan and cover with boiling salted water. Simmer until tender. Drain and chill. Combine remaining ingredients and serve over endive. Makes 1 serving. Serve at mealtime only. Supplement as required.

Each serving is equivalent to: 1 cup Vegetables; 1 ounce Fish; Basic French Dressing (see page 302)

Salmon Loaf

3 slices enriched white bread,
    made into crumbs
½ cup evaporated skimmed milk
½ cup water
12 ounces drained canned salmon,
    flaked
1 tablespoon margarine, melted

1 tablespoon dehydrated onion
    flakes, reconstituted in 1
    tablespoon water
1 teaspoon lemon juice
2 medium eggs, beaten
4 medium eggs, hard-cooked

In a large bowl, combine bread crumbs, milk, and water. Let stand 10 minutes. In a medium bowl, combine salmon, margarine, onion flakes, lemon juice, and beaten eggs. Add to bread mixture; mix thoroughly. Spoon half the mixture into a 9x5x3-inch nonstick loaf pan. Shell the hard-cooked eggs and arrange in a row through the center of the salmon mixture. Cover with remaining salmon mixture.

Bake at 350°F. for 45 to 50 minutes or until loaf is firm and browned. Divide evenly. Makes 6 midday meal servings.

Each serving is equivalent to: ½ serving Bread; ⅙ serving Milk (1 tablespoon plus 1 teaspoon evaporated skimmed milk); 2 ounces Fish; 1 Egg; ½ serving Fat

Salmon Salad

Garlic French Dressing
(see page 302)
½ cup plain unflavored yogurt
1 tablespoon prepared mustard
1 teaspoon seasoned salt
1 pound drained canned salmon,
flaked
8 ounces cooked peas
1 cup thinly sliced celery
¼ cup diced dill pickle
Romaine or iceberg lettuce leaves

In a bowl combine Garlic French Dressing, yogurt, mustard, and seasoned salt. Add salmon, peas, celery, and pickle. Toss to combine. Chill. Divide evenly and serve on lettuce leaves. Makes 4 midday meal servings.

Each serving is equivalent to: Garlic French Dressing (see page 302); ¼ serving Milk (2 tablespoons yogurt); 4 ounces Fish; 2 ounces Limited Vegetable; ¼ cup plus 1 tablespoon Vegetables

Sardine Luncheon Platter

½ cup canned button mushrooms
½ cup cooked cauliflower florets
¼ cup julienned celery
5 cherry tomatoes
2 ounces drained canned sardines
1 ounce cooked beets, sliced
1 medium egg, hard-cooked and
cut in quarters
¼ recipe Garlic French Dressing
(1 serving, see page 302)
¼ cup sliced pimento

Arrange the first 7 ingredients on a platter. Top with dressing. Garnish with pimento. Makes 1 midday meal serving.

Each serving is equivalent to: 1¾ cups Vegetables; 1 ounce Limited Vegetable; 2 ounces Fish; 1 Egg; Garlic French Dressing (see page 302)

Scalloped Salmon or Tomato Herring

1 pound drained canned salmon or
   tomato herring
½ teaspoon dill weed
Freshly ground black pepper to
   taste
4 slices enriched white bread,
   toasted and made into crumbs

1 tablespoon lemon juice
1 cup skim milk
½ cup evaporated skimmed milk
2 tablespoons margarine
Lemon wedges to garnish

Layer half the salmon in a 1-quart baking dish. Sprinkle with dill weed
and pepper. Top with half the crumbs. Add remaining salmon;
sprinkle with lemon juice and cover with remaining crumbs. Combine
skim and evaporated skimmed milk in a measuring cup and pour over
fish. Dot evenly with margarine. Bake at 350°F. for 35 minutes or until
top is golden brown. Garnish with lemon wedges. Divide evenly.
Makes 4 midday meal servings.

Each serving is equivalent to: 4 ounces Fish; 1 serving Bread; ½
serving Milk (¼ cup skim milk and 2 tablespoons evaporated skimmed milk); 1½ servings Fat

Tuna Sandwich Spread

4 ounces drained canned tuna,
   flaked
1 tablespoon mayonnaise
1 teaspoon dehydrated onion
   flakes, reconstituted in 1
   teaspoon water

1 teaspoon prepared mustard
2 tablespoons diced celery
1 frankfurter roll, toasted

In a small bowl combine tuna, mayonnaise, onion flakes, and mustard. Mash together to form a spread. Fold in celery. Serve on
frankfurter roll. Makes 1 midday meal serving.

Each serving is equivalent to: 4 ounces Fish; 3 servings Fat; 2
tablespoons Vegetables; 2 servings Bread (once-a-week selection)

Tuna Tetrazzini on Broccoli

¼ recipe Mushroom White Sauce
(1 serving, see page 297)
1 ounce grated American or
Cheddar cheese

2 ounces drained canned tuna,
flaked
½ cup cooked enriched broad
noodles
½ cup cooked chopped broccoli

In top of double boiler, over boiling water, combine Mushroom White Sauce and cheese. Cook, stirring constantly, until cheese melts. Remove from heat. Stir in tuna. Make a layer of hot noodles on a serving dish. Top with hot broccoli. Spoon tuna mixture over broccoli and noodles. Makes 1 midday meal serving.

Each serving is equivalent to: Mushroom White Sauce (see page 297; 1 ounce Hard Cheese; 2 ounces Fish; 1 serving Choice Group; ½ cup Vegetables

Tuna-Vegetable Pie

1 pound 2 ounces peeled cooked
potatoes, sliced
1½ pounds drained canned tuna,
flaked
1½ recipes "Ravigote" Sauce
(6 servings, see page 297)

1 teaspoon paprika
2 cups cooked diced carrots
6 ounces cooked peas

In bowl mash the potatoes; add tuna, "Ravigote" Sauce, and paprika. Spread half of mixture in a 1½-quart shallow, nonstick casserole. In separate bowl combine carrots and peas; arrange over tuna mixture in casserole. Spread remaining tuna mixture over vegetable layer. Bake at 350°F. for 30 minutes or until piping hot. Divide evenly. Makes 6 midday meal servings.

Each serving is equivalent to: 1 serving Choice Group; 4 ounces Fish; "Ravigote" Sauce (see page 297); ⅓ cup Vegetables; 1 ounce Limited Vegetable

LEGUMES

Legumes are an economical, efficient, and low-cost source of protein. We've provided general tips on cooking them, along with the best of our recipes. Try our soups: Black Turtle Bean, fragrant with cumin and coriander; hearty Split Pea and Minestrone, and Bean and Potato Soup. Our stews include beans, rice, and vegetables. Other favorites include a Pilaf of Chick Peas and Kasha, and Lentils Creole with a diced raw onion. Our salads are made with beans and tuna, kidney beans with eggs and cauliflower, even garlicky garbanzos. Then, too, you'll find such superior food specialties as Soybean Vegeloaf and Burgers. You'll love these legumes!

Rules for Using Legumes

1. Amounts (net drained, cooked weight):
   Women, Men, and Youth: 6 ounces at the Midday Meal
   Women and Youth: 8 ounces at the Evening Meal
   Men: 12 ounces at the Evening Meal
2. Select up to 3 times weekly, if desired:
   beans
      kidney, lima, pink, white, or soybeans
      (dried or canned dried)
   lentils
      (dried or canned dried)
   peas
      black-eyed (cowpeas), chick (garbanzos) or split
      (dried or canned dried)
3. Canned legumes packed with sugar are "illegal."
4. A ½ serving of legumes combined with chicken, veal, fish, egg, or

cheese must be considered a legumes meal. A½ serving of legumes combined with a selection from the "Beef" Group category must be counted as a "Beef" Group meal.

5. *Cooking Procedures:*

Follow package directions. Cook until tender; drain, reserving liquid if desired; weigh portions. Cooked legumes may be combined with other ingredients. Cooking liquid and added ingredients may be consumed.

Unless package states otherwise, all legumes should be washed and picked through to remove any undesirable particles.

Overnight Salt Soak Method—Soak beans using 3 to 4 times as much salted water as beans. The salt helps the beans to absorb the water more evenly, and they then keep their shape better. Remove any beans that float to the surface. Beans should be soaked overnight or at least 6 to 8 hours. Beans can be cooked in the water in which they were soaked or in fresh water to cover plus 1 inch.

One-Hour Hot Soak Method—In a saucepan, cover beans with hot water and bring to a boil. Boil 2 minutes; then set aside for about one hour. Drain. Add enough water to cover plus 1 inch.

Bring to a boil and cook until tender, adding more water if necessary. Cooking time depends on type and age of bean and place of origin. Drain, weigh, and use as recipe directs.

Bean, Rice, and Vegetable Stew

1 cup chicken bouillon
½ cup sliced carrots
2 ounces onion, chopped
1 bay leaf
1 garlic clove, crushed
12 ounces cooked dried chick peas (garbanzos)

1 cup canned medium tomatoes, chopped
1 cup frozen chopped broccoli
¼ teaspoon seasoned salt
⅛ teaspoon pepper
1 cup cooked brown rice

In saucepan combine bouillon, carrots, onion, bay leaf, and garlic. Simmer 10 minutes. Add chick peas, tomatoes, broccoli, seasoned salt, and pepper. Simmer 15 minutes. Add rice. Cook over low heat 4 minutes or until thoroughly heated. Divide evenly. Makes 2 midday meal servings.

Each serving is equivalent to: ⅔ serving Something Extra (½ cup bouillon); 1¼ cups Vegetables; 1 ounce Limited Vegetable; 6 ounces Legumes; 1 serving Choice Group

Chick Peas and Kasha Pilaf

1 ounce dry buckwheat groats (kasha)

3 ounces drained, canned dried chick peas (garbanzos) reserve ¼ cup liquid

1 packet instant chicken broth and seasoning mix

1 pimento or chili pepper, chopped

¼ cup plain unflavored yogurt

In a small saucepan cover kasha with boiling salted water. Cover saucepan and cook over low heat about 15 minutes or until kasha is tender. Drain any excess liquid. Set kasha aside. In saucepan, heat liquid from chick peas. Add broth mix and stir to dissolve. Add kasha and pimento; heat thoroughly. Remove from heat; stir in yogurt. Makes 1 midday meal serving. Supplement as required.

Each serving is equivalent to: 1 serving Choice Group; 3 ounces Legumes; 1 serving Something Extra (1 packet broth mix); ¼ cup Vegetables; ½ serving Milk (¼ cup yogurt)

Garbanzo Beans in Pita

Pita, a round Middle Eastern bread, is available at many supermarkets.

6 pita breads

1 pound, 2 ounces drained canned dried chick peas (garbanzos), lightly mashed

2 tablespoons minced fresh parsley

1 tablespoon lemon juice

1 small garlic clove, mashed

¼ teaspoon cayenne pepper

¼ teaspoon cumin

¼ teaspoon ground coriander

2 cups shredded lettuce

3 medium tomatoes, chopped

1 medium cucumber, pared and diced

6 ounces onion, diced

¼ cup plus 2 tablespoons plain unflavored yogurt

Cut a small piece of each pita bread off and reserve. Open breads to form a pouch. Set aside. In bowl combine chick peas, parsley, lemon juice, garlic, cayenne, cumin, and coriander. In separate bowl combine remaining ingredients. Divide each mixture into 6 portions. Stuff each pita bread with one portion of chick pea mixture and top each with one portion of vegetable-yogurt mixture. Serve each with reserved end used as a garnish. Makes 6 midday meal servings. Supplement as required.

Each serving is equivalent to: 2 servings Bread (once-a-week selection); 3 ounces Legumes; ⅔ cup Vegetables; 1 ounce Limited Vegetable; ⅛ serving Milk (1 tablespoon yogurt)

Garbanzo Dip

Combine 12 ounces drained canned dried chick peas (garbanzos), 1 teaspoon sesame oil, 1 small garlic clove, and as much water as necessary to moisten, in blender container. Process until smooth. Season with salt, freshly ground pepper, and curry powder. Serve dip surrounded with 2 cups crisp raw vegetables. Divide evenly. Makes 2 midday meal servings.

Each serving is equivalent to: 6 ounces Legumes; ½ serving Fat; 1 cup Vegetables

Variation: Follow above recipe and stir in 2 tablespoons imitation mayonnaise. Add 1½ servings Fat to equivalent listing.

Black Turtle Bean Sunday Supper Soup

Fragrant with cumin and coriander.

2¼ pounds cooked, dried black turtle beans	2 garlic cloves, crushed
2 cups water	1 tablespoon minced fresh parsley
1½ cups diced carrots	1½ teaspoons salt
6 ounces onion, diced	1 teaspoon cumin seed
2 medium tomatoes, diced	½ teaspoon ground coriander
½ cup diced celery	3 cups cooked brown rice
	6 lemon slices

In a large saucepan combine all ingredients except rice and lemon. Cover and simmer 1 hour or until beans are very soft; add more water to adjust consistency if desired. Divide evenly into deep bowls, each containing ½ cup hot brown rice. Float a lemon slice on each serving. Makes 6 midday meal servings.

Each serving is equivalent to: 6 ounces Legumes; ½ cup Vegetables; 1 ounce Limited Vegetable; 1 serving Choice Group

Fava Bean and Meat Stew

12 ounces cooked lamb, diced
4 ounces onion, chopped
2 garlic cloves, minced
2 cups Beef Stock (see page 163)
1 tablespoon plus 1 teaspoon
    tomato paste

1 pound cooked dried fava beans
3 tablespoons chopped fresh
    parsley
Dash thyme

In nonstick saucepan, combine lamb, onion, and garlic; cook until onion is browned. Stir in stock and tomato paste. Add beans, parsley, and thyme; cook until most of the liquid has evaporated. Divide evenly. Makes 4 evening meal servings.

Each serving is equivalent to: 3 ounces "Beef" Group; 1 ounce Limited Vegetable; ⅔ serving Something Extra (½ cup stock); $1/_{12}$ serving Bonus (1 teaspoon tomato paste); 4 ounces Legumes

Kidney Bean and Egg Salad

¼ cup imitation mayonnaise
2 teaspoons prepared mustard
4 ounces onion, finely diced
1 cup diced celery
12 ounces drained, canned dried
    red kidney beans
1 medium cucumber, pared and
    diced

4 lettuce leaves
4 medium eggs, hard-cooked and
    quartered
1 medium cucumber, pared and
    sliced
1 teaspoon capers

In bowl combine first 4 ingredients in order given. Add kidney beans and diced cucumber; chill. Divide evenly onto lettuce leaves; surround each with one egg and ¼ of the cucumber slices. Garnish with capers. Makes 4 midday meal servings.

Each serving is equivalent to: 1½ servings Fat; 1 ounce Limited Vegetable; ½ cup Vegetables; 3 ounces Legumes; 1 Egg

Variation:
Soybean and Egg Salad—Omit mustard and substitute 1 tablespoon lemon juice. Replace kidney beans with 12 ounces cooked dried soybeans.

Mexicali Bean Dip

Serve this with vegetable "dippers."

12 ounces drained canned dried red kidney beans, reserve 2 tablespoons liquid
¼ teaspoon garlic powder
¼ teaspoon cumin seed, crushed
4 ounces shredded Cheddar cheese
¼ cup vegetable oil

In saucepan, heat beans, mashing with a wooden spoon. Stir in garlic powder and cumin. Add reserved bean liquid. Stir in cheese until melted. Remove from heat; stir in oil. Divide evenly. Makes 4 midday meal servings.

Each serving is equivalent to: 3 ounces Legumes; 1 ounce Hard Cheese; 3 servings Fat

Quick-and-Easy Bean Salad with Yogurt

12 ounces drained canned dried red kidney beans
1 medium green pepper, seeded and diced
½ cup diced celery
2 ounces diced onion
1 garlic clove, minced
¼ cup plain unflavored yogurt
2 tablespoons vegetable oil
1 tablespoon lemon juice
2½ cups mixed salad greens (chicory, iceberg, and romaine lettuce)
1 medium tomato, sliced
2 tablespoons chopped fresh chives
2 tablespoons chopped fresh parsley
Salt and pepper to taste

In bowl combine beans, green pepper, celery, onion, and garlic. In small cup combine yogurt, oil, and lemon juice; pour over bean mixture. Chill until ready to use. Arrange greens on serving platter; top with bean mixture and surround with tomato slices. Sprinkle with chives, parsley, salt, and pepper; serve at once. Divide evenly. Makes 4 midday meal servings. Supplement as required.

Each serving is equivalent to: 3 ounces Legumes; 1 cup Vegetables; ½ ounce Limited Vegetable; ⅛ serving Milk (1 tablespoon yogurt); 1½ servings Fat

Lentils and Rice

Delicious with salad and yogurt dressing (see "Sauces and Salad Dressings," page 294). Small red lentils can be purchased in Middle East stores. If not available, the green ones may be used.

4 ounces onion, minced
½ teaspoon cumin
¼ cup Chicken Stock (see page 140
12 ounces cooked dried red lentils (see Note)

2 cups cooked brown rice (see Note)
½ teaspoon salt
1 tablespoon plus 1 teaspoon vegetable oil (optional)

In saucepan cook onion and cumin in stock until liquid is evaporated. Add lentils, rice, and salt. Cook until thoroughly heated. Remove from heat. Stir in oil, if desired. Serve hot or cold. Divide evenly. Makes 4 midday meal servings. Supplement as required.

Each serving is equivalent to: 1 ounce Limited Vegetable; $1/12$ serving Something Extra (1 tablespoon stock); 3 ounces Legumes; 1 serving Choice Group; 1 serving Fat (optional)

Note: Cook lentils with 2 crushed garlic cloves. Discard garlic; drain and reserve liquid. Weigh lentils. Use reserved liquid for cooking the rice, adding more water if necessary. Measure rice.

Lentil and Squash Curry

1 cup sliced mushrooms
1 cup sliced zucchini
4 ounces onion, diced
¼ teaspoon curry powder
1 pound cooked dried lentils
1 cup chicken bouillon

1 tablespoon minced fresh parsley
¾ teaspoon salt
½ teaspoon lemon juice
Freshly ground pepper to taste
1 tablespoon plus 1 teaspoon
    vegetable oil (optional)

In saucepan combine mushrooms, zucchini, onion, and curry powder. Cook 4 minutes. Add remaining ingredients except oil. Cover and simmer 15 minutes or until vegetables are tender. Remove from heat; stir in oil, if desired. Divide evenly. Makes 4 evening meal servings. Supplement as required.

Each serving is equivalent to: ½ cup Vegetables; 1 ounce Limited Vegetable; 4 ounces Legumes; ⅓ serving Something Extra (¼ cup bouillon); 1 serving Fat (optional)

Lentils Creole Style

4 ounces onion, finely diced,
    reserve 2 tablespoons
1 medium tomato, finely chopped
½ medium green pepper, seeded
    and chopped
¼ cup chopped pimento

8 ounces cooked dried lentils
1 packet instant chicken broth and
    seasoning mix
½ teaspoon Worcestershire sauce
Salt and pepper to taste

Combine onions, tomato, green pepper, and pimento in nonstick skillet. Cook until tender-crisp. Add lentils, broth mix, Worcestershire, salt, and pepper. Cook, stirring occasionally, until thoroughly heated. Divide evenly; top each portion with 1 tablespoon reserved onion. Makes 2 evening meal servings. Supplement as required.

Each serving is equivalent to: 2 ounces Limited Vegetable; ½ cup Vegetables; 4 ounces Legumes; ½ serving Something Extra (½ packet broth mix)

Lentils with Prunes

In saucepan combine 3 ounces cooked dried lentils, 2 dried medium prunes, and 2 tablespoons water. Heat, stirring often, until liquid is evaporated. Makes 1 midday meal serving. Supplement as required.

Each serving is equivalent to: 3 ounces Legumes; ½ serving Fruit

Lentil Soup

2 cups water
6 ounces cooked dried lentils
1 canned medium tomato,
  chopped
¼ cup diced celery
¼ cup diced carrots
¼ medium green pepper, diced

1 ounce diced parsnips
1 packet instant chicken broth and
  seasoning mix
1 teaspoon chopped fresh parsley
½ teaspoon dill weed
Salt and pepper to taste

In saucepan combine all ingredients and simmer until vegetables are tender. Add more water to adjust consistency, if desired. Divide evenly. Makes 2 midday meal servings. Supplement as required.

Each serving is equivalent to: 3 ounces Legumes; ½ cup plus 1 tablespoon Vegetables; ½ ounce Limited Vegetable; ½ serving Something Extra (½ packet broth mix)

Variation: Add ¼ cup spinach with other vegetables. Cook as directed. Add 2 tablespoons Vegetables to equivalent listing.

Lima Bean and Carrot Soup

1 pound cooked dried lima beans
2 cups sliced carrots
6 ounces sliced onion
2 tablespoons minced fresh
  parsley

1 tablespoon Worcestershire
  sauce
1 teaspoon salt
White pepper to taste
1 cup evaporated skimmed milk
Chopped watercress to garnish

In large saucepan, combine first 7 ingredients. Add water to cover. Bring to a boil; lower heat and simmer about 20 minutes or until vegetables are tender. Pour bean mixture into blender container, in two batches, if necessary; process until pureed. Return to saucepan. Stir in evaporated skimmed milk. Heat, but do not boil. Divide evenly and serve garnished with watercress. Makes 4 evening meal servings. Supplement as required.

Each serving is equivalent to: 4 ounces Legumes; ½ cup Vegetables; 1½ ounces Limited Vegetable; ½ serving Milk (¼ cup evaporated skimmed milk)

Three-Bean Soup

1½ pounds cooked dried navy beans, reserve cooking liquid

2 cups cut green beans

1 to 2 garlic cloves, minced

½ teaspoon basil

Salt and pepper to taste

2 cups cooked frozen fresh lima beans

2 cups diced zucchini

4 canned medium tomatoes, chopped

2 cups cooked enriched noodles

In large saucepan combine reserved cooking liquid and enough water to make 2 quarts liquid. Add navy and green beans, garlic, basil, salt, and pepper; bring to boil, reduce heat and simmer 45 minutes. Add lima beans, zucchini and tomatoes. Simmer 30 minutes longer. Divide evenly into 8 soup bowls, each containing ¼ cup hot noodles. Makes 8 midday meal servings. Supplement as required.

Each serving is equivalent to: 3 ounces Legumes; 1 serving Choice Group; ¾ cup Vegetables

Pinto Beans Texas Style

4 ounces onion, chopped

12 ounces cooked dried pinto beans

4 canned medium tomatoes, crushed

2 tablespoons chili sauce

1 teaspoon prepared mustard (optional)

½ teaspoon Worcestershire sauce

Salt and cayenne pepper to taste

1 cup cooked brown rice

Brown onion in nonstick skillet. Add remaining ingredients except rice. Heat; stirring occasionally. Serve over hot rice. Divide evenly. Makes 2 midday meal servings.

Each serving is equivalent to: 2 ounces Limited Vegetable; 6 ounces Legumes; 1 cup Vegetables; 1½ servings Something Extra (1 tablespoon chili sauce); 1 serving Choice Group

Portuguese-Style Pinto Bean Soup

1 pound cooked dried pinto beans, reserve cooking liquid
1 quart cooking liquid (or cooking liquid plus water to equal 1 quart)
12 ounces pared potato, diced

4 ounces diced onion
½ cup tomato paste
1 garlic clove, minced
½ teaspoon allspice
Salt and freshly ground pepper to taste

In a large saucepan, combine all ingredients except salt and pepper. Bring to a boil. Lower heat; cover and simmer about 30 minutes or until vegetables are tender. Season with salt and pepper. Divide evenly. Makes 4 evening meal servings. Supplement as required.

Each serving is equivalent to: 4 ounces Legumes; 1 serving Choice Group; 1 ounce Limited Vegetable; ½ serving Bonus (2 tablespoons tomato paste)

Variation: To make 4 delicious complete evening meal servings, add 8 ounces diced ham during the last 15 minutes of cooking. Add 2 ounces "Beef" Group (cured) to equivalent listing.

Soybean Casserole

2 cups chopped celery
2 ounces chopped onion
¼ medium green pepper, seeded and chopped
½ packet instant chicken broth and seasoning mix dissolved in ¼ cup hot water
2 tablespoons plus 2 teaspoons flour

2 cups skim milk
1½ pounds cooked dried soybeans
1 teaspoon salt
2 slices enriched white bread, made into crumbs
1 tablespoon plus 1 teaspoon margarine

In saucepan cook celery, onion, and green pepper about 3 minutes. Add dissolved broth mix; cook 5 minutes. Blend in flour. Slowly add milk and cook, stirring constantly until mixture thickens. Add beans and salt. Mix well. Pour into a 1-quart nonstick baking dish. Sprinkle evenly with bread crumbs. Dot evenly with margarine. Bake at 350°F. for 30 minutes or until golden brown. Divide evenly. Makes 4 midday meal servings.

Each serving is equivalent to: ½ cup plus 1½ teaspoons Vegetables; ½ ounce Limited Vegetable; 2⅛ servings Something Extra (⅛ packet broth mix and 2 teaspoons flour); ½ serving Milk (½ cup skim milk); 6 ounces Legumes; ½ serving Bread; 1 serving Fat

Soybean Cheese Casserole

1 cup chicken bouillon
4 ounces chopped onion
1 medium green pepper, seeded
  and chopped
1 garlic clove, minced
4 canned medium tomatoes,
  crushed
2 tablespoons tomato paste

1 teaspoon basil
¼ teaspoon oregano
Salt and pepper to taste
12 ounces cooked dried soybeans
4 ounces sharp Cheddar cheese,
  grated
2 slices enriched white bread,
  made into crumbs

In saucepan combine bouillon, onion, green pepper, and garlic. Cook until vegetables are tender. Add tomatoes, tomato paste, and seasonings. Cook until slightly thickened; add soybeans. Transfer mixture to a 1½-quart casserole. In a small bowl, combine cheese and crumbs. Sprinkle over tomato bean mixture. Bake at 350°F. for 40 minutes or until golden. Divide evenly. Makes 4 midday meal servings.

Each serving is equivalent to: ⅓ serving Something Extra (¼ cup bouillon); 1 ounce Limited Vegetable; ½ cup plus 2 tablespoons Vegetables; ⅛ serving Bonus (1½ teaspoons tomato paste); 3 ounces Legumes; 1 ounce Hard Cheese; ½ serving Bread

Soybean Stuffed Peppers

4 medium green peppers, halved
    and seeded
1 pound cooked dried soybeans,
    mashed
1 cup diced celery
2 medium tomatoes, diced
1 tablespoon water
1 teaspoon dehydrated onion
    flakes

Dash garlic powder
Salt to taste
Pepper to taste
2 slices enriched white bread,
    made into crumbs
1 tablespoon plus 1 teaspoon
    imitation (or diet) margarine,
    melted

In large saucepan cook pepper halves in boiling salted water 3 minutes or until tender-crisp. Drain; set aside to cool. In medium bowl combine next 8 ingredients; divide evenly into 8 portions and fill each pepper half. In a small bowl combine bread crumbs and margarine. Sprinkle an equal amount of crumb mixture over each pepper half. Place peppers in large nonstick baking pan. Bake at 350°F. 25 to 30 minutes or until peppers are soft. Makes 4 evening meal servings, 2 halves each. Supplement as required.

    Each serving is equivalent to: 1 cup Vegetables; 4 ounces Legumes; ½ serving Bread; ½ serving Fat

Soybean Vegeloaf

1½ cups chicken bouillon
1 cup sliced mushrooms
¾ cup finely chopped celery
1 medium green pepper, seeded
    and finely chopped
3 ounces onion, finely chopped
1 garlic clove, minced
1 pound, 2 ounces cooked dried
    soybeans

2 cups grated carrots
¼ cup flour
¼ cup chopped fresh parsley
½ teaspoon oregano
½ teaspoon thyme
Dash ground cloves
6 medium eggs, slightly beaten
3 slices whole wheat bread, made
    into crumbs

In saucepan combine bouillon, mushrooms, celery, green pepper, onion, and garlic. Cook 5 minutes. Cool slightly. Stir in remaining ingredients in order given until well combined. Press mixture into a large nonstick loaf pan. Bake at 350°F. for 40 minutes or until golden. Divide evenly. Makes 6 midday meal servings.

Each serving is equivalent to: 2⅓ servings Something Extra (¼ cup bouillon and 2 teaspoons flour); ¾ cup Vegetables; ½ ounce Limited Vegetable; 3 ounces Legumes; 1 Egg; ½ serving Bread

Soyburgers

12 ounces ground beef
12 ounces cooked, dried soybeans, mashed

1 tablespoon dehydrated onion flakes
½ teaspoon salt
⅛ teaspoon pepper

Combine all ingredients in bowl. Divide into 4 equal patties. Place on rack; bake at 375°F. for 25 minutes or until done to taste. Serve hot. Makes 4 midday meal servings, 1 patty each.

Each serving is equivalent to: 2 ounces "Beef" Group; 3 ounces Legumes

Split Pea Minestrone

Generally a heaping cup of split peas will make about 1 pound cooked. Cook peas according to package directions, drain and reserve liquid; weigh peas.

2 cups sliced zucchini
1½ cups sliced mushrooms
6 ounces chopped onion
½ cup diced celery
3 cups Ham or Chicken Stock (see page 140 or 163)

1 pound cooked dried split peas
½ teaspoon salt
½ teaspoon basil
Black pepper to taste
12 ounces peeled, cooked potatoes, diced (optional)

In a large saucepan combine zucchini, mushrooms, onions, and celery. Cook about 5 minutes. Add remaining ingredients, except potatoes. Simmer, stirring occasionally, about 45 minutes or until soup thickens. Add water to adjust consistency if necessary. Add potatoes, if desired. Cook 10 minutes. Divide evenly. Makes 4 evening meal servings. Supplement as required.

Each serving is equivalent to: 1 cup Vegetables; 1½ ounces Limited Vegetable; 1 serving Something Extra (¾ cup stock); 4 ounces Legumes; 1 serving Choice Group (optional)

Split Pea Soup

¾ cup diced carrots
3 ounces diced onion
12 ounces cooked dried split peas
2 cups water

2 packets instant chicken broth
  and seasoning mix
½ bay leaf

In saucepan cook carrots and onion for 3 minutes. Add remaining ingredients. Cover and simmer, stirring often, for 25 to 30 minutes or until desired consistency. Divide evenly. Makes 2 midday meal servings.

Each serving is equivalent to: ¼ cup plus 2 tablespoons Vegetables; 1½ ounces Limited Vegetable; 6 ounces Legumes; 1 serving Something Extra (1 packet broth mix)

Baked Beans with Frankfurters

12 ounces cooked dried white
  beans
1 medium apple or small pear,
  cored, pared, and diced
1 medium green pepper, seeded
  and diced
1 ounce finely diced onion or
  scallion

2 tablespoons catsup
1 teaspoon prepared mustard
Few drops hot sauce
5 canned medium tomatoes,
  crushed
6 ounces frankfurters, sliced

In a shallow 2-quart casserole combine first 7 ingredients. Top with tomatoes and frankfurters. Bake at 350°F. for 30 minutes. Divide evenly. Makes 4 midday meal servings.

Each serving is equivalent to: 3 ounces Legumes; ¼ serving Fruit; ¾ cup Vegetables; ¼ ounce Limited Vegetable; ¾ serving Something Extra (1½ teaspoons catsup); 1½ ounces Frankfurters

Variation: Substitute 6 ounces sliced Canadian bacon for frankfurters. Substitute 1½ ounces "Beef" Group (cured) for Frankfurters in equivalent listing.

Bean Salad Turkish Style

**6 ounces peeled cooked potatoes,
    diced**
1 cup cooked diced carrots
2 medium tomatoes, diced
1 garlic clove, minced
8 ounces cooked dried white beans
¼ cup water

½ cup chopped fresh parsley
**Salt and freshly ground pepper to
    taste**
**2 teaspoons vegetable oil
    (optional)**
2 cups shredded lettuce

In saucepan combine potatoes, carrots, tomatoes, and garlic. Cook 3 minutes. Add beans and water. Cook until most of the water is evaporated and beans are hot. Stir in parsley and season with salt and pepper. Remove from heat. Stir in oil if desired. Serve on lettuce. Divide evenly. Makes 2 evening meal servings. Supplement as required.

Each serving is equivalent to: 1 serving Choice Group; 2¼ cups Vegetables; 4 ounces Legumes; 1 serving Fat (optional)

Bean and Potato Soup

**1½ pounds cooked dried white
    beans, reserve cooking liquid**
**2 quarts cooking liquid (or
    cooking liquid plus water to
    equal 2 quarts)**
12 ounces pared potatoes, diced

2 cups chopped celery
4 ounces diced onion
2 small garlic cloves, minced
Salt and white pepper to taste
2 cups cooked brown rice
Chopped fresh parsley to garnish

In a large saucepan combine beans, liquid, potatoes, celery, onion, garlic, salt, and pepper. Bring to a boil. Lower heat, cover and simmer for 30 minutes or until vegetables are tender. If desired, remove cover and cook until thickened, stirring occasionally. Adjust seasonings. Divide evenly into 8 soup bowls, each containing ¼ cup hot rice. Garnish each serving with chopped parsley. Makes 8 midday meal servings. Supplement as required.

Each serving is equivalent to: 3 ounces Legumes; 1 serving Choice Group; ¼ cup Vegetables; ½ ounce Limited Vegetable

White Bean and Tuna Salad

Tomato wedges and cooked green beans are fine additions to this salad plate.

2 tablespoons vegetable oil
2 teaspoons lemon juice or red
  wine vinegar
6 ounces cooked dried white beans
¼ cup chopped fresh parsley

½ ounce scallions, chopped
Salt and pepper to taste
4 ounces drained canned tuna
2 lettuce leaves

In bowl combine oil and lemon juice or vinegar. Add beans, parsley, scallions, salt, and pepper. Toss to combine. Chill. Break tuna into chunks. Divide bean mixture evenly onto lettuce leaves. Top each with half the tuna. Makes 2 midday meal servings.

Each serving is equivalent to: 3 servings Fat; 3 ounces Legumes; ¼ ounce Limited Vegetable; 2 tablespoons Vegetables; 2 ounces Fish

VEGETABLES

One can't help but marvel at the myriad vegetables that nature has produced. Literally hundreds of thousands of edible plants flourish around the world, but only a relatively few kinds are ordinarily used as food. Our chapter on vegetables includes most of the popular vegetables, and a lively sprinkling of those less well-known. Please do try the strange and exotic vegetables you might be lucky enough to find at your markets. They will perk up your menu. For the same reason, cook some of the vegetables which you usually eat raw—celery, cucumber, and tomato, for instance. And, in reverse, try eating raw some vegetables which you normally cook, such as broccoli, cauliflower, or zucchini.

Rules for Using Vegetables

1. Use vegetables raw or cooked, fresh, frozen (without sauce) or canned.
2. Select at least 2 servings daily.
   Serving Size: ½ cup or 1 medium (e.g., tomato) or 4 ounces Limited Vegetable (see rule 4).
3. Vegetables must be eaten at the Midday and Evening Meals. They may also be eaten at any other time. Vary selections.
4. Limited Vegetables
   Serving Size: 4 ounces
   The following vegetables are optional and must be weighed. Do not exceed a daily combined total of 4 ounces, drained weight.

artichoke	Brussels sprouts
artichoke hearts	celeriac (celery root)
beets	Chinese pea pods (snow peas)

Jerusalem artichokes	winter squash
jicima	acorn
leeks	banana
okra	buttercup
onions	butternut
parsnips	calabaza
peas	Danish turban
pumpkin	Des Moines
rutabagas (yellow turnips)	gold nugget
salsify (oyster plant)	hubbard
scallions	kushaw
shallots	peppercorn
water chestnuts	table queen

5. Vegetables are "illegal" if they contain added sugar (with the exception of canned peas).

Crudités

For party-goers or party-givers who want taste without waist, these raw crisp vegetables, called crudités in France, are a favorite hors d'oeuvre. Prepare them ahead and refrigerate until party time.

Beans, Green or Wax—Use uncooked whole, or parboil and cut on diagonal.

Bean Sprouts—Prepare as Vinaigrette (see page 256).

Broccoli—Rinse tiny raw florets in ice water containing 1 teaspoon lemon juice or vinegar. Drain and dry.

Carrots—Cut off slivers or strips using a paring knife. To make curls, roll up strips, secure with toothpick, and put in ice water to set the curl.

Cauliflower—Dip tiny raw florets in ice water containing 1 teaspoon lemon juice or vinegar. Drain and dry.

Celeriac (celery root)—Pare and cut in long strips, blanch 1 or 2 minutes in water containing lemon juice, drain and serve. (Limited Vegetable)

Celery—Cut tender ribs into long, slim fingers. Use raw or poach lightly in chicken bouillon. Celery sticks look pretty served with the green leaves left on.

Chinese Cabbage—Use halved stalks or rolled-up leaf sections.

Chinese Snow Peas—Serve them whole and crisp. (Limited Vegetable)

Cucumbers—Pare or, if young, rinse and use. With tines of a fork, make parallel gashes from top to bottom around the whole cucumber, then slice in rounds or cut in long, thin strips. Sprinkle with chopped fresh dill or chives, if desired.

Fennel—Cut into slices and serve raw.

Kale—Serve this curly-leaved member of the cabbage family raw. Cut off and discard root ends. Rinse and dry leaves.

Kohlrabi—Pare it just as you would turnip, then slice and serve.

Lettuce—Rinse crisp firm leaves of chicory and an assortment of other available greens.

Mushrooms—Dip whole mushroom caps in lemon juice or cut through cap and stem in pretty slices and dip in lemon juice. Serve raw.

Parsley—Use crisp sprigs, rinsed and dried.

Peppers—Use both red and green for color contrast. Seed and cut into strips or rings.

Pimentos—Use for bright red color; nice shredded and used as light stuffing in celery ribs.

Radishes—Prepare radish roses or accordions (see page 280).

Scallions—Trim off root end, but leave plenty of green leaf. Cut the thick ones in half, lengthwise. (Limited Vegetable)

Spinach—Rinse several times to remove sand. Drain well and serve raw. Cut out tough ribs with scissors, if necessary.

Squash: Summer—Use young thin-skinned zucchini. Cut into fingers or slices and serve.

Tomatoes—Use whole cherry tomatoes, or serve medium tomatoes, cut in quarters and sprinkled with basil, fresh dill, or minced fresh garlic.

Watercress—Use fresh sprigs, rinsed and dried.

Suggested platter of crudités for 1 serving:
½ cup raw broccoli florets
½ cup carrot strips or curls
½ cup raw cauliflower florets
½ cup barely cooked crisp green beans
3 cherry tomatoes

¼ medium red pepper, cut into strips
1 ounce scallions
Celery sticks
Radish roses
Sprigs of watercress and parsley

Suggested dips for individual servings:
    1 serving Pimento Dressing (see page 336)
        or
    1 serving Basic French Dressing (see page 302)
        or
    1 serving Hollandaise Sauce (see page 299)

Vegetable Stock

2 cups diced celery ribs and leaves
1 cup shredded lettuce
4 ounces onion studded with cloves
¼ cup each carrots, turnips, and
** parsnips**

Bouquet Garni (see page 318)
Dash each white and cayenne
** pepper**
½ teaspoon salt

In a kettle combine all ingredients and add enough water to cover. Bring to boil. Lower heat and cover partially with a lid. Simmer about 1½ hours or until vegetables are tender. Strain and chill. Use liquid as base for soup with cooked leftover vegetables. There are as many variations as your imagination can dream up.

Artichokes

When purchasing artichokes look for compact green leaves. Loose or discolored leaves are signs of overmaturity or poor quality. When preparing artichokes, wash, drain, and cut off stem. Remove any tough, dry outer leaves. Using a kitchen scissors or knife remove the thorny tip of each leaf. To avoid discoloration until cooking, place artichokes in water to cover with 3 tablespoons lemon juice or vinegar added to each quart of water.

Use a stainless steel or enameled saucepan to keep artichokes from discoloring during cooking. Adding lemon juice to the cooking liquid will also keep them from discoloring; but this can cause a loss in flavor. Therefore, salted water is the preferred liquid for home preparation. Cook artichokes in boiling liquid to cover or in a steamer until tender.

Asparagus

Purchase asparagus that has straight stalks, with tightly closed tips. When preparing asparagus, gently rinse several times. Remove the bottom part of the stalk where it snaps easily. Using a vegetable peeler, remove outer scales from each stalk. Using string, tie asparagus into serving-size bunches. Use only a few inches of water to cook. Stand asparagus upright in a steamer and cover, or in the bottom part of a double boiler, inverting the top of a double boiler over the asparagus tips. The steam will cook the upper part of the stalk and tips. Cook approximately 12 to 15 minutes or until stalks are tender. You may also lie stalks down in a wide-bottom pan and add ½ inch of boiling salted water; cover pan and simmer 10 to 12 minutes, or until tender. Regardless of cooking method, asparagus should be removed from water immediately when tender, untied, and served or allowed to cool for later use.

Asparagus Guacamole

A pretty salad when served as a dip with orange sections, bite-size pieces of vegetables, or tortillas.

24 medium asparagus spears, cooked and chopped
1½ medium tomatoes, chopped
2 ounces onion, chopped
¼ cup canned green chili peppers

1 tablespoon plus 1 teaspoon vegetable oil
1 teaspoon lemon juice
1 garlic clove, crushed
½ teaspoon salt
¼ teaspoon freshly ground pepper

Combine all ingredients in blender container; process until smooth. Chill. Divide evenly. Makes 4 servings. Serve at mealtime only.

Each serving is equivalent to: ¾ cup Vegetables; ½ ounce Limited Vegetable; 1 serving Fat

Asparagus Vinaigrette

6 cooked asparagus spears   **¼ recipe Basic French Dressing
(1 serving; see page 302)**

Arrange asparagus spears on plate and top with Basic French Dressing. Chill. Makes 1 serving. Serve at mealtime only.

Each serving is equivalent to: ½ cup Vegetables; Basic French Dressing (see page 302).

Sprouting Beans

The best-known and most commonly used bean sprout is the mung bean, but any dried bean or seed can be sprouted. Some examples are: alfalfa, aduki, garbanzos, and lentils.

One pound of beans for sprouting will make 5 to 7 pounds of this fresh vegetable. Buy dried mung or soybeans for sprouting. Discard split or discolored beans. Soak ¼ cup rinsed beans overnight in water to cover. Drain, rinse, place in a quart jar, and tie cheesecloth over the opening. To grow white tender sprouts, store bottle on its side in a dark place or cover with papers to exclude light. Rinse and drain beans several times a day to keep them moist, for about 4 days, or until sprouts are 1 to 2 inches long; ¼ cup of mung beans will yield about ¾ of a pound of sprouts.

Treat sprouted beans like any fresh vegetable. Store in refrigerator as soon as they are ready for eating and use as soon as possible. Sprouted beans may be eaten raw or cooked. To cook, place sprouts in a pan with a small amount of boiling salted water. Cover and cook to desired degree of tenderness. They can also be served blanched. Place in a strainer and pour boiling water over them. Drain and serve. To freshen canned bean sprouts, transfer them to a strainer and rinse several times under running water. Then soak in ice water, using lots of ice cubes. This should crisp them in about an hour.

Bean sprouts add a crunchy texture to sandwich fillings and are delicious in tossed salads.

Bean Sprout Casserole

2 cups blanched or canned bean
　sprouts, rinsed
2 cups drained canned whole
　kernel corn
½ medium green pepper, seeded
　and diced

¼ cup diced pimento
Salt and pepper to taste
Basic White Sauce (see page 296)
Paprika to garnish

In a medium bowl combine bean sprouts, corn, green pepper, pimento, salt, and pepper. Transfer to a 1-quart ovenproof casserole. Top with Basic White Sauce; sprinkle with paprika. Bake at 350°F. for 25 minutes or until piping hot. Divide evenly. Makes 4 servings. Serve at mealtime only.

　　Each serving is equivalent to: ½ cup plus 2 tablespoons Vegetables; 1 serving Choice Group; Basic White Sauce (see page 296)

Bean Sprout Curry

1 medium apple, pared, cored,
　and diced
1 cup diced celery
4 ounces onion, finely diced
2 packets instant chicken broth
　and seasoning mix
2 teaspoons curry powder

1½ cups water
8 dried medium prunes, pitted
　and diced
2 tablespoons cornstarch,
　dissolved in 2 tablespoons water
2 cups canned bean sprouts,
　rinsed

In a medium saucepan combine apple, celery, onion, broth mix, and curry powder. Cook over medium heat, stirring frequently until onions are transparent. Add water and prunes. Bring to boil; lower heat and simmer 15 to 20 minutes or until celery is tender-crisp. Stir in cornstarch; cook until thickened. Add bean sprouts; toss to combine. Heat for about 1 minute. Divide evenly. Makes 4 servings.

　　Each serving is equivalent to: ¾ serving Fruit; ¾ cup Vegetables; 1 ounce Limited Vegetable; 2 servings Something Extra (½ packet broth mix and 1½ teaspoons cornstarch)

Bean Sprout Vinaigrette

In bowl combine 1 cup bean sprouts, ¼ cup diced celery, ¼ medium cucumber, pared and diced, and 2 tablespoons sliced radishes. In separate bowl or measuring cup, combine 1½ teaspoons soy sauce, 1 teaspoon sesame oil, 1 teaspoon lemon juice, and ½ teaspoon minced chives. Pour over salad, and toss. Makes 1 serving. Serve at mealtime only.

Each serving is equivalent to: 1½ cups Vegetables; 1 serving Fat

Banana, Beet, and Water Chestnut Salad

1 medium banana, sliced	4 cups shredded lettuce
2 tablespoons lemon juice	2 tablespoons vegetable oil
8 ounces drained canned sliced beets	1 tablespoon red wine vinegar
	1 tablespoon prepared mustard
4 ounces drained canned water chestnuts, sliced	¼ teaspoon salt
	⅛ teaspoon pepper

Place banana in a medium bowl. Sprinkle with lemon juice. Add beets and water chestnuts; toss lightly to combine. Arrange lettuce on a large serving platter; top with banana mixture. Place remaining ingredients in a small jar with tight-fitting cover; shake well to combine. Pour over banana mixture. Divide evenly. Makes 4 servings. Serve at mealtime only.

Each serving is equivalent to: ½ serving Fruit; 3 ounces Limited Vegetable; 1 cup Vegetables; 1½ servings Fat

Icy Borscht from the Blender

8 ounces drained canned beets, with ¼ cup liquid	½ cup plain unflavored yogurt
1½ cups beef or chicken bouillon	½ medium cucumber, pared and diced
1 teaspoon lemon juice	

Combine beets with liquid, bouillon, and lemon juice in blender container; process until smooth. Chill. Before serving, stir in yogurt and cucumber. Divide evenly. Makes 2 servings.

Each serving is equivalent to: 4 ounces Limited Vegetable; 1 serving Something Extra (¾ cup bouillon); ½ serving Milk (¼ cup yogurt); 2 tablespoons Vegetables

Variations:

1. Add 1 medium tomato, peeled and diced, to blender container. Continue as above. Add ¼ cup Vegetables to equivalent listing.

2. Add 6 ounces peeled cooked potato, diced just before serving. Add 1 serving Choice Group to equivalent listing.

Stir-Cooked Broccoli and Water Chestnuts

To brighten up your Chinese meal.

1 medium bunch broccoli (6 cups)
¼ cup chicken bouillon
2 tablespoons soy sauce
1 garlic clove, minced

4 ounces drained canned water chestnuts, sliced
1 tablespoon plus 1 teaspoon vegetable oil (optional)

Cut broccoli into florets and cut stems into pieces about the same size as the florets. Place in a large saucepan; cover with water. Bring to a boil; lower heat and cook about 3 minutes. Drain. In a wok or a large nonstick skillet combine chicken bouillon, soy sauce, and garlic. Bring to a boil; add broccoli and water chestnuts. Cook, stirring constantly, about 3 to 4 minutes or until broccoli is tender-crisp. Remove from heat; stir in oil if desired. Divide evenly. Makes 4 servings. If oil is used, serve at mealtime only.

Each serving is equivalent to: 1½ cups Vegetables; $1/12$ serving Something Extra (1 tablespoon bouillon); 1 ounce Limited Vegetable; 1 serving Fat (optional)

Brussels Sprouts

Wash fresh Brussels sprouts in salted water. Remove a thin slice from stem end and make a crosswise cut in each stem. Remove any loose or discolored leaves. Brussels sprouts may be cooked in boiling salted water, steamed, or cooked in a pressure cooker until tender. This is a limited vegetable and must be weighed.

Quick-and-Easy Brussels Sprouts

12 ounces Brussels sprouts
1 tablespoon plus 1 teaspoon margarine

Salt and freshly ground pepper to taste

Add Brussels sprouts to saucepan with boiling salted water to cover. Return water to a boil; reduce heat and simmer for 12 minutes or until tender. Drain. Toss with margarine; sprinkle with salt and pepper. Divide evenly. Makes 4 servings. Serve at mealtime only.

Each serving is equivalent to: 3 ounces Limited Vegetable; 1 serving Fat

Burdock

Burdock is a root vegetable, well known in Japan as "gobo." It grows wild throughout most of the United States and has a long, tapering, tender, edible root. It is crisp and crunchy in texture, and delicious both raw in salads and cooked as a vegetable. Burdock is a limited vegetable and must be weighed.

To prepare, split the root and remove the outer layer. Use the smooth white core inside.

Cabbage

Choose firm green or red cabbage heads. Cabbage may be eaten raw or cooked. Allow 1 pound fresh cabbage for 2 cups cooked. Quarter or shred cabbage and cook in boiling salted water only until tender.

Chinese Cabbage

A staple of the Oriental diet, Chinese cabbage is also known as "celery cabbage" because of its shape. It has long, wide, white stalks with a crinkly, leafy, light green edge. Eat raw or cook in boiling salted water until tender. Serve as a vegetable.

Creamy Cole Slaw

6 cups shredded cabbage
2 cups grated carrots
½ cup plain unflavored yogurt
¼ cup mayonnaise
Artificial sweetener to equal 3
  teaspoons sugar

½ teaspoon salt
¼ teaspoon onion powder
¼ teaspoon dehydrated onion
  flakes
⅛ teaspoon celery seed
Dash white pepper

In a large bowl, combine cabbage and carrots. In a small bowl, combine remaining ingredients. Pour over cabbage mixture. Toss lightly. Chill. Divide evenly. Makes 6 servings. Serve at mealtime only.

Each serving is equivalent to: 1⅓ cups Vegetables; ⅙ serving Milk (1 tablespoon plus 1 teaspoon yogurt); 2 servings Fat

Cactus

The pads and fleshy stems of this plant can be gathered at any season. To prepare, place the pads in the oven at 375°F. for 40 minutes; then split the skin and pull it off. The remaining soft flesh is mucilaginous, like okra, and can be used as a thickener in soups or stews, or served as a vegetable.

Cardoon

Cardoon is a long, celerylike vegetable with dark green leaves. It is said to taste like asparagus but is not nearly as flavorful. The innermost tender shoots may be eaten raw in salads, but cardoon is more often cooked like celery and served hot, as a vegetable.

Carrot and Pineapple Mold

1 envelope unflavored gelatin
½ cup water
1 cup coarsely grated carrots
1 cup orange-flavored dietetic soda

½ cup canned crushed pineapple, no sugar added
Artificial sweetener to equal 2 teaspoons sugar
⅛ teaspoon peppermint extract

In a medium saucepan soften gelatin in water. Place over low heat; cook, stirring constantly, until gelatin is dissolved. Remove from heat. Add remaining ingredients and stir to combine. Pour into a 3-cup mold and chill until firm. Unmold. Divide evenly. Makes 2 servings.

Each serving is equivalent to: 1 serving Something Extra (½ envelope gelatin); ½ cup Vegetables; ½ serving Fruit

Cauliflower

Buy cauliflower with white, tightly formed florets. Avoid discolored or spreading florets, as these are signs of age. Cut away outer leaves and stem. Separate the florets, rinse, drain and dry on paper towels. Raw cauliflower is delicious served with a dip. (See Yogurt-Onion Mix Dressing, page 311.)

Celeriac

Whether your vegetable market calls it "celery root," "celery knob," or "celeriac," don't pass up this delicious root vegetable. Although it is more popular in Europe, Americans are eating celeriac cold in salads, and hot, as a side dish with beef or poultry, and using it as a flavoring in soups and stews. Small size celeriac is usually more flavorful than the large size, which tends to be woody. To cook: wash, pare, and slice the root. Cook in a small amount of boiling salted water for about 20 minutes or until tender. This is a limited vegetable on the Food Plan and must be weighed.

Cooked Celery

3 cups cut celery
Salt to taste

Pepper to taste

Cut celery as desired. In saucepan combine celery with water to cover. Cook until celery is tender. Drain and season with salt and pepper. Divide evenly. Makes 4 servings.

Each serving is equivalent to: ¾ cup Vegetables

Celery and Lima Beans in "Creamy" Chive Sauce

¾ cup cooked sliced celery
½ cup cooked fresh lima beans

2 tablespoons evaporated
   skimmed milk
½ teaspoon chives

Combine all ingredients in a small saucepan. Cook until thoroughly heated; DO NOT BOIL. Makes 1 serving. Serve at mealtime only.

Each serving is equivalent to: ¾ cup Vegetables; 1 serving Choice Group; ¼ serving Milk (2 tablespoons evaporated skimmed milk)

Celery in Mushroom Sauce

¾ cup cooked sliced celery
½ cup cooked sliced mushrooms

¼ recipe Basic White Sauce
   (1 serving, see page 296)

Combine all ingredients in an individual baking dish. Bake at 375°F. for 15 minutes or until hot and bubbly. Makes 1 serving. Serve at mealtime only. Each serving is equivalent to: 1¼ cups Vegetables; Basic White Sauce (see page 296)

Cucumbers

Gherkins
This is a variety of tiny cucumber.

Kirbies
This is a variety of small cucumber.

Creamy Cucumber Soup

This summer soup is a perfect beginning for a fish dinner.

3 medium cucumbers	¼ teaspoon dill weed
Salt to taste	2¼ cups Chicken Stock (see page
¼ cup margarine	140
2 tablespoons flour	¼ teaspoon white pepper
2 cups hot skim milk	Chopped fresh chives to garnish

Cut ½ of one cucumber into 6 equal slices. Reserve for garnish. Pare, seed, and grate remaining cucumbers. Sprinkle with salt and let stand 20 minutes. Drain and set aside. In top of double boiler over hot water melt margarine, stir in flour, and cook 5 minutes. Add milk, dill, and cucumbers. Cook 30 minutes. Remove from heat and process mixture in blender container until smooth. Transfer to bowl and add stock, salt, and pepper. Refrigerate 3 hours or until well chilled. Stir; divide evenly into 6 bowls; garnish each with chives and one cucumber slice. Makes 6 servings. Serve at mealtime only.

Each serving is equivalent to: ¼ cup Vegetables; 2 servings Fat; 1½ servings Something Extra (1 teaspoon flour and ¼ cup plus 2 tablespoons stock); ⅓ serving Milk (⅓ cup skim milk)

Minty Hot Cucumber

Serve as a side dish for salmon or lamb.

1 medium cucumber, pared, seeded, and cut into 1-inch pieces	**1 teaspoon lemon juice** **1 teaspoon chopped fresh mint** **½ teaspoon salt**

Place cucumber in a small saucepan with enough water to cover. Bring to boil, reduce heat, and simmer 5 minutes or until soft. Drain. In bowl toss cucumber with remaining ingredients. Divide evenly. Makes 2 servings.

Each serving is equivalent to: ¼ cup Vegetables

Chinese Winter Melon

This is a large round melon with light green skin. It may weigh 20 to 30 pounds. The meat is white, with yellow seeds, and has a delicate flavor.

Baked Eggplant Casserole

The Turkish name for this dish is Patlijan.

2 medium eggplants, pared and sliced 1 inch thick (8 cups)	**3 medium green peppers, seeded and sliced ¼ inch thick**
1 tablespoon salt	**½ cup chopped fresh parsley**
6 ounces sliced onion	**2 garlic cloves, minced**
4 medium tomatoes, peeled and sliced	**1½ cups tomato sauce, no sugar added**

Sprinkle eggplant with salt and let stand for 20 minutes. Rinse, drain, and dry with paper towels. In a large casserole layer ½ of all ingredients, in order given, beginning with eggplant. Repeat layers using remaining ingredients. Bake at 425°F. for 40 minutes or until vegetables are soft. Divide evenly. Makes 6 servings.

Each serving is equivalent to: 2 cups Vegetables; 1 ounce Limited Vegetable; ½ serving Bonus (¼ cup tomato sauce)

Baked Stuffed Eggplant

1 medium eggplant, cut in half
    lengthwise (4 cups)
1 cup tomato puree, divided
1½ teaspoons chopped fresh
    parsley
1 teaspoon dehydrated onion
    flakes, reconstituted in 1
    tablespoon water

½ garlic clove, minced
¼ teaspoon basil
⅛ teaspoon fennel seeds
⅛ teaspoon pepper
4 ounces grated Cheddar cheese
1 cup cooked enriched rice

Place eggplant, cut side down, in a baking pan. Add ¼ inch water and bake at 350°F. until eggplant is soft. Remove eggplant and allow to cool slightly. Scoop out pulp leaving a ½-inch shell. Set aside. In saucepan combine next 7 ingredients and simmer 10 minutes. In bowl combine pulp, cheese, rice, and ½ cup tomato sauce. Divide evenly and stuff into eggplant shells. Place in casserole, stuffed side up, and cover with remaining sauce. Bake at 375°F. for 25 minutes or until stuffing is hot and cheese is melted. Divide evenly. Makes 2 midday meal servings.

Each serving is equivalent to: 2 cups Vegetables; 1 serving Bonus (½ cup tomato puree); 2 ounces Hard Cheese; 1 serving Choice Group

Crisp Eggplant Slices, Italian Style

1 medium egg, slightly beaten
1 teaspoon imitation mayonnaise
Salt and pepper to taste
1 slice enriched white bread, made
    into crumbs

1 ounce grated Parmesan cheese
¼ teaspoon oregano
1 cup sliced eggplant, ¼ inch thick

In a small bowl combine egg, mayonnaise, salt, and pepper. In separate bowl mix together bread crumbs, cheese, and oregano. Dip each slice of eggplant in egg mixture, then dip into crumb mixture to evenly coat each side. Place in shallow baking dish. Sprinkle with any extra egg and crumb mixture. Bake at 450°F. for 15 minutes or until crispy, turning once. Makes 1 midday meal serving.

Each serving is equivalent to: 1 Egg; ½ serving Fat; 1 serving Bread; 1 ounce Hard Cheese; 1 cup Vegetables

Eggplant Parmigiana

2 cups pared eggplant slices, ¾ inch thick
Salt, pepper, and garlic powder to taste

1½ ounces grated Mozzarella cheese
½ ounce grated Parmesan cheese
¾ cup tomato sauce, no sugar added

Sprinkle eggplant with salt, pepper, and garlic powder. Place on baking sheet and broil 4 inches from source of heat for 8 minutes or until tender, turning once. Combine cheeses. In a 1-quart casserole layer ½ of the eggplant, ½ the sauce, and ½ the cheese. Repeat layers. Cover and bake at 350°F. for about 15 minutes. Remove cover and bake 15 minutes longer. Divide evenly. Makes 2 midday meal servings. Supplement as required.

Each serving is equivalent to: 1 cup Vegetables; 1 ounce Hard Cheese; ¾ serving Bonus (¼ cup plus 2 tablespoons tomato sauce)

Fennel

This vegetable is also called "anise" or "fennocchi." It has a licorice flavor and is similar in appearance to celery but with feathery leaves and a large, bulbous root. Fennel is used raw in salads or cooked as a vegetable.

Green Beans

When shopping for green beans, look for firm pods. Snip off the ends and cut the pods into 1-inch pieces or long diagonal "French-style" slivers, or leave them whole. Simmer beans in enough boiling salted water to cover for about 10 minutes or until beans are tender-crisp; drain. Season with salt and pepper. Serve hot or chilled.

Frozen Beans

Frozen beans are a convenient way to always have beans on hand. Cook beans according to package directions.

Three-Bean Salad with Oil Dressing

¼ cup vegetable oil
¼ cup cider vinegar
¼ cup tomato juice
1 tablespoon chopped fresh
  parsley
1 tablespoon chives
Artificial sweetener to equal 2
  teaspoons sugar

1 teaspoon tarragon
⅛ teaspoon garlic powder
2 cups cooked fresh lima beans
2 cups cooked cut wax beans
2 cups cooked cut green beans
Salt and white pepper to taste

In a large bowl combine oil, vinegar, tomato juice, parsley, chives, sweetener, tarragon, and garlic powder. Add beans, salt, and pepper; toss lightly. Chill at least two hours before serving. Divide evenly. Makes 4 servings. Serve at mealtime only.

Each serving is equivalent to: 3 servings Fat; $1/16$ serving Bonus (1 tablespoon tomato juice); 1 serving Choice Group; 1 cup Vegetables

Grape Leaves

The edible leaves of the grapevine are often used for wrapping fish, fowl, rice, or mixtures. Fresh leaves gathered in June will be full grown but still tender. To prepare them for use, blanch for one minute; drain and dry. Grape leaves are also available packed in brine. Remove the tough stem ends; rinse and dry leaves before filling.

Heart of Palm

This vegetable is variously referred to as "swamp cabbage," "palmetto cabbage," and "cabbage palm." It is the heart of a tropical palm tree and weighs about 3 to 4 pounds. Rarely seen fresh, it is widely available canned. Its most common use is in salads.

Jerusalem Artichoke

The Jerusalem artichoke is a small, knobby, thin-skinned tuber of the sunflower species. It resembles a potato but has a sweeter, nutlike flavor and is more watery. It is used raw in salads, and cooked as a vegetable. It may also be combined with fruit in desserts. Jerusalem artichoke is a limited vegetable and must be weighed.

It is best to cook the Jerusalem artichoke with the skin on, because it is bumpy and very difficult to pare and darkens quickly when the skin is removed.

Jicima

This delicious vegetable is of Mexican heritage. When pared and sliced, it is creamy white, similar in color to potatoes. Its delicate sweetness adds a mellow flavor to crisp green salads and makes it an excellent vegetable to serve with dips. Cooked, it can be used as a hot vegetable with your main course. This is a limited vegetable and must be weighed.

Kale and Potato Stew

Enjoy this as a side dish as they do in northern Europe.

1¼ cups chicken bouillon   **3 ounces pared potato, diced**
1 cup kale   **1 ounce sliced onion**

Combine all ingredients in saucepan; cover and cook until potato is tender. Makes 1 serving. Serve at mealtime only.

Each serving is equivalent to: 1⅔ servings Something Extra (1¼ cups bouillon); 1 cup Vegetables; 1 serving Choice Group; 1 ounce Limited Vegetable

Kohlrabi

Only a few dozen vegetables are popular around the world, which still leaves hundreds of thousands of lesser known types. Kohlrabi, which looks like a turnip at its base and tastes like mild cabbage, is practically unknown here, although it is popular among the Germans as well as the Scandinavians and other northern Europeans. Enjoy its delicate cabbage-like flavor with any salmon or tuna casserole.

Here is an easy method of preparing kohlrabi.
Pare and slice 2 small bulbs of kohlrabi. Put slices in steamer and steam for about 25 minutes; or cover slices with boiling water in saucepan and cook for about 20 minutes. Drain. Serve with a teaspoon of margarine, a dash of nutmeg and minced parsley or chives, salt, and pepper. Divide evenly. Makes 2 servings. Serve at mealtime only.

Each serving is equivalent to: ½ cup Vegetables; ½ serving Fat

Kohlrabi Tops

If the top leaves are fresh, rinse them, cut off the tough spine, and serve raw in salad, or cover leaves with boiling water and cook uncovered until leaves wilt. Chop fine or process them in blender container. Use to make soup or serve along with the bulb.

Lettuce and Greens

Lettuce, which has been cultivated for more than 2,500 years, was once known as the "water plant" because it refreshed travelers. It is deliciously refreshing for us, too. The most popular kinds are crisp-head (iceberg), butterhead (bibb, limestone), cos (romaine), loose leaf, curly endive, chicory, escarole, and Belgian endive. Raw spinach, watercress, and arugula are also frequently used in salads. You might want to try some wild and even lesser known greens, too; they will add variety to your salads.

All greens should be rinsed thoroughly, to restore lost moisture and to remove soil. Dry quickly and tear into bite-size pieces. If greens are prepared in advance, wrap them in paper or cloth toweling and refrigerate until ready to use. Whenever possible, use more than one type of green in a salad.

Arugula
This salad green, which is similar to watercress, is frequently found in Italian markets.

Beet Greens
These are the tops or leaves of the beet plant. They may be eaten raw or cooked and used in the same manner as Swiss Chard (see page 286).

Collard Greens
These greens are from a plant that is a member of the cabbage family. Cook and use in the same manner as spinach.

Comfrey Leaves
This green grows wild and can be used raw in salads, or cooked in soups and stews or served as a vegetable.

Dandelion Greens
This familiar weed belongs to the chicory family. The tender inner leaves have a slightly bitter flavor. These greens are delectable raw in salads or cooked as a green vegetable. Discard the mature outer leaves; they are tough and bitter.

Fiddlefern
The coiled tips of young fern fronds are a springtime delicacy. The

season is very short, usually around the first two weeks in May. The ferns are best if picked in the morning. Although they will keep for a couple of days in the refrigerator, they taste better when used the same day. The flavor hints of asparagus and mushrooms combined. Fiddlefern may be served raw as a salad green, or steamed and eaten as a vegetable.

Rub off the fuzz from the fronds; then steam or boil them in salted water for approximately 20 to 30 minutes or until tender.

Lamb Quarters
This plant, which grows wild throughout much of the United States and Canada, is sometimes called "pig weed," "goose foot," or "wild spinach." It tastes very much like spinach, although it is considerably milder.

Mustard Greens
Mustard greens include several species of the mustard plant, grown for their young leaves. The leaves vary in shape but are similar in flavor. They are used raw in salads, or cooked as a vegetable.

Nasturtium Leaves
This plant, nicknamed "Indian cress," is a member of the watercress family. Its pale green leaves have the flavor of watercress but are more delicate and less peppery. Nasturtium leaves make a delightful salad, either alone or combined with other greens.

The leaves may be blanched and used as a substitute in recipes calling for grape leaves.

Peppergrass
This plant is one of the many members of the mustard family. It grows wild throughout much of the United States and Canada. The young leaves are delicious in salads, or cooked and mixed with other cooked greens.

Poke Greens
These greens—which are also called "poke weeds"—grow wild in much of the United States, Canada, and Mexico. After the dandelion, the poke green is probably our best-known edible wild plant. Use only the first tender leaves found in the spring. They can be served raw or cooked like other greens.

Sorrel
Sorrel is the name applied to several plants. The two which are best known—and most often used in cooking—are called "garden sorrel" and "sour grass." The acid-flavored leaves are used raw in salads, or cooked as greens in soups or as a vegetable puree. In Holland, sorrel is used as a substitute for spinach.

To prepare, wash the greens and remove the stems. If the leaf is large, remove the vein. Cook sorrel in boiling salted water for about 5 minutes. Use 1 cup of water for each quart of well-packed leaves.

Turnip Greens
These are the tops from the young turnip plant. The greens may be served raw in salads, or cooked and eaten as a vegetable.

Black Mushrooms

To prepare, pour boiling water over dried black mushrooms, then let them soak for 15 minutes or more. When the mushrooms are soft, squeeze to remove excess water and cut off tough stems. Mushrooms are now ready for slicing or cutting in wedges to use in recipes.

Baked Stuffed Mushrooms Florentine

2 cups large mushrooms
1 cup cooked, chopped spinach
2 teaspoons dehydrated onion flakes, reconstituted in 1 tablespoon water
2 teaspoons vegetable oil
½ packet (½ teaspoon) instant chicken broth and seasoning mix
½ teaspoon Worcestershire sauce
Salt and pepper to taste

Wash mushrooms. Remove and finely chop stems; reserve caps. In bowl combine chopped stems and remaining ingredients. Stuff mushroom caps with spinach mixture. Place mushrooms, stuffed side up, in an 8x8-inch baking pan; cover. Bake at 375°F. for 10 minutes. Remove cover; bake 10 minutes longer or until mushrooms are tender. Divide evenly. Makes 4 servings.

Each serving is equivalent to: ¾ cup Vegetables; ½ serving Fat; ⅛ serving Something Extra (⅛ packet broth mix)

Cooked Mushrooms

3 cups fresh mushrooms, about 1
    pound
2½ cups water

1 tablespoon lemon juice or red
    wine vinegar
¾ teaspoon salt

Wipe mushrooms with damp cloth and dry thoroughly. If ends are discolored, trim a thin slice from the bottom. If the mushrooms are small, use them whole; otherwise, cut lengthwise in halves or slices. In a saucepan bring water to a boil; add mushrooms, lemon juice or vinegar, and salt. Cover and bring to quick boil; simmer about 10 minutes. Drain and reserve liquid. The mushroom liquid is good stock for soups or sauces. Divide evenly. Makes 4 servings.

Each serving is equivalent to: ¾ cup Vegetables

Variations:

A Blanc—Use the mushrooms in salads, casseroles, or in any dish calling for cooked white mushrooms. Small white mushrooms skewered with toothpicks are a nice hors d'oeuvre.

"Nuts"—Place 3 cups whole cooked mushrooms on a shallow pan. Broil for 25 minutes or until they become crisp. Salt and serve. Divide evenly. Makes 4 servings.

Caraway Mushroom Consommé

2 ounces finely diced onion
¼ cup finely diced turnips
¼ cup finely diced carrots
¼ cup finely diced celery
1 packet instant beef broth and
    seasoning mix

2 cups mushroom liquid (see
    Cooked Mushrooms, above)
1 cup water
2 teaspoons caraway seeds
1 teaspoon marjoram
1 bay leaf
Salt to taste

In a medium saucepan combine onion, turnips, carrots, celery, and broth mix; cook, stirring occasionally, until vegetables are tender; add mushroom liquid, water, caraway seeds, marjoram, bay leaf, and salt. Bring to boil, reduce heat; simmer for 40 minutes. Strain and discard solids. Divide broth evenly into 4 bowls. Makes 4 servings.

Each serving is equivalent to: ¾ serving Something Extra (¼ packet broth mix and ½ teaspoon caraway seeds)

Mushroom Relish

3 tablespoons vegetable oil
2 tablespoons red wine vinegar
2 tablespoons Dijon mustard
1½ teaspoons chopped fresh parsley
1 garlic clove, minced
Artificial sweetener to equal 1 teaspoon sugar
1 teaspoon chives
Salt and pepper to taste
3 cups cooked mushrooms

In medium bowl combine oil, vinegar, mustard, parsley, garlic, sweetener, chives, salt, and pepper. Mix well, add mushrooms, and let marinate overnight. Divide evenly. Makes 4 servings. Serve at mealtime only.

Each serving is equivalent to: 2¼ servings Fat; ¾ cup Vegetables

Mushroom Salad

½ cup cooked mushrooms
½ cup carrot sticks
½ cup cooked green beans
1 medium tomato, diced
1 tablespoon vegetable oil
1 tablespoon red wine vinegar
1 teaspoon tarragon
1 teaspoon Worcestershire sauce
Artificial sweetener to equal ½ teaspoon sugar
½ teaspoon dehydrated parsley flakes
Salt and pepper to taste

Arrange mushrooms, carrots, green beans, and tomato on a serving plate. In a small bowl combine remaining ingredients. Pour over salad. Makes 1 serving. Serve at mealtime only.

Each serving is equivalent to: 2 cups Vegetables; 3 servings Fat

Mushroom Sandwich Spread

1 cup cooked sliced mushrooms	1 teaspoon chopped chives
¾ cup finely diced green pepper	Salt and pepper to taste
¼ cup diced pimento	2 slices enriched white bread,
2 tablespoons imitation	toasted
mayonnaise	

In a medium bowl combine all ingredients except bread; mix thoroughly. Divide evenly and spread on toast slices. Makes 2 servings. Serve at mealtime only.

Each serving is equivalent to: 1 cup Vegetables; 1½ servings Fat; 1 serving Bread

Okra

Look for young, tender, crisp pods. Scrub pods and slice, if desired. Cook in a small amount of boiling salted water 10 to 15 minutes or until tender. Do not overcook. Okra has a gluey sap that helps thicken sauces. Dishes that use okra as a thickening agent are called "gumbos." Okra is also available frozen and canned. This is a Limited Vegetable and must be weighed.

Okra Soup

Traditionally this is served over cooked rice.

3 cups Chicken Stock (see page 140)	1 teaspoon minced fresh parsley
8 ounces fresh or frozen okra	1 bay leaf
1 tablespoon chopped celery	1 clove
1 teaspoon dehydrated onion	Salt and pepper to taste
flakes	1 cup tomato puree

Combine all ingredients except tomato puree in saucepan and cook for 25 minutes. Add tomato puree. Heat and serve. Divide evenly. Makes 4 servings.

Each serving is equivalent to: 1 serving Something Extra (¾ cup stock); 2 ounces Limited Vegetable; ¾ teaspoon Vegetables; ½ serving Bonus (¼ cup tomato puree)

Onions

There are many kinds of onions, of various colors and sizes. They are part of the same family as shallots, leeks, scallions, garlic, and chives. Onions are used to flavor roasts, casseroles, salads, vegetables, soups, and stews.

Onions can be peeled more easily if boiling water is poured over them and they are allowed to stand for a few minutes. Onions are a limited vegetable and must be weighed.

Cooked Onions

Drop peeled onions into boiling salted water. Cook 15 to 35 minutes, depending on the size of the onion. Onions are cooked when they are transparent and can be pierced easily with a fork. Weigh and serve.

Sliced onions may be cooked the same way but require less time.

To brown onions, preheat a nonstick skillet. Add onions and cook, stirring constantly with a wooden spoon to avoid scorching. Weigh and serve.

Garlic

Garlic in all forms is allowed on our Food Plan. Most of our recipes call for fresh garlic, but dehydrated minced garlic, garlic powder, and garlic salt are all acceptable substitutes. To peel and crush the fresh clove, put it on a wooden board. Crush with the side of a cleaver or knife. Remove the skin with a fork or toothpick.

Leeks

Leeks are closely related to scallions and garlic. They are often used as a flavoring in soups or chowders, and their delicate flavor makes them a delicious vegetable, too. Wash in several changes of water to remove sand. Trim off the root end, discard the green stem. Cook in a small amount of boiling salted water until tender, about 15 minutes. Drain and season to taste. Weigh and serve.

Scallions

Scallions, known as "spring" or "raw green" onions in various parts of the country, may be eaten fresh or cooked. Finely chopped, they're great in salads or as additional seasoning ingredient in casseroles. Scallions are a limited vegetable and must be weighed.

Shallots

The shallot is a mild-flavored cousin of the onion, leek, and garlic, and grows in clove form, similar to garlic. Fresh shallots are used raw in salads and as an additional seasoning ingredient cooked in dishes. Shallots are a limited vegetable and must be weighed.

Onion Soup

1 pound onions, thinly sliced
4½ cups Beef Stock (see page 163)
1 teaspoon steak sauce
Dash celery salt and pepper

4 slices enriched white bread,
   toasted and cut into quarters
4 ounces grated hard cheese

Combine all ingredients except toast and cheese in a large saucepan. Cover and bring to a boil; lower heat. Simmer about 20 minutes or until onions are soft. Divide evenly into 4 ovenproof soup bowls. Top each with 4 toast quarters. Sprinkle each with 1 ounce cheese. Bake at 350°F. until cheese melts. Makes 4 midday meal servings. Supplement as required.

Each serving is equivalent to: 4 ounces Limited Vegetable; 1½ servings Something Extra (1 cup plus 2 tablespoons stock); 1 serving Bread; 1 ounce Hard Cheese

Stuffed Onions

1 pound small onions, cut in half
1 cup diced mushrooms
1 packet instant chicken broth and
   seasoning mix
¼ teaspoon thyme

⅛ teaspoon salt
⅛ teaspoon pepper
2 slices enriched white bread,
   made into crumbs
2 tablespoons vegetable oil

Remove center of onions by pushing in end of onion with fingers to make a pocket; dice inside portion and reserve pockets. In a nonstick skillet combine diced onions, mushrooms, broth mix, thyme, salt, and pepper; cook until onions are brown. Transfer to a large bowl. Add bread crumbs and oil; mix thoroughly. Divide mixture evenly and stuff into onion pockets. Place in a baking dish; add about ¼ inch water to dish. Bake at 350°F. for 25 minutes. Divide evenly. Makes 8 servings. Serve at mealtime only.

Each serving is equivalent to: 2 ounces Limited Vegetable; 2 tablespoons Vegetables; ⅛ serving Something Extra (⅛ packet broth mix); ¼ serving Bread; ¾ serving Fat

Parsley

Parsley is nature's complement to pungent onion and garlic, and is also used as a garnish. American markets usually carry two varieties: American and Italian. The curly American kind is frequently used as a garnish, whereas Italian parsley, which has flat, jagged leaves that resemble celery tops, is most often used as a flavoring. To store parsely, break off the bottom part of stem, remove string which ties leaves into a bunch, and give them a quick bath in cold water. Drain leaves, dry in paper or cloth towels, and store in covered container in refrigerator.

Parsnips

An excellent vegetable! It looks like a white carrot and can be cooked like a carrot. Scrape to clean; weigh, slice, and drop into water containing vinegar or lemon juice, to prevent discoloring.

Drain and transfer to saucepan containing small amount of boiling water. Cover and cook until tender. Serve with a pinch of chopped fresh parsley.

Orange-Glazed Parsnips

1 pound pared parsnips, diced
2 tablespoons frozen orange juice
  concentrate
2 tablespoons margarine

½ teaspoon grated orange rind
Dash ginger
1 cup orange sections, no sugar
  added

In saucepan cook parsnips with water to cover until tender. Drain. In top of double boiler over boiling water combine orange juice concentrate, margarine, orange rind, and ginger; cook until margarine is melted. Add parsnips and cook 10 minutes or until parsnips are glazed. Add orange sections and continue cooking 5 minutes. Divide evenly. Makes 4 servings. Serve at mealtime only.

Each serving is equivalent to: 4 ounces Limited Vegetable; ¾ serving Fruit; 1½ servings Fat

Chinese Pea Pods

Chinese pea pods are also known as "snow peas," or "sugar peas." The pea within the pod is extremely small, and both the peas and the pods are edible. They are available fresh and frozen. Fresh snow peas are most plentiful from May through September. To prepare pea pods, break off tips and remove string on both sides. To retain the delicate flavor and color, cook in a minimum amount of liquid just until tender-crisp. This is a limited vegetable and must be weighed.

Chili Peppers

Peppers are eaten all over the world. In the United States, the sweet mild red or green pepper is usually preferred. However, there is another category, hot (or "chili") peppers, which come in a remarkable range of sizes, shapes, and colors. They have a fiery, pungent taste. Some are considerably hotter than others and there are literally hundreds of hybrids. They are available fresh, canned, dried, or powdered.

To prepare fresh chili peppers: Rinse, open the pods, remove the seeds, and scrape the pulp from the skin. Do not touch your face, eyes, or lips unless you wash your hands thoroughly, since the oil from hot peppers will cause discomfort if it comes in contact with the skin or other membranes.

To prepare dried chili peppers: Plump them in boiling water for 20 to 30 minutes. Drain and reserve the water. Cool chilis and remove seeds. Scrape the pulp from the skin and add to reserved liquid.

Sweet, Green, or Bell Peppers

To roast peppers: Wash and dry peppers and place on pan 5 inches from boiler heat. Broil, turning with tongs, until skin is black and charred on all sides, about 15 minutes. Remove, place in paper bag, and let peppers steam 5 to 10 minutes or until cool enough to handle. Peel away charred skin and discard seeds and membranes.

To skin fresh peppers: Place peppers in 350°F. oven, turning occasionally until the skin is scorched and can be removed easily.

To freeze peppers: Cut off stem ends, cut peppers in half, and discard seeds and membranes. Dice; spread on wax paper in baking pan and freeze. Remove from freezer, pack in freezer container, and label. You can easily remove a small amount from container for use in a recipe. Usually, no defrosting is necessary.

To prepare peppers for stuffing: Cut off the stem end and scoop out seeds and membranes. Drop peppers in a large pot of boiling water and parboil until nearly tender, about 10 minutes. Remove and turn upside down to drain. Fill peppers, bake in shallow pan or muffin or custard cups at 350°F. for about 20 minutes or until filling is hot.

Pumpkin Fritters

2 ounces canned pumpkin
1 medium egg
1 slice enriched white bread,
　quartered
2 tablespoons skim milk

1 tablespoon water
Artificial sweetener to equal 2
　teaspoons sugar
¼ teaspoon baking powder
⅛ teaspoon cinnamon

Combine all ingredients in blender container; process until smooth. Drop by spoonfuls onto a preheated nonstick skillet. When bottom is browned, turn to brown other side. Serve hot. Makes 1 morning or midday meal serving. Supplement as required.

Each serving is equivalent to: 2 ounces Limited Vegetable; 1 Egg; 1 serving Bread; ⅛ serving Milk (2 tablespoons skim milk)

Quick-and-Easy Pumpkin Soup

What goes well with roast loin of pork? The answer is as easy as pumpkin soup.

1 pound canned pumpkin
3 cups chicken bouillon
Artificial sweetener to equal 2
   teaspoons sugar

¼ teaspoon cinnamon
⅛ teaspoon nutmeg
⅛ teaspoon ginger

Combine all ingredients in a large saucepan. Bring to a boil; lower heat and simmer 5 minutes. Divide evenly. Makes 4 servings.

Each serving is equivalent to: 4 ounces Limited Vegetable; 1 serving Something Extra (¾ cup bouillon)

Variation: For "Cream" of Pumpkin Soup, follow recipe above. Add 1 cup evaporated skimmed milk; heat but do not boil. Add ½ serving Milk (¼ cup evaporated skimmed milk) to equivalent listing.

Radishes

The red radish most frequently seen in the market is one of several varieties available. There are also white radishes, black radishes, and the large Japanese radish called "daikon."

To cook radishes: Pare and slice, if desired. Cover with boiling water and cook until tender.

To make radish roses: Slice off the top. Make 4 or 5 cuts about ¼ inch deep all around radish to create petals. Place in bowl of ice water and refrigerate for an hour or two, or until "rose" opens. Drain and use as garnish.

To make radish accordions: Trim a thin slice from each end, then make parallel slashes ⅛ inch apart along one side of radish, being careful not to cut through to opposite side. Refrigerate, as for radish roses.

Rutabaga

Deep yellow flesh and strong flavor distinguish this cousin of the turnip. Rutabaga is often sold with a wax coating. This is pared off when you remove the skin. In saucepan, cover pared, diced rutabaga with boiling salted water and cook until tender, about 20 to 30 minutes. Rutabaga is delicious plain and is a special treat when combined with potato. This is a limited vegetable on the Food Plan and must be weighed.

Rutabaga-Potato Mash

4 ounces cooked rutabaga, mashed

3 ounces peeled cooked potato, mashed
1 teaspoon margarine

Combine rutabaga and potato in saucepan; heat. Remove from heat, add margarine, and serve. Makes 1 serving. Serve at mealtime only.

Each serving is equivalent to: 4 ounces Limited Vegetable; 1 serving Choice Group; 1 serving Fat

Salsify

This fleshy root is also known as an oyster plant because to some people its flavor is reminiscent of the oyster. Salsify is shaped like a carrot or parsnip and can be white or black. The black variety is large and reputed to have a better flavor. Salsify is a limited vegetable and must be weighed.

To prepare, remove the tops and scrub the root. Pare and cover with acidulated water (1 quart water with 1 tablespoon lemon juice) to prevent discoloration until ready to use. Boil until tender, drain, season, and serve.

Sauerkraut with Prunes

To garnish a roast.

2 cups canned sauerkraut, rinsed	4 dried medium prunes, pitted
¾ cup chicken bouillon	and diced
2 ounces minced onion	Dash white pepper

Combine sauerkraut, bouillon, and onion in a medium saucepan. Bring to a boil; lower heat and simmer about 20 minutes or until onion is tender. Add prunes; cook about 10 minutes longer or until most of the liquid has evaporated. Season with pepper. Divide evenly. Makes 4 servings.

Each serving is equivalent to: ½ cup Vegetables; ¼ serving Something Extra (3 tablespoons bouillon); ½ ounce Limited Vegetable; ¼ serving Fruit

Creamy Spinach

Wash fresh spinach several times to remove sand. Drain and dry on paper towels. Remove and discard tough stems.

6 cups spinach leaves	Dash nutmeg
¼ cup evaporated skimmed milk	Salt and pepper to taste
1 tablespoon plus 1 teaspoon	
margarine	

Place spinach in boiling salted water to cover. Cook 4 minutes or until tender. Drain well. In top of double boiler over boiling water combine milk, margarine, and spinach. Cook until margarine is melted. Season with nutmeg, salt, and pepper. Divide evenly. Makes 4 servings. Serve at mealtime only.

Each serving is equivalent to: 1½ cups Vegetables; ⅛ serving Milk (1 tablespoon evaporated skimmed milk); 1 serving Fat

Squash

Summer Squash:

Caserta
Chayote or Mirliton
Cocozelle
Scallop, Cymling,
    or Pattypan

Spaghetti
Straight or crookneck
Vegetable marrow
Zucchini

Summer squash should be fresh in appearance with a tender rind. The seeds should be soft and fully edible.

To cook, cut summer squash in slices and steam until tender. Drain and serve with measured amounts of margarine.

Winter Squash:

Acorn or Table Queen
Banana
Buttercup
Butternut

Calabaza
Hubbard
Kushaw
Turban

Winter squash should feel heavy for its size. Avoid squash with cuts and soft spots.

To cook, cut winter squash in half. Remove seeds and place in pan containing small amount of water. Bake at 400°F. until tender, about 45 minutes. The pulp should be removed from the shell and weighed.

It may be mashed and seasoned with salt, pepper, cinnamon, nutmeg, or artificial sweetener. Margarine in measured amounts may also be added.

Baked Acorn Squash

1 12-ounce acorn squash*	Brown sugar substitute to equal 1
2 teaspoons margarine	tablespoon brown sugar
	Cinnamon to taste (optional)

Cut squash in half; remove and discard seeds. Place cut side down in a shallow baking dish containing ½ inch water. Bake at 400°F. for 30 minutes or until squash is tender. Scoop out pulp and weigh 8 ounces. Reserve any remaining pulp for another use. In bowl mash pulp and combine with margarine, sweetener, and cinnamon, if desired. Divide evenly into 2 individual ovenproof casseroles; bake 20 minutes or until hot. Makes 2 servings. Serve at mealtime only.

Each serving is equivalent to: 4 ounces Limited Vegetable; 1 serving Fat

*After removing seeds and skin, a 12-ounce acorn squash weighs about 8 ounces.

Mashed Butternut Squash

Cut one butternut squash in half; remove and discard the seeds and stringy portion. Place in baking pan, cut side down; add ¼ inch water to pan, and cover. Bake at 400°F. for 50 minutes or until soft. Remove squash from shell. Weigh 8 ounces. Place in a bowl, mash with fork or electric beater. Stir in 1 tablespoon margarine and a dash each of cinnamon and salt. Divide evenly. Makes 2 servings. Serve at mealtime only.

Each serving is equivalent to: 4 ounces Limited Vegetable; 1½ servings Fat

Variation:

Mashed Butternut Squash in Orange Shells—Prepare Mashed Butternut Squash as above, omitting margarine; stir in ¼ cup orange juice. Remove fruit from 2 small orange halves;* divide squash

*Fruit may be divided evenly and eaten with Mashed Butternut Squash in Orange Shells or reserved to be eaten at another time. If consumed with Mashed Squash, add ½ serving Fruit to equivalent listing.

mixture evenly into shells. If desired, reheat in oven at 375°F. for 15 minutes. Makes 2 servings (one filled shell each).

Each serving is equivalent to: 4 ounces Limited Vegetable; ¼ serving Fruit

Savory Winter Squash Stew

Examples of winter squash include acorn, banana, buttercup, butternut, and hubbard. Here's a good way to cook it.

1 pound pared and seeded winter squash, cut in large cubes
1 cup water
4 canned medium tomatoes, chopped

2 medium green peppers, seeded and cut in strips
1 small garlic clove, minced
¼ teaspoon savory
Salt to taste
Pepper to taste

In saucepan combine squash and water. Cover; cook 15 minutes or until water is almost evaporated. Add remaining ingredients and simmer 20 minutes. Divide evenly. Makes 4 servings.

Each serving is equivalent to: 4 ounces Limited Vegetable; ¾ cup Vegetables

Zucchini Boats

1½ cups (10-ounce package) frozen chopped spinach
2 medium zucchini (about 2 cups)
2 teaspoons chopped fresh parsley
1 teaspoon Italian seasoning, or ½ teaspoon oregano, ¼ teaspoon marjoram, and ¼ teaspoon basil

½ teaspoon dehydrated onion flakes
½ teaspoon salt
½ garlic clove
⅛ teaspoon pepper
8 ounces cooked ground veal, chicken, or turkey, crumbled

Cook spinach according to package directions: let cool. Squeeze out as much liquid as possible; transfer spinach to blender container.

Place zucchini in a medium saucepan with salted water to cover. Cook for 5 to 7 minutes or until zucchini skin yields to light touch of fork. Remove zucchini from liquid and cut in half lengthwise. Gently scoop out seeds, leaving a firm shell; add seeds to blender container with spinach. Add seasonings and process until mixture is pureed. Transfer to a medium mixing bowl. Stir in crumbled veal, chicken, or turkey. Divide mixture evenly and fill zucchini shells. Bake at 350°F. for 15 to 20 minutes or until thoroughly heated. Makes 2 midday meal servings, 2 zucchini boats each.

Each serving is equivalent to: 1¾ cups Vegetables; 4 ounces Veal or Poultry

Zucchini Salad

2 cups thinly sliced zucchini
2 medium tomatoes, cut in wedges
1 cup thinly sliced mushrooms
4 ounces thinly sliced onion

Basic French Dressing
(see page 302)
2 cups lettuce leaves

In bowl combine all ingredients except lettuce; chill. Arrange lettuce on serving platter. Top with salad. Divide evenly. Makes 4 servings. Serve at mealtime only.

Each serving is equivalent to: 1½ cups Vegetables; 1 ounce Limited Vegetable; Basic French Dressing (see page 302)

Swiss Chard

This often neglected but delicious vegetable is a type of beet that does not develop the fleshy root of the ordinary beet but is grown for the leaves and stalk. Wash carefully and remove the root ends. Cut the stalks in 2-inch pieces; cut up the leaves if they are large. Cook in a small amount of boiling water 5 to 10 minutes for the leaves and 10 to 15 minutes for the stalks. Add a little minced fresh garlic or lemon juice before serving.

Tomatoes

To skin fresh tomatoes, stroke each tomato with the dull edge of a knife until the skin wrinkles and can be removed. If the skin doesn't come off easily, immerse tomato in boiling water for a minute or two, then plunge it into cold water, drain, and peel. If garden tomatoes are out of season and the hothouse varieties leave you cold, try canned ones. Canned whole peeled tomatoes are an excellent substitute in recipes calling for fresh tomatoes.

White Turnips

If you have never tried raw white turnips, here's a new taste treat. Wash them well and serve whole like apples, or grate or slice and add to a salad. Cooked and browned turnips make a nice change from potatoes when serving a roast.

Water Chestnuts

The crunchiness of the water chestnut is welcome in many dishes. Stuff sliced water chestnuts into cooked prunes as an hors d'oeuvre or meat accompaniment, dice them and use with apples in a salad; serve them with cooked green beans or other vegetables, and, of course, use them in Chinese dishes. Place unused water chestnuts in a small jar, cover with water, and refrigerate. They will keep a week or two if you remember to change the water daily. This is a limited vegetable and must be weighed.

Creamy Vegetable Soups

Purees of vegetables are just one step away from creamy soups. In saucepan heat ½ cup of a cooked pureed vegetable (asparagus, broccoli, carrot, cauliflower, celery, zucchini, etc.) with ¾ cup chicken bouillon. Stir in 2 tablespoons evaporated skimmed milk and reheat, but do not boil. Garnish with chopped fresh parsley, dill, or watercress. Makes 1 serving.

Each serving is equivalent to: ½ cup Vegetables; 1 serving Something Extra (¾ cup bouillon); ¼ serving Milk (2 tablespoons evaporated skimmed milk)

Variations:
1. Add 3 ounces peeled cooked potatoes, diced. Serve at mealtime only. Add 1 serving Choice Group to equivalent listing.
2. Dissolve 1 teaspoon cornstarch in 1 tablespoon water and stir into vegetable-bouillon mixture. Simmer, stirring often, for 2 minutes or until soup has thickened. Continue as above. Add 1 serving Something Extra (1 teaspoon cornstarch) to equivalent listing.
3. Omit evaporated skimmed milk and heat as directed. Chill soup and stir in ¼ cup plain unflavored yogurt. In equivalent listing change milk equivalent to ½ serving Milk (¼ cup yogurt).

Gazpacho

2 fresh or canned medium
  tomatoes, chopped
½ medium cucumber, pared and
  chopped
½ medium green pepper, seeded
  and chopped
1 ounce diced onion
½ slice enriched white bread, torn
  into pieces (optional)

3 tablespoons water
1 tablespoon vegetable oil
2 teaspoons red wine vinegar
½ teaspoon chili powder or to taste
1 garlic clove
Dash artificial sweetener
Dash cumin
Salt and pepper to taste

Combine all ingredients in a blender container or food processor; process to desired consistency. Add more water to adjust consistency, if desired. Chill. Divide evenly. Makes 2 servings. Serve at mealtime only.

Each serving is equivalent to: ¾ cup Vegetables; ½ ounce Limited Vegetable; ¼ serving Bread (optional); 1½ servings Fat

Mexi-Cauliflower Romaine and Pepper Salad

To make a complete midday meal, for each serving slice 2 hard-cooked medium eggs and toss together with salad. Also pretty with shredded drained canned beets garnished with chopped fresh parsley.

½ medium head romaine lettuce (4 cups)

2 cups thinly sliced cauliflower florets

1 medium green pepper, seeded and cubed

2 tablespoons vegetable oil

1 tablespoon plus 1 teaspoon chili sauce

1 tablespoon lemon juice or vinegar

1 tablespoon water

½ teaspoon prepared white horseradish

Dash salt and cayenne pepper

Separate lettuce leaves from head; rinse with cool water and dry well. Stack leaves and cut crosswise to make ¼- to ½-inch shreds. Place in large salad bowl; add cauliflower and green pepper. In a small jar with tight-fitting lid, combine remaining ingredients; cover and shake well. Pour over vegetables; toss to combine. Divide evenly. Makes 4 servings. Serve at mealtime only.

Each serving is equivalent to: 1½ cups plus 2 tablespoons Vegetables; 1½ servings Fat; ½ serving Something Extra (1 teaspoon chili sauce)

Minestrone (Vegetable Soup Italian Style)

1 cup sliced zucchini or shredded spinach

1 cup shredded cabbage or coarsely chopped cauliflower

1 cup sliced celery

1 cup sliced carrots

4 ounces diced scallions or onion

4 packets instant chicken broth and seasoning mix

1 garlic clove, minced

3 cups water

1 cup tomato puree

½ teaspoon basil

¼ teaspoon thyme

2 crushed peppercorns

2⅔ cups cooked enriched elbow macaroni

In a large saucepan combine zucchini, cabbage, celery, carrots, scallions, broth mix, and garlic. Cook 3 to 5 minutes over medium

heat, stirring occasionally. Add remaining ingredients except macaroni. Bring to a boil; cover. Lower heat; simmer 20 minutes or until
vegetables are tender. Stir in macaroni; cook until thoroughly heated.
Divide evenly. Makes 4 servings. Serve at mealtime only.

Each serving is equivalent to: 1 cup Vegetables; 1 ounce Limited
Vegetable; 1 serving Something Extra (1 packet broth mix); ½ serving
Bonus (¼ cup tomato puree); 1 serving Choice Group

Variations:
1. Omit macaroni and add 2 cups cooked barley, whole kernel
corn, fresh lima beans, or enriched rice.
2. Omit macaroni and add 12 ounces diced pared potato to saucepan with water and remaining ingredients.
3. Omit macaroni and float 1 slice enriched white bread, diced, on
each serving. Change equivalent listing from 1 serving Choice Group
to 1 serving Bread.

Oriental Vegetable Mix

2 cups shredded cabbage
2 cups bean sprouts
1 cup diagonally sliced celery
4 ounces drained canned water
    chestnuts, sliced
2 ounces finely chopped scallion

1 cup chicken bouillon
2 tablespoons soy sauce
½ teaspoon dry mustard,
    dissolved in 1 tablespoon water
    (optional)

In a large skillet cook first 5 ingredients 3 minutes. Add bouillon and
simmer, stirring often, until most of the liquid has evaporated. Stir in
soy sauce and mustard if desired. Divide evenly. Makes 4 servings.

Each serving is equivalent to: 1¼ cups Vegetables; 1½ ounces
Limited Vegetable; ⅓ serving Something Extra (¼ cup bouillon)

Ratatouille

Ratatouille can be folded into omelets, or topped with Swiss cheese and baked until cheese melts and bubbles, or served with cottage cheese or scrambled eggs for the midday meal. Delicious too with fresh crisp vegetables.

1¼ cups sliced zucchini, cut in ¼-inch slices
1¼ cups pared diced eggplant, cut in ½-inch dice
6 ounces sliced onion
1 medium green pepper, seeded and cut in ½-inch dice
1 packet instant chicken broth and seasoning mix

1 garlic clove, minced
4 canned medium tomatoes, coarsely chopped
1 cup tomato puree
1 teaspoon basil
1 teaspoon oregano
Salt and freshly ground pepper to taste

Combine first 6 ingredients in saucepan, cook 5 minutes. Add remaining ingredients and cook over medium heat, stirring often for about 1¼ hours or until vegetables are tender. Divide evenly. Makes 4 servings.

Each serving is equivalent to: 1¼ cups Vegetables; 1½ ounces Limited Vegetable; ¼ serving Something Extra (¼ packet broth mix); ½ serving Bonus (¼ cup tomato puree)

Vegetables à la Grecque

1 quart water
½ cup lemon juice
1 teaspoon salt
½ teaspoon thyme
½ teaspoon rosemary
½ teaspoon savory
10 peppercorns

2 garlic cloves, crushed
1 bay leaf
3 cups vegetables (cauliflower, carrots, celery, green beans, broccoli, etc.)
Basic French Dressing (see page 302)

In saucepan combine first 9 ingredients and simmer 15 minutes. Add vegetables, return water to boil; reduce heat and simmer until vegetables are tender-crisp. Allow vegetables to cool in liquid; drain.* Toss vegetables with Basic French Dressing. Chill. Divide evenly. Makes 4 servings. Serve at mealtime only.

Each serving is equivalent to: ¾ cup Vegetables; Basic French Dressing (see page 302)

*Reserve liquid if desired; liquid may be used again for cooking additional vegetables.

Vegetable Purees

Bean and Pumpkin Puree

In blender container or food processor combine 4 ounces cooked dried kidney or white beans and 4 ounces cooked pumpkin. Process until pureed, pushing mixture down with spatula if necessary. Transfer to a small saucepan; cook over low heat, stirring constantly, until thoroughly heated. Makes 1 evening meal serving. Supplement as required.

Each serving is equivalent to: 4 ounces Legumes; 4 ounces Limited Vegetable

Pureed Broccoli and Cauliflower

In saucepan combine 2 cups each of chopped broccoli and cauliflower; cook in boiling salted water until tender. Drain; place in blender container or food processor; process until pureed, pushing mixture down with spatula if necessary. Season with salt, pepper, nutmeg, and lemon juice. Serve hot. Divide evenly. Makes 4 servings.

Each serving is equivalent to: 1 cup Vegetables

Pureed Carrots

In blender container or food processor combine 1 cup cooked carrots, 1 tablespoon evaporated skimmed milk, and 1 teaspoon margarine.

Process until pureed, pushing mixture down with spatula if necessary. Transfer to a small baking dish; bake at 350°F. for 15 minutes or until thoroughly heated. Makes 1 serving. Serve at mealtime only.

Each serving is equivalent to: 1 cup Vegetables; ⅛ serving Milk (1 tablespoon evaporated skimmed milk); 1 serving Fat

Pureed Potatoes and Turnips

If you or the kids don't like green vegetables, turnips, or parsnips, and prefer potatoes, puree them together! You'll get the flavor of potatoes plus the food value of the vegetable, and the potato taste survives almost any combination. In a medium saucepan combine ½ cup pared, diced white turnip and 3 ounces pared, diced potato. Cover them with boiling salted water and cook until very soft, about 25 minutes. Drain. Mash, beat, or puree vegetables in food mill, blender container, or food processor. Add 1 tablespoon evaporated skimmed milk and 1 teaspoon margarine, if desired. Season to taste with salt and white pepper. Makes 1 serving. Serve at mealtime only.

Each serving is equivalent to: ½ cup Vegetables; 1 serving Choice Group; ⅛ serving Milk (1 tablespoon evaporated skimmed milk); 1 serving Fat (optional)

Watercress Vegetable Puree

In blender container or food processor combine ½ cup cooked green beans, ½ cup cooked sliced zucchini, ¼ cup cooked sliced celery, ¼ cup cooked chopped watercress, and 2 ounces cooked sliced onion. Process until pureed, pushing mixture down with spatula if necessary. Season to taste with salt and curry powder. Transfer to small saucepan; cook over low heat, stirring constantly, until thoroughly heated. Divide evenly. Makes 2 servings.

Each serving is equivalent to: ¾ cup Vegetables; 1 ounce Limited Vegetable

SAUCES AND SALAD DRESSINGS

Sauces and salad dressings, some with fats and others without, are combined in this chapter for easy reference. Hot or cold, sweet, sour (or both at once), thick or thin, in all colors (white, red, yellow, brown), bland or nippy, bumpy or smooth—there's really something for everyone here. You must try our foolproof "Hollandaise" Sauce. Enjoy, within your Menu Plan limits, of course.

Rules for Using Fats

1. Select 3 servings daily, at mealtime only.
   A serving is:
   margarine, liquid vegetable oil, *1 level teaspoon*
   margarine, imitation (or diet) liquid vegetable oil, *2 level teaspoons*
   mayonnaise, *1 level teaspoon*
   mayonnaise, imitation, *2 level teaspoons*
   vegetable oil (corn, cottonseed, safflower, sesame, soybean, sunflower), *1 level teaspoon*
2. You may mix-and-match fats; i.e., you may have 1 teaspoon margarine and 2 teaspoons mayonnaise daily, or 4 teaspoons imitation (or diet) margarine and 1 teaspoon vegetable oil daily.
3. Margarine—liquid vegetable oil margarine is a product in which the first ingredient listed is liquid vegetable oil, not hydrogenated and not partially hydrogenated; e.g., liquid corn oil margarine.

4. Any product labeled "mayonnaise" and any oil labeled "vegetable oil" may be used.
5. *Cooking Procedures:*
   May be mixed with other ingredients and baked in a casserole.
   May be melted over direct heat in a flameproof container, or in a double boiler.
   After a food item has been broiled, pierce or cut slightly, if possible. Spread fat over food, and broil for no longer than one minute.
   May never be used for sauteéing or frying.

Basic Brown Sauce

A cornerstone of continental cooking, this sauce may be varied in many ways.

2 tablespoons plus 2 teaspoons margarine
2 tablespoons plus 2 teaspoons flour
¼ cup tomato puree
2 cups water
2 packets instant beef broth and seasoning mix

2 teaspoons dehydrated onion flakes, reconstituted in 2 teaspoons water
1½ teaspoons browning sauce
4 peppercorns
2 cloves
1 small bay leaf
Dash thyme
Dash garlic powder

Melt margarine in top of double boiler, over boiling water; using a wooden spoon or wire whisk, add flour, and cook 7 minutes, stirring frequently. Stir in tomato puree. Slowly add water, stirring constantly. Add remaining ingredients; cover and cook 30 minutes or until thickened, stirring often. Divide evenly. Makes 4 servings. Serve at mealtime only.

Each serving is equivalent to: 2 servings Fat; 2½ servings Something Extra (2 teaspoons flour and ½ packet broth mix); ⅛ serving Bonus (1 tablespoon tomato puree)

Variations:

Cherry Sauce—Prepare Basic Brown Sauce as above. Add 1 cup canned pitted cherries, no sugar added. Divide evenly. Makes 4 servings. Serve at mealtime only. Add ½ serving Fruit to equivalent listing.

Mustard Sauce—Prepare Basic Brown Sauce as above. Dissolve 2½ teaspoons dry mustard in ½ cup evaporated skimmed milk and add to Brown Sauce. Serve hot. Divide evenly. Makes 4 servings. Serve at mealtime only. Add ¼ serving Milk to equivalent listing.

Basic White or Béchamel Sauce

A basic sauce you can perk up in many ways.

2 tablespoons margarine	**Dash white pepper**
2 tablespoons flour	**1 cup skim milk**
⅛ teaspoon salt	

Melt margarine in top of double boiler over hot water. Add flour, salt, and pepper, and cook over moderate heat about 2 minutes, stirring constantly. Gradually add milk. Cook, stirring constantly until mixture thickens. Keep warm in double boiler. Makes about 1 cup. Divide evenly into 4 servings. Serve at mealtime only.

Each serving is equivalent to: 1½ servings Fat; 1½ servings Something Extra (1½ teaspoons flour); ¼ serving Milk (¼ cup skim milk)

Variations:

Caper White Sauce—For boiled or poached fish. Stir in 1½ tablespoons capers and ½ teaspoon wine extract.

Curry Sauce—Add 1 teaspoon curry powder, or to taste, with the flour.

Diavolo Sauce—To melted margarine in basic recipe, add 1 teaspoon dehydrated onion flakes reconstituted, before stirring in flour and seasonings. Use only ¾ cup skim milk; add ¼ cup tomato puree and ¼ to ½ teaspoon hot sauce. Reduce milk equivalent to ³/₁₆ serving

Milk (3 tablespoons skim milk) and add ⅛ serving Bonus (1 table-spoon tomato puree) to equivalent listing.

Dill Sauce—Add ¾ teaspoon dill weed and dash of nutmeg with salt and pepper in the basic recipe. Substitute Fish Stock (see page 207) for half of the skim milk. Delicious with poached fish. Reduce milk equivalent to ⅛ serving Milk (2 tablespoons skim milk) in equivalent listing.

Enriched White Sauce—Use only ½ cup skim milk; add ¼ cup evaporated skimmed milk and 2 tablespoons Double Strength Chicken Stock (see page 140) and cook as directed in basic recipe. In equivalent listing add ¹/₁₂ serving Something Extra (1½ teaspoons Double-Strength Stock) and change (¼ cup skim milk) to (2 tablespoons skim milk and 1 tablespoon evaporated skimmed milk).

Florentine Sauce—After adding milk, stir in ½ cup finely chopped spinach. Cook as directed in basic recipe. Add 2 tablespoons Vegetables to equivalent listing.

Herb Sauce—Add 1 teaspoon chopped fresh parsley, ½ teaspoon minced fresh chives, and ¼ teaspoon tarragon with the flour.

Horseradish White Sauce—To basic recipe add 1½ tablespoons prepared white horseradish and ½ teaspoon prepared mustard. Serve with chicken, beef, or lamb.

Hot Tartar Sauce—Add 1 ounce diced onion and ¼ medium green pepper, seeded and diced, to margarine before adding flour. After sauce has thickened, stir in ¼ cup imitation mayonnaise, 1½ tea-spoons lemon juice, 2 tablespoons chopped dill pickle, and 2 tea-spoons chopped fresh parsley. Use for seafood, broccoli, or aspara-gus. Add ¼ ounce Limited Vegetable, 1 tablespoon Vegetables, and 1½ servings Fat to equivalent listing.

Mushroom White Sauce—Add 1 ounce diced onion and ¼ cup sliced mushrooms to margarine before adding flour. When sauce thickens, add a dash Worcestershire sauce. Add ¼ ounce Limited Vegetable and 1 tablespoon Vegetables to equivalent listing.

"Ravigote" Sauce—Add 1 ounce diced onion to margarine before adding flour. When sauce thickens, add 1 teaspoon each tarragon, chervil, and chives. Add ¼ ounce Limited Vegetable to equivalent listing.

Thin Basic White Sauce—Increase skim milk to 2 cups in basic recipe. Add ¼ serving Milk (¼ cup skim milk) to equivalent listing.

Fines Herbes Spread

Use as a sandwich spread or serve melted on hot cooked vegetables, fish, or broiled meat. This may be varied in many ways by using different combinations of herbs.

2 tablespoons unsalted margarine
¼ teaspoon chives
¼ teaspoon chopped fresh parsley
¼ teaspoon tarragon

¼ teaspoon marjoram
⅛ teaspoon grated lemon rind
Dash salt and pepper

In a small bowl combine all ingredients. Chill. Divide evenly. Makes 4 servings. Serve at mealtime only.

Each serving is equivalent to: 1½ servings Fat

Mustard Sauce for Vegetables

3 tablespoons imitation (or diet)
  margarine
1 teaspoon prepared mustard
1 teaspoon flour
¼ cup water
Salt and white pepper to taste

Combine margarine and mustard in top of double boiler and heat over boiling water to melt margarine. Stir in flour; cook about 1 minute. Add water; cook, stirring constantly until mixture thickens. Season to taste. Divide evenly. Makes 3 servings. Serve at mealtime only.

Each serving is equivalent to: 1½ servings Fat; ⅓ serving Something Extra (⅓ teaspoon flour)

Prune Sauce

Cornstarch may be substituted for flour in many recipes that use flour as a thickening agent. Generally you will need less cornstarch than flour to thicken a sauce. It is an especially good thickener for clear fruit sauces and sauces to be served with Oriental foods. It is a good idea to dissolve cornstarch in a cold liquid before adding to other ingredients.

1¼ cups water
12 dried large prunes, pitted and
    diced
1 tablespoon cornstarch, dissolved
    in 3 tablespoons water

Artificial sweetener to equal ½
    teaspoon sugar
⅛ teaspoon ginger
Dash salt
1 tablespoon wine vinegar
2 teaspoons margarine

In a small saucepan combine water and prunes. Bring to a boil; lower heat and simmer 10 minutes. Drain and measure liquid. Add more water if necessary to equal 1¼ cups liquid. Return to saucepan with prunes. In a small bowl or custard cup combine cornstarch, sweetener, ginger, and salt. Gradually stir into prune mixture. Cook over medium heat, stirring constantly until sauce comes to a boil. Remove from heat. Blend in vinegar and margarine. Serve over warm meat. If sauce thickens while standing, stir in water, a teaspoon at a time, until desired consistency. Divide evenly. Makes 4 servings. Serve at mealtime only.

Each serving is equivalent to: 1 serving Fruit; ¾ serving Something Extra (¾ teaspoon cornstarch); ½ serving Fat

"Hollandaise"

Great over hot asparagus.

1 tablespoon cornstarch
½ cup water
1 packet instant chicken broth and
    seasoning mix

¼ cup imitation (or diet)
    margarine
2 tablespoons mayonnaise
1 teaspoon lemon juice
Dash hot sauce

In a small saucepan, dissolve cornstarch in water. Add broth mix. Stir over medium heat until thickened. Remove from heat. Stir in margarine until melted. Add mayonnaise; stir until blended. Add lemon juice and hot sauce; stir to combine. Divide evenly. Makes 6 servings. Serve at mealtime only.

Each serving is equivalent to: ⅔ serving Something Extra (½ teaspoon cornstarch and ⅙ packet broth mix); 2 servings Fat

Lemony Mayonnaise

Delicious with vegetables or on a salad.

2 tablespoons imitation mayonnaise	¼ teaspoon grated lemon rind Dash salt

Combine all ingredients in a small bowl. Divide evenly. Makes 2 servings. Serve at mealtime only.

Each serving is equivalent to: 1½ servings Fat

Rémoulade Sauce

Serve with crabmeat or sliced tomatoes.

2 tablespoons imitation mayonnaise ¼ teaspoon finely chopped dill pickle	¼ teaspoon chopped capers ¼ teaspoon prepared mustard Dash chopped fresh parsley Dash tarragon

Combine all ingredients in a small bowl. Divide evenly. Makes 2 servings. Serve at mealtime only.

Each serving is equivalent to: 1½ serving Fat; ⅛ teaspoon Vegetables

Russian Mayonnaise

2 tablespoons imitation mayonnaise 1 tablespoon plain unflavored yogurt 1 tablespoon chili sauce	2 teaspoons tarragon vinegar 2 teaspoons lemon juice ¼ teaspoon prepared white horseradish Dash salt and pepper

Combine all ingredients in a small bowl. Divide evenly. Makes 2 servings. Serve at mealtime only.

Each serving is equivalent to: 1½ serving Fat; ¹/₁₆ serving Milk (1½ teaspoons yogurt); ¾ serving Something Extra (1½ teaspoons chili sauce)

Seafood Dressing—I

Delicious on cold lobster tails or shrimp.

¼ cup imitation mayonnaise
¼ cup chili sauce
¼ teaspoon minced capers

Dash each basil, tarragon, and savory

Combine all ingredients in a small bowl. Chill before serving. Divide evenly. Makes 4 servings, about 2 tablespoons each. Serve at mealtime only.

Each serving is equivalent to: 1½ servings Fat; 1½ servings Something Extra (1 tablespoon chili sauce)

Seafood Dressing—II

¼ cup imitation mayonnaise
¼ cup evaporated skimmed milk
  or plain unflavored yogurt

2 teaspoons lemon juice or vinegar
2 teaspoons catsup (optional)

Combine all ingredients in a small bowl. Chill before serving. Divide evenly. Makes 4 servings, about 2 tablespoons each. Serve at mealtime only.

Each serving is equivalent to: 1½ servings Fat; ⅛ serving Milk (1 tablespoon evaporated skimmed milk or yogurt); ¼ serving Something Extra (½ teaspoon catsup) (optional)

Tartar Sauce

Serve with broiled, poached, or baked fish.

**2 tablespoons imitation
mayonnaise
1 tablespoon chopped dill pickle
½ teaspoon chopped fresh parsley
½ teaspoon prepared mustard**

**Dash each of salt, Worcestershire
sauce, lemon juice, and hot
sauce**

Combine all ingredients in a small bowl. Divide evenly. Makes 2
servings. Serve at mealtime only.

Each serving is equivalent to: 1½ servings Fat; 1½ teaspoons
Vegetables

Basic French or Vinaigrette Dressing

This dressing can be varied in dozens of ways with a change of
seasoning, vinegar, and herbs, and the addition of finely diced vegetables.

**¼ cup vegetable oil
¼ cup wine or tarragon vinegar**

**¼ teaspoon salt
Dash white pepper**

Combine all ingredients in a jar with tight-fitting cover. Shake vigor-
ously before using. Divide evenly. Makes 4 servings. Serve at mealtime only.

Each serving is equivalent to: 3 servings Fat

Variations:

Garlic French Dressing—Prepare Basic French or Vinaigrette
Dressing. Add 1 crushed garlic clove to the dressing; refrigerate.
Remove garlic before serving.

Garlic Italian Dressing—Add 1 teaspoon Italian seasoning or ¼
teaspoon each of oregano, basil, thyme, and rosemary to Garlic

French Dressing. Two teaspoons prepared mustard may also be added.

Lemony Vinaigrette Dressing—Prepare Basic French or Vinaigrette Dressing. Add 2 tablespoons lemon juice and ¼ teaspoon grated lemon rind.

Lemony Vinaigrette Dressing with Sesame Seeds—Prepare Lemony Vinaigrette Dressing. Stir in 1 tablespoon toasted sesame seeds just before serving. Poppy seeds or caraway may be used instead of sesame seeds. These do not require toasting. Add ¾ serving Something Extra (¾ teaspoon seeds) to equivalent listing.

Lorenzo Dressing—Prepare Basic French or Vinaigrette Dressing. Blend 1 tablespoon plus 1 teaspoon chili sauce or catsup into the dressing. Add ½ serving Something Extra (1 teaspoon chili sauce) to equivalent listing.

Sweet Vinaigrette—Prepare Basic French or Vinaigrette Dressing. Add juice from 2 servings of canned fruit, no sugar added. Pour over the canned fruit. Add ½ serving Fruit to equivalent listing.

Sweet and Sour Sauce

¼ cup cider vinegar
¼ cup catsup
¼ cup water
2 to 3 tablespoons Worcestershire
    sauce
1 tablespoon lemon juice
½ teaspoon salt

Artificial sweetener to equal 4
    teaspoons sugar
1 tablespoon cornstarch, dissolved
    in 1 tablespoon water
1 tablespoon vegetable oil
    (optional)

In a small saucepan combine vinegar, catsup, water, Worcestershire, lemon juice, salt, and sweetener. Bring to a boil; stir in cornstarch. Cook, stirring constantly, until sauce thickens and clears. Remove from heat and stir in oil, if desired. Serve with roasted pork. Divide evenly. Makes 6 servings. Serve at mealtime only.

Each serving is equivalent to: 1½ servings Something Extra (2 teaspoons catsup and ½ teaspoon cornstarch); ½ serving Fat (optional)

Barbecue Fruit Sauce

Try this sauce when baking skinned and boned chicken breasts.

4 ounces onion, finely chopped
3 tablespoons cider vinegar
1 tablespoon prepared mustard
2 teaspoons Worcestershire sauce

8 canned peach halves with ½ cup
  juice, no sugar added
½ cup catsup

In a medium saucepan, cook onion over medium heat 1 to 2 minutes, stirring frequently. Add vinegar, mustard, and Worcestershire; cook, stirring constantly, about 3 minutes. Add peach juice and catsup. Lower heat and simmer, stirring occasionally, for 15 to 20 minutes or until mixture thickens. Place peaches in a small ovenproof casserole and heat. Serve sauce and peaches at the same meal. Divide evenly. Makes 4 servings.

Each serving is equivalent to: 1 ounce Limited Vegetable; 1 serving Fruit; 3 servings Something Extra (2 tablespoons catsup)

Creole Sauce

Use over cooked vegetables, pasta, meat, or fish. Also good as omelet filling.

4 ounces onion, thinly sliced
½ cup chopped celery
1 medium green pepper, seeded
  and thinly sliced
4 canned medium tomatoes,
  chopped, with liquid
1 cup sliced mushrooms

¾ cup Beef Stock (see page 163)
1 tablespoon minced pimento
Salt and pepper to taste
Bouquet garni (1 bay leaf, 10
  parsley sprigs, 2 cloves, 1 garlic
  clove, sliced, tied in
  cheesecloth)

In medium saucepan cook onion, celery, and green pepper over moderate heat 5 minutes or until tender. Add tomatoes, mushrooms, stock, pimento, salt, and pepper. Add bouquet garni to sauce. Simmer covered, about 25 minutes, stirring occasionally. Add water, about ¼ cup at a time, as necessary, to adjust consistency. Remove and discard bouquet garni. Serve hot. Divide evenly. Makes 4 servings.

Each serving is equivalent to: 1 ounce Limited Vegetable; 1 cup Vegetables; ¼ serving Something Extra (3 tablespoons stock)

Variation: Omit bouquet garni and add dash hot sauce, chili powder, or crushed red pepper.

Cocktail Sauce

**2 tablespoons plus 2 teaspoons
  chili sauce**
**2 tablespoons plus 2 teaspoons
  catsup**

**1 tablespoon plus 1 teaspoon
  tomato puree**
1 teaspoon lemon juice
**½ teaspoon prepared horseradish
Dash salt**

In a small bowl combine all ingredients. Divide evenly. Makes 4 servings.

Each serving is equivalent to: 2 servings Something Extra (2 teaspoons chili sauce and 2 teaspoons catsup); $1/24$ serving Bonus (1 teaspoon tomato puree)

Fat-Free Salad Dressings

1. In small saucepan combine 1 cup red wine vinegar and ½ cup chopped fresh basil, dill, tarragon, or thyme. Bring to a boil. Cool and pour into a jar with tight-fitting cover. Let stand at room temperature 10 to 14 days. Strain and use as desired.
2. Omit herbs from preceding recipe and add 4 crushed garlic cloves. Allow to stand at room temperature 3 to 5 days.
3. Serve freshly squeezed lemon juice over your salad.

Fat-Free White Sauce

2 cups skim milk
¼ cup flour, dissolved in ¼ cup
   water

Dash lemon juice
Salt and white pepper to taste

In medium saucepan combine milk and flour. Heat, stirring constantly until sauce is thickened. Season with remaining ingredients.
Divide evenly. Makes 4 servings.

Each serving is equivalent to: ½ serving Milk (½ cup skim milk); 3
servings Something Extra (1 tablespoon flour)

Japanese Soy-Sauce Dip

Serve hot as a dip for seafood and vegetables.

In saucepan combine ½ cup Beef Stock (see page 163), 2 tablespoons soy sauce, 1 teaspoon prepared white horseradish, and 1 teaspoon sherry extract, if desired. Bring to a boil. Divide evenly. Makes
2 servings.

Each serving is equivalent to: ⅓ serving Something Extra (¼ cup
stock)

Mustard Sauce

2 tablespoons plus 2 teaspoons
   flour
2 tablespoons dry mustard
½ cup water, divided
1 packet instant chicken broth and
   seasoning mix
1½ ounces finely chopped shallots
   or scallions

1 tablespoon lemon juice
1 tablespoon white vinegar
¼ teaspoon thyme
1 small bay leaf
1½ cups skim milk
Salt and white pepper to taste

In a small bowl combine flour, mustard, and ¼ cup water to make a
paste. Set aside. In a medium saucepan combine remaining water and

broth mix; add shallots or scallions, lemon juice, vinegar, thyme, and bay leaf. Simmer until most of liquid has evaporated. Remove and discard bay leaf. Add milk; heat gently. Using a wire whisk, beat mustard-flour mixture into milk mixture. Cook, stirring constantly, until thickened. Continue cooking about 5 minutes; do not boil. Season with salt and pepper. Divide evenly. Makes 6 servings.

Each serving is equivalent to: 1½ servings Something Extra (1⅓ teaspoons flour and ¹/₆ packet broth mix); ¼ ounce Limited Vegetable; ¼ serving Milk (¼ cup skim milk)

Tomato Sauce

½ medium green pepper, seeded and finely chopped
2 ounces chopped onion
1 garlic clove, minced
2¾ cups canned medium tomatoes, crushed
1 cup tomato puree
¾ cup beef bouillon
½ cup tomato paste
1½ teaspoons basil
¾ teaspoon salt
½ teaspoon chopped fresh parsley
½ teaspoon oregano
⅛ teaspoon pepper

In medium saucepan combine green pepper, onion, and garlic. Cook 2 to 3 minutes. Add remaining ingredients; simmer about 35 minutes or until sauce reaches desired consistency, stirring often. Divide evenly. Makes 4 servings.

Each serving is equivalent to: ¾ cup Vegetables; ½ ounce Limited Vegetable; 1 serving Bonus (¼ cup tomato puree and 2 tablespoons tomato paste); ¼ serving Something Extra (3 tablespoons bouillon)

Variations:
1. Prepare Tomato Sauce. Stir in ½ cup evaporated skimmed milk. Heat, but do not boil. Add ¼ serving Milk (2 tablespoons evaporated skimmed milk) to equivalent listing.
2. Prepare Tomato Sauce. Remove from heat. Stir in 1 tablespoon plus 1 teaspoon vegetable oil. Serve at mealtime only. Add 1 serving Fat to equivalent listing.
3. Prepare Tomato Sauce. Stir in 4 ounces grated Parmesan

cheese. Divide evenly. Makes 4 midday meal servings. Supplement as required. Add 1 ounce Hard Cheese to equivalent listing.

4. Prepare Tomato Sauce. Stir in 8 ounces cooked ground beef, crumbled, and ½ cup water. Divide evenly. Serve each portion topped with 1 ounce grated hard cheese. Makes 4 midday meal servings. Add 2 ounces "Beef" Group and 1 ounce Hard Cheese to equivalent listing.

5. Add ¼ cup diced carrots and ¼ cup diced celery when cooking vegetables in Tomato Sauce recipe. Omit basil and oregano and add 1 teaspoon thyme. Add 2 tablespoons Vegetables to equivalent listing.

Creamy Yogurt Thousand Island Dressing

½ cup plain unflavored yogurt
1 tablespoon plus 1 teaspoon chili sauce
1 tablespoon chopped dill pickle
2 teaspoons dehydrated onion flakes
½ teaspoon lemon juice
½ teaspoon prepared mustard
¼ teaspoon salt

Combine all ingredients in a small bowl. Cover and chill. Divide evenly. Makes 4 servings.

Each serving is equivalent to: ¼ serving Milk (2 tablespoons yogurt); ½ serving Something Extra (1 teaspoon chili sauce); ¾ teaspoon Vegetables

Tangy Yogurt Dressing

In a bowl combine ½ cup plain unflavored yogurt, 2 teaspoons lemon juice, ¼ teaspoon grated lemon rind, and ¼ teaspoon celery seed. Chill. Divide evenly. Makes 4 servings.

Each serving is equivalent to: ¼ serving Milk (2 tablespoons yogurt)

Tart Yogurt Dressing

½ cup plain unflavored yogurt   1 teaspoon salt
¼ cup cider vinegar   Dash freshly ground pepper
1 tablespoon vegetable oil

Place ingredients in jar with tight-fitting cover; shake to combine. Divide evenly. Serve over shredded cabbage, sliced tomatoes, salad greens, or cooked vegetables. Makes 3 servings. Serve at mealtime only.

Each serving is equivalent to: ⅓ serving Milk (2 tablespoons plus 2 teaspoons yogurt); 1 serving Fat

Yogurt Asparagus Dressing

Combine 1 cup cooked asparagus, ½ cup plain unflavored yogurt, 1 garlic clove, ½ teaspoon lemon juice, and ¼ teaspoon lemon rind in blender container or food processor. Process until smooth. Divide evenly. Delicious as a dressing or spread. Makes 4 servings.

Each serving is equivalent to: ¼ cup Vegetables; ¼ serving Milk (2 tablespoons yogurt)

Yogurt Bleu Cheese Dressing

In bowl combine ½ cup plain unflavored yogurt, 1 ounce crumbled Bleu cheese, ½ teaspoon cider vinegar, and a dash of salt. Blend; chill. Serve over green salad. Makes 1 midday meal serving. Supplement as required.

Each serving is equivalent to: 1 serving Milk (½ cup yogurt); 1 ounce Hard Cheese

Yogurt Cinnamon Fruit Dressing

Drain the juice from 1 serving canned fruit, no sugar added, into a bowl. Stir in ½ cup plain unflavored yogurt. Add artificial sweetener to equal 2 teaspoons sugar, if desired, and cinnamon to taste. Use as dressing for the fruit. Makes 1 serving.

Each serving is equivalent to: 1 serving Fruit; 1 serving Milk (½ cup yogurt)

Yogurt Cucumber Sauce

½ cup plain unflavored yogurt
¼ medium cucumber, pared, seeded, and diced
1 teaspoon lemon juice or cider vinegar
¼ teaspoon dill weed

¼ teaspoon paprika
⅛ teaspoon salt or to taste
2 tablespoons imitation mayonnaise (optional)
½ teaspoon aromatic bitters (optional)

In a bowl combine yogurt and cucumber. Stir in lemon juice or cider vinegar, dill weed, paprika, and salt. Blend in imitation mayonnaise and aromatic bitters if desired. Excellent with salmon or cold poached fish. Divide evenly. Makes 4 servings. If mayonnaise is used, serve at mealtime only.

Each serving is equivalent to: ¼ serving Milk (2 tablespoons yogurt); 1½ teaspoons Vegetables; ¾ serving Fat (optional)

Yogurt Dill Sauce for Salmon or Fish Mousse

½ cup plain unflavored yogurt
1 tablespoon plus 1 teaspoon imitation mayonnaise
1½ teaspoons minced fresh dill or ½ teaspoon dill weed

½ teaspoon prepared white horseradish
Dash each salt, white pepper, and hot sauce

Combine all ingredients in a bowl. Divide evenly. Makes 4 servings. Serve at mealtime only.

Each serving is equivalent to: ¼ serving Milk (2 tablespoons yogurt); ½ serving Fat

Yogurt Herbal Dressing

In a bowl combine ½ cup plain unflavored yogurt with 1 tablespoon chives, 1 tablespoon minced fresh parsley, ½ minced garlic clove, if desired, and ⅛ teaspoon grated lemon rind. Chives can be replaced with any other fresh herb. One teaspoon minced capers can be added. Divide evenly. Serve over cooked vegetables. Makes 4 servings.

Each serving is equivalent to: ¼ serving Milk (2 tablespoons yogurt)

Yogurt Horseradish Sauce

In a bowl combine ½ cup plain unflavored yogurt, 1 tablespoon prepared white horseradish, ¼ teaspoon prepared mustard, ⅛ teaspoon salt, and a dash of hot sauce. Divide evenly. Serve with sliced turkey or tongue. Makes 4 servings.

Each serving is equivalent to: ¼ serving Milk (2 tablespoons yogurt)

Yogurt Mustard Sauce

In a bowl blend 1 tablespoon prepared mustard and 2 teaspoons cider vinegar with ½ cup plain unflavored yogurt. Divide evenly. Serve with cold beef. Makes 4 servings.

Each serving is equivalent to: ¼ serving Milk (2 tablespoons yogurt)

Yogurt Onion-Mix Dressing

In a bowl stir 1 packet instant onion broth and seasoning mix into ½ cup plain unflavored yogurt. Divide evenly. Makes a piquant dip for raw vegetables. Makes 4 servings.

Each serving is equivalent to: ¼ serving Something Extra (¼ packet broth mix); ¼ serving Milk (2 tablespoons yogurt)

Yogurt Tomato Dressing

In a bowl combine ½ cup plain unflavored yogurt, ½ cup tomato puree, 1 teaspoon basil, and ¼ teaspoon celery seed. Refrigerate 1 hour before using. Divide evenly. Makes 4 servings.

Each serving is equivalent to: ¼ serving Milk (2 tablespoons yogurt); ¼ serving Bonus (2 tablespoons tomato puree)

OPTIONAL

To provide new taste lifts, we've added a number of specialty foods, seasonings, condiments, and "something extra." Sip our spritzers, herb teas, and soups. For cocktail parties, shake-up time will be "shape-up" time if you stick to such allowed treats as our Red-Blooded Mary Mix and our Iceberg Floats. But study the next few pages and you'll soon be exercising your own options.

Beverages

Water. Artificially sweetened carbonated beverages, club soda, coffee, and tea, in reasonable amounts.

Bonus

Select up to 1 serving daily, if desired.
   clam juice, 1 cup (8 fluid ounces)
   mixed clam and tomato juice, 1 cup (8 fluid ounces)
   mixed vegetable juice, 1 cup (8 fluid ounces)
   tomato juice, 1 cup (8 fluid ounces)
   tomato paste, ¼ cup
   tomato puree, ½ cup
   tomato sauce (no sugar added), ½ cup

Seasonings and Condiments

Use reasonable amounts of the following: artificial sweeteners, baking powder, baking soda, browning sauce, dehydrated vegetable flakes, extracts, flavorings, herbs, horseradish, hot sauce, lemon juice, lime juice, mustard, pepper, pepper sauce, rennin tablets, salt, seasonings, seaweed, soy sauce, spices, steak sauce, vinegar, and Worcestershire sauce.

1. Seasonings and condiments are "legal," except for those which list sugar and/or sorbitol, dextrose, corn syrup, starch, or dextrin as the first or second ingredient.
2. Any type of vinegar is "legal," except those with sugar added.
3. Fresh fruit rinds are "legal," as seasonings.
   Dehydrated fruit rinds are "legal" as seasonings, if neither sugar nor starch is listed as the first or second ingredient.

Something Extra

Select up to 3 servings daily, if desired.

arrowroot, cornstarch, flour, *1 level teaspoon*
bouillon and broth:
  bouillon cube, *1*
  instant bouillon, *1 level teaspoon*
  instant broth and seasoning mix, *1 packet*
catsup, chili sauce, *2 level teaspoons*
cocoa, unsweetened, *1 level teaspoon*
concentrated yeast extract, *1 level teaspoon*
gelatin, unflavored, *½ envelope (about 1½ level teaspoons)*
seeds:
  caraway, poppy, sesame, *1 level teaspoon*

Specialty Foods

In general you need not be concerned about counting calories. However, if the following items are used, calories MUST be counted. Limit intake to a total of 15 calories per day.

A Specialty Food is "legal" if it is labeled low calorie or dietetic, and/or contains artificial sweetener. These foods must have nutrition labeling indicating calories per serving. This group is allowed daily, in the total amount of 15 calories.

Check labels carefully for calorie count. Do not use if label does not indicate calories.

beverages, noncarbonated or dry mix, low calorie

catsup, salad dressings or sauces, low calorie

gelatin, flavored, low calorie

jams, jellies, or preserves, low calorie

syrups or toppings, low calorie

In addition, one serving of the following items may be substituted once daily, for one milk serving.

flavored milk beverages, low calorie, 1 packet or serving

flavored milk puddings, low calorie, ½ cup

Pep Up Your Meals with Spices and Herbs

Allspice—Delicate West Indian spice. Flavor resembles a blend of nutmeg, cinnamon, and cloves. Whole, it's a favorite seasoning for pickles, stews, and boiled fish.

Basil—Means "king," and this herb adds the crowning touch to all tomato dishes. Gives zest to eggs, fish, soups, stews, and salads.

Bay Leaf—This dried laurel leaf provides the classic seasoning for stews, soups, pickles, sauces, and fish. Remove the leaf before serving.

Bitters—A liquid blend of herbs and spices, often used in drinks. Add a few drops to tomato or clam juice. For unusual flavor, try a few drops in scrambled eggs.

Bouquet Garni or Bouquet of Herbs—A combination of herbs either tied together or wrapped in cheesecloth and tied into bags. Usually added during the last half hour of cooking and removed before serving.

Capers—Pickled buds of the caper bush. They taste like sharp gherkins. Use in sauces and salads.

Cardamom—Native to India. The seeds are delicious in coffee; the pods are used in pickling. Powdered or ground, it is nice sprinkled on melon and other fruits.

Cayenne—Small hot red pepper, ground and used sparingly to season eggs, meats, and fish.

Celery Seed—Pungent seed, used in stews, cole slaw, potato salad, and salad dressings.

Chervil—Delicate herb of the carrot family. Combines well with other herbs. Delicious fresh or dry, in salads, soups, egg and cheese dishes.

Chili Powder—The ancient Aztecs are credited for this blend of chili, allspice, red peppers, cumin seed, oregano, garlic powder, and salt. Use sparingly in cocktail sauces, eggs, stews, and meat loaf.

Chive—Has a mild onionlike flavor. Adds color and flavor to cottage cheese, eggs, potatoes, vegetable dishes, and soups.

Cinnamon—Bark of the cinnamon tree. Ground and mixed with artificial sweetener, it's a favorite on French toast, pancakes, and puddings.

Cloves—Nail-shaped dried flower bud. Once available only to the rich, today it can be enjoyed by everyone. Whole, it is used in baking ham, in pickling, and in drinks. Many desserts call for it in ground form.

Coriander—Use this pungent herb sparingly. Gives character to pickles and stuffing to be served with poultry. It is one of the many spices found in curry powder.

Cumin—Aromatic seeds used whole or ground, in egg and cheese dishes, sauerkraut, meats, rice, pickles, and Mexican foods.

Curry Powder—A blend of spices from India. Used in curries of meat, fish, eggs, and chicken, and to perk up leftover stews.

Dill—The tender fresh or dried leaves, as well as the seeds, add a delightful flavor to eggs, cheeses, salads, and potatoes. A favorite in Scandinavian cookery.

Fennel—Has a slight licorice taste. Gives special flavor to apples and steamed fish.

Garlic—This indispensable seasoning is available fresh, dehydrated, minced, flaked, and in salt and powder form.

Ginger—The fresh root is a staple of Oriental cookery. Dried and ground, it is used in soups, stews, and desserts.

Italian Seasoning—You can buy this blend of herbs or can make your own by combining basil, oregano, rosemary, red pepper, garlic, marjoram, thyme, and sage. Used over fish, meats, poultry, liver, enriched rice, and pasta.

Mace—The lacy covering of the inner shell holding the nutmeg. Delicious in spinach.

Marjoram—One of the best-known herbs. Gives nice flavor to peas, green beans, and limas.

Mint—Everyone knows this aromatic herb. Delicious with lamb and in cool drinks and hot tea.

Mustard—The whole seed is used in pickling; ground, with a little water added, it's the hot mustard used in Oriental cookery. Prepared mustard is the favorite with frankfurters and is delicious in sauces and salad dressings.

Nutmeg—Traditionally used in desserts. Also adds a special flavor to spinach and Brussels sprouts.

Oregano—Wild marjoram, stronger in flavor than its cultivated cousin. Widely used in Mexican and Italian dishes.

Paprika—A member of the pepper family. Available in mild and fiery flavor. Used for color and flavor.

Parsley—Used in foods for flavor and for garnish. Can be fresh, frozen, or dried. Fresh is available with either a curly or a flat leaf. Save the stems to use when preparing soup stock.

Pepper—Available black or white. Used whole in pickling and soups; ground, in most meat, poultry, fish, egg, and vegetable dishes.

Poultry Seasoning—A mixture of several spices used to season poultry and meats.

Pumpkin Pie Spice—A mixture of cinnamon, ginger, cloves, and nutmeg, used to season pumpkin and fruit desserts.

Rosemary—"Rosemary is for remembrance," and its sweet fresh flavor makes lamb stews, boiled potatoes, turnips, and cauliflower memorable.

Saffron—The world's most expensive spice, so make a little go a long way. Place a pinch in boiling water, before adding rice, to develop golden color and appetizing flavor.

Sage—Used in poultry seasoning, it is the perfect compliment to fowl, pork, and fish dishes.

Savory—Lightly aromatic; good with green beans, meats, chicken, and scrambled eggs.

Tarragon—Add this anise-flavored herb to vinegar, salad dressings, and sauces for meat, poultry, and seafood.

Thyme—Has a pungent flavor. Use sparingly, in clam chowder, onions, eggplant, tomatoes, and celery.

Turmeric—This slightly bitter-tasting herb adds a saffronlike natural coloring to rice, chicken, and seafood.

Vanilla Beans—The source of vanilla extract, used to enhance flavor of custards, puddings, and beverages.

Bouquet Garni

Bouquet Garni #1
Tie together between 2 celery ribs:

4 parsley or chervil sprigs
⅓ bay leaf
2 thyme sprigs

1 leek, white portion only, stuck with 2 cloves

Bouquet Garni #2
Wrap the following herbs in a 4-inch square of cheesecloth and tie into a bag:

½ teaspoon dehydrated parsley
   flakes
¼ teaspoon each thyme and
   marjoram
Small piece of bay leaf
½ teaspoon dried celery leaves

Add Bouquet Garni during last half hour of cooking. Remove before serving.

Directions for Making a Basic Gelatin Mixture

In a saucepan sprinkle 1 envelope unflavored gelatin over ½ cup cold liquid. Place over low heat and stir until gelatin is dissolved. Remove from heat and add remaining liquid called for. Pour mixture into mold. Chill until firm, about 3 to 4 hours. To unmold, dip mold in warm water to depth of gelatin. Loosen around edge with the tip of a paring knife. Place serving dish on top of mold and turn upside down. Shake, holding dish tightly to the mold. If gelatin does not unmold, repeat process.
   1 envelope gelatin is equivalent to: 2 servings Something Extra

Herbal Teas and Soup

For each serving:
   Herb—In teapot place 1 or 2 tablespoons chopped fresh herbs. Add 1 cup boiling water. Cover and steep for about 5 minutes or more. Strain and serve. Use as a tea or mix with 1 packet instant broth and seasoning mix and serve as soup. If broth mix is used each serving is equivalent to 1 serving Something Extra.
   Mexican—In saucepan combine a stick of cinnamon and 1 cup

water and bring to boil. Boil several minutes; remove from heat and add 1 teaspoon tea leaves or 1 tea bag. Steep about 5 minutes. Strain and serve.

Mint—In teapot place ⅛ teaspoon dried mint or 1 tablespoon fresh mint leaves and 1 teaspoon tea leaves or 1 tea bag. Add 1 cup boiling water and steep about 5 minutes. Strain and serve.

Tomato Products

1. Tomato puree is available canned. It is made from the peeled and seeded pulp of the tomato.
2. Tomato sauce is available canned without added sugar. It is a combination of tomatoes, salt, pepper, and seasonings.
3. Tomato paste is available canned. It is a rich concentration of tomatoes cooked down until most of the moisture has been removed.
4. Tomato juice is available canned or bottled. It is the juice extracted from ripe tomatoes.

Tips for Leftovers: Leftover puree, sauce, and paste are often wasted in the kitchen, yet all can be frozen. Try freezing them in ice cube trays. Store the cubes in freezer containers. You can then "lift out" as many cubes as you require, defrost them, and measure the amount needed for the recipe.

Creamy Cold Tomato Soup

2 cups tomato puree
1¾ cups evaporated skimmed
  milk
3 to 4 ice cubes

¼ teaspoon oregano or thyme
¼ cup plain unflavored yogurt
1 ounce chopped onion or scallion
  (optional)

In blender container, combine tomato puree, milk, ice cubes, and oregano or thyme. Process until ice is crushed. Divide evenly into 4 soup bowls. Spoon 1 tablespoon yogurt on each serving. Sprinkle each with ¼ ounce of the onion or scallion, if desired. Serve immediately. Makes 4 servings.

Each serving is equivalent to: 1 serving Bonus (½ cup tomato puree); 1 serving Milk (¼ cup plus 3 tablespoons evaporated skimmed milk and 1 tablespoon yogurt); ¼ ounce Limited Vegetable (optional)

Hot Tomato-Beef Drink

1 cup tomato juice
¾ cup beef bouillon

⅛ teaspoon hot sauce
Lemon slices to garnish

In a medium saucepan combine tomato juice, bouillon, and hot sauce. Bring to a boil. Serve, evenly divided, in mugs. Garnish with lemon slices. Makes 2 servings.

Each serving is equivalent to: ½ serving Bonus (½ cup tomato juice); ½ serving Something Extra (¼ cup plus 2 tablespoons bouillon)

Hot Tomato Bouillon

4½ cups tomato juice
3 cups beef bouillon
1 tablespoon Worcestershire sauce

Dash hot sauce
6 mint sprigs

Combine all ingredients, except mint, in large saucepan. Bring to a boil. Lower heat and simmer 5 minutes. Serve, evenly divided, in bowls or soup mugs. Garnish with mint. Makes 6 servings.

Each serving is equivalent to: ¾ serving Bonus (¾ cup tomato juice); ⅔ serving Something Extra (½ cup bouillon)

Parsley Icebergs

Hot sauce to taste
16 parsley sprigs

2 quarts tomato or mixed
vegetable juice

Fill a 16-compartment ice cube tray with water. Add hot sauce and a parsley sprig to each compartment. Freeze until solid. Divide juice equally into 8 tall glasses. Place 2 "icebergs" in each glass. Makes 8 servings.

Each serving is equivalent to: 1 serving Bonus (1 cup tomato or mixed vegetable juice)

Red-Blooded Mary Mix

Only you and the bartender will know that the vodka is missing.

¾ cup tomato juice
1 teaspoon Worcestershire sauce
¼ teaspoon lime juice
Hot sauce to taste

Salt and freshly ground pepper to
taste
1 lime wedge

Combine all ingredients except lime wedge in cocktail shaker. Shake; serve in glass over ice. Garnish with lime wedge. Makes 1 serving.

Each serving is equivalent to: ¾ serving Bonus (¾ cup tomato juice)

Spritzers

Here's our version of a spritzer. Try it at your next party. Pour ½ cup club soda over 3 ice cubes in a 6-ounce glass. Add 1 teaspoon sherry extract and a slice of lemon or lime.

"OLD FAVORITES"

No matter how many new things—and people—come into our lives, we retain a special fondness for favorites from the past. So we have nostalgically selected seventy-one of the most popular recipes from the 1973 edition of this cookbook, ranging from appetizers to desserts. These "friends" wear well, for they fit right into our present Food Program. Meet your "old favorites" gathered in one delicious chapter. (Even if they're *new* to you, you'll enjoy them!)

Cinnamon Toast

1 slice enriched white bread,
  lightly toasted
1 teaspoon margarine

Artificial sweetener to equal 2
  teaspoons sugar
¼ teaspoon cinnamon
Dash nutmeg (optional)

Spread margarine on toast. In small cup combine sweetener, cinnamon, and nutmeg, if desired; sprinkle on toast. Broil for about ½ minute. Makes 1 serving. Serve at mealtime only.

Each serving is equivalent to: 1 serving Bread; 1 serving Fat

Not-So-Danish Pastry

⅓ cup cottage cheese
Artificial sweetener to equal 1
  teaspoon sugar
½ teaspoon extract, any flavor

Dash cinnamon
1 slice enriched white bread,
  toasted

In small bowl combine cottage cheese with sweetener, extract, and cinnamon. Spread on toast and place under broiler until hot and bubbly. Makes 1 morning meal serving.

Each serving is equivalent to: ⅓ cup Soft Cheese; 1 serving Bread

Variations:

1. Omit extract; add ¼ teaspoon imitation butter flavoring and ¼ teaspoon dehydrated orange peel to cottage cheese mixture. Proceed as above.

2. Omit sweetener, extract, and cinnamon; combine cheese with ½ teaspoon caraway seeds and salt to taste; spread on toast. Proceed as above. Add ½ serving Something Extra (½ teaspoon caraway seeds) to equivalent listing.

Cheese Latkes (Pancakes)

You don't have to be Jewish to enjoy latkes. They're a great treat with or without the blueberry topping. Other fruits may be substituted, if desired, so try your favorite!

1 medium egg, beaten
⅓ cup cottage cheese
⅓ cup skim milk
¼ teaspoon salt

1 slice enriched white bread, made into crumbs
Blueberry Topping (see following recipe)

In bowl combine all ingredients except Blueberry Topping. Using a tablespoon, drop mixture by the spoonful onto a preheated nonstick skillet. Brown lightly; turn with a spatula to brown other side. Serve warm with Blueberry Topping. Makes 1 midday meal serving.

Each serving is equivalent to: 1 Egg; ⅓ cup Soft Cheese; ⅓ serving Milk (⅓ cup skim milk); 1 serving Bread; Blueberry Topping (recipe follows)

Blueberry Topping

½ cup blueberries
1 tablespoon water

Artificial sweetener to equal 2 teaspoons sugar

Combine ingredients in saucepan and simmer until berries are soft. Serve with Cheese Latkes. Makes 1 serving.

Each serving is equivalent to: 1 serving Fruit

Coconut Bread Pudding

1 cup skim milk
1 medium egg
Artificial sweetener to equal 6
  teaspoons sugar
1 teaspoon coconut extract
  (optional)

½ teaspoon vanilla extract
1 slice enriched white bread, cut
  into cubes
Cinnamon to taste

Combine all ingredients except bread and cinnamon in blender container; process until frothy. Pour mixture into a small baking dish. Press bread cubes into mixture. Sprinkle with cinnamon. Set baking dish into a pan containing approximately ½ inch of hot water. Bake at 350°F. for about 50 minutes or until a knife inserted comes out clean. Makes 1 morning or midday meal serving. Supplement as required.

Each serving is equivalent to: 1 serving Milk (1 cup skim milk); 1 Egg; 1 serving Bread

Note: For a fluffier pudding, separate egg. Beat white separately until stiff peaks form. Fold into blended mixture and bake as above.

Variation: *Orange Bread Pudding*—Instead of 1 cup skim milk use ½ cup orange juice and ½ cup skim milk. Omit coconut extract and cinnamon. Add 1½ teaspoons dehydrated orange peel and ¼ teaspoon orange extract. Follow above directions.

Each serving is equivalent to: ½ serving Milk (½ cup skim milk); 1 serving Fruit; 1 Egg; 1 serving Bread

Matzo "Fry" (a Matzo Omelet)

Here's another recipe to enjoy during the Passover holiday.

1 matzo board
2 medium eggs, well beaten
2 tablespoons water

¼ teaspoon salt
Dash pepper
Cinnamon to taste (optional)

Break matzo into 2-inch pieces and place in colander. Pour boiling water over matzo and drain quickly to prevent sogginess. In bowl combine eggs, water, salt, pepper, and matzo. Heat a 7-inch nonstick skillet. Add matzo-egg mixture and cook over low heat until golden brown on one side, then turn carefully and brown the other side. Sprinkle with cinnamon, if desired. Divide evenly. Makes 2 morning or midday meal servings. Supplement as required.

Each serving is equivalent to: 1 serving Bread; 1 Egg

Pizzaiolas

A delicious midday meal! Hide the seasoning under the cheese, where the heat won't scorch it and make it bitter.

1 slice enriched white bread
¼ cup tomato puree

Dash each of oregano, garlic
**   powder, and basil or Italian**
**   seasoning**
2 ounces hard cheese, grated

Toast bread lightly; spread with puree and sprinkle on seasonings. Top with cheese. Broil until cheese is melted. Makes 1 midday meal serving.

Each serving is equivalent to: 1 serving Bread; ½ serving Bonus (¼ cup tomato puree); 2 ounces Hard Cheese

Variation: Omit tomato puree. Place 1 sliced medium tomato on bread before adding remaining ingredients. Omit Bonus from equivalent listing and add ½ cup Vegetables.

Reuben Sandwich

1 slice rye bread
2 ounces cooked turkey, sliced
¼ cup drained sauerkraut
1 ounce Swiss cheese, sliced

½ medium dill pickle, sliced
Watercress to garnish
Radish roses to garnish

Lightly toast bread. Arrange turkey on toast. Spread sauerkraut over turkey and top with cheese. Place on baking sheet; bake at 450°F. or place under preheated broiler and heat until cheese is melted. Garnish with pickle slices, watercress, and radish roses. Makes 1 midday meal serving.

Each serving is equivalent to: 1 serving Bread; 2 ounces Poultry; ½ cup Vegetables; 1 ounce Hard Cheese

Luncheon Featuring a Mug of Soup, Croutons and a Lot of "Kisses"

Here's a hearty luncheon to serve on a blustery day when puttering in the kitchen is exactly what you feel like doing. A tossed salad is all you need to complete the meal.

Soup

¾ cup tomato juice
¼ cup clam juice
Dash garlic powder (optional)

Dash chopped fresh parsley
¼ medium dill pickle, sliced
   (optional)

In saucepan combine all ingredients except pickle. Bring to a boil, reduce heat, and simmer 2 minutes. Serve in a mug and garnish with pickle slices if desired. Makes 1 serving.

Each serving is equivalent to: 1 serving Bonus (¾ cup tomato juice and ¼ cup clam juice); 2 tablespoons Vegetables (optional)

Croutons

1 medium egg yolk
1 ounce grated Parmesan cheese
Dash salt
Dash pepper

Dash dry mustard
2 thin slices enriched white bread
   (see page 79)

In bowl beat yolk; stir in cheese, salt, pepper, and mustard to make a paste. Cut bread slices into quarters. Divide egg yolk mixture evenly into 8 portions. Mound onto bread. Place on a baking sheet and bake at 250°F. for 20 minutes or until cheese melts. Croutons must be consumed at the same meal as Meringue Kisses (recipe follows), which contain the remaining egg white.

For serving equivalents, see following recipe.

Meringue Kisses

1 medium egg white
Artificial sweetener to equal 4
   teaspoons sugar

¼ teaspoon flavored extract
⅛ teaspoon cream of tartar
Dash salt

Line a baking sheet with parchment paper, aluminum foil, or brown paper. In bowl beat egg white until foamy; add remaining ingredients and continue beating until stiff. Using a teaspoon, drop mixture onto paper leaving about 2 inches between meringues. Bake at 250°F. for 40 minutes or until lightly golden. Turn off oven and let stand 10 minutes. Using a spatula, remove meringues from paper. Serve in hot soup. Makes 1 midday meal serving. Meringue Kisses must be consumed at the same meal as Croutons (see preceding recipe), which contain the remaining egg yolk.

Each serving is equivalent to: 1 Egg; 1 ounce Hard Cheese; 1 serving Bread

Hot and Cold Soups

Beef Broth

In a small saucepan heat ¾ cup beef bouillon and a dash each of garlic powder, chopped fresh parsley, and Worcestershire sauce. Makes 1 serving.

Each serving is equivalent to: 1 serving Something Extra (¾ cup bouillon)

Bouillon Spritzer

Freeze ¾ cup beef bouillon. Crush frozen bouillon and combine with 1 cup club soda. Serve in chilled glass garnished with a lemon wedge. Makes 1 serving.

Each serving is equivalent to: 1 serving Something Extra (¾ cup bouillon)

Chicken Soup

In a small saucepan heat ¾ cup chicken bouillon with 2 tablespoons cooked diced carrots, 2 tablespoons cooked diced celery, 1 teaspoon dehydrated onion flakes, ½ teaspoon chopped fresh parsley, and salt and pepper to taste. Makes 1 serving.

Each serving is equivalent to: 1 serving Something Extra (¾ cup bouillon); ¼ cup Vegetables

"Old-Fashioned" Vegetable Soup

In small saucepan heat ¾ cup liquid from cooked or canned vegetables,* 2 tablespoons each cooked diced celery and carrots, 2 tablespoons chopped fresh herbs, and 1 packet instant chicken broth and seasoning mix. Makes 1 serving.

Each serving is equivalent to: ¼ cup Vegetables; 1 serving Something Extra (1 packet broth mix)

Note: Do not use liquid from Limited Vegetables for this recipe. See page 249 for list of Limited Vegetables.

"Wonton" Soup

Add ¼ cup shredded spinach or lettuce to Chicken Soup or "Old-Fashioned" Vegetable Soup (see preceding recipes) and allow to wilt. Makes 1 serving.

Each serving is equivalent to: ¼ cup Vegetables; Chicken Soup or "Old-Fashioned" Vegetable Soup (see recipes)

Tomato Soup

In saucepan combine 2 cups tomato juice, ¼ cup diced celery, 1 packet instant beef broth and seasoning mix, 1 tablespoon dehydrated onion flakes, 1 teaspoon lemon juice, artificial sweetener to equal 1 teaspoon sugar, dash cayenne pepper, and salt to taste. Bring to boil, reduce heat, and simmer 10 to 12 minutes or until celery is tender. Transfer to blender container and process. Wet rims of 2 mugs and dip in salt; evenly divide soup into mugs. Garnish each with chopped fresh parsley. Makes 2 servings.

Each serving is equivalent to: 1 serving Bonus (1 cup tomato juice); 2 tablespoons Vegetables; ½ serving Something Extra (½ packet broth mix)

Madrilene (Jellied Tomato Soup)

In saucepan sprinkle 1 envelope of unflavored gelatin over ¼ cup water and allow to soften. Heat, stirring to dissolve gelatin. Add to 1 recipe Tomato Soup (see preceding recipe). Refrigerate until chilled. Garnish with chopped fresh parsley or chives. Divide evenly. Makes 2 servings.

Each serving is equivalent to: 1½ servings Something Extra (½ envelope gelatin and ½ packet broth mix); Tomato Soup (see recipe)

Chicken Liver Pâté

1 pound chicken livers, halved
8 ounces sliced onion
1 packet instant chicken broth and
    seasoning mix

¾ teaspoon poultry seasoning
Salt to taste
Pepper to taste
Lettuce leaves

Place liver and onion in a small saucepan. Cover and cook over low heat about 20 minutes or until onions are tender and liver is cooked. Do not overcook; centers should remain pink. Transfer to blender container or food processor. Add remaining ingredients except lettuce leaves. Process until smooth. Chill and serve on lettuce leaves. Divide evenly. Makes 2 evening meal servings.

Each serving is equivalent to: 6 ounces Liver; 4 ounces Limited Vegetable; ½ serving Something Extra (½ packet broth mix)

Cioppino

2 cups tomato juice
3 tablespoons red wine vinegar
2 tablespoons dehydrated onion flakes
2 tablespoons dehydrated bell pepper flakes
1 tablespoon chopped fresh parsley
1 tablespoon drained capers

2 teaspoons basil
2 teaspoons lemon juice
Artificial sweetener to equal 2 teaspoons sugar
1 teaspoon rosemary
¼ teaspoon garlic powder
1 pound assorted boned fish and shellfish, cut in 1-inch pieces

In saucepan combine all ingredients except fish. Bring to a boil, reduce heat, and simmer until reduced by half. Add fish, cover, and simmer until fish is done. Divide evenly. Makes 2 evening meal servings.

Each serving is equivalent to: 1 serving Bonus (1 cup tomato juice); 6 ounces Fish

Gefilte Fish

12 ounces boned whitefish, chopped
12 ounces boned pike, chopped
4 ounces onion, chopped
¼ cup chopped celery
2 teaspoons salt
¼ teaspoon garlic powder

¼ teaspoon pepper
¼ cup skim milk
1 envelope unflavored gelatin
2 cups water
1 packet instant chicken broth and seasoning mix
1 cup cooked sliced carrots

Put fish, onion, and celery through a meat grinder twice, or process in food processor until ground. In bowl combine fish mixture with salt, garlic powder, and pepper. Gradually add milk and combine. Shape into 4 equal oval patties. Poach in simmering salted water for 15 minutes. Remove patties with a slotted spoon and place on serving dish. Allow to cool; cover and refrigerate. In another saucepan sprinkle gelatin over water and allow to soften. Add broth mix and heat, stirring to dissolve. Chill until slightly firm. Dice and arrange gelatin and carrots around poached fish. Divide evenly. Makes 4 midday meal servings.

Each serving is equivalent to: 4 ounces Fish; 1 ounce Limited Vegetable; ¼ cup plus 1 tablespoon Vegetables; $^1/_{16}$ serving Milk (1 tablespoon skim milk); ¾ serving Something Extra (¼ envelope gelatin and ¼ packet broth mix)

Chips for Your Fish and . . .

3 ounces pared potato, cut into matchstick pieces

Onion salt to taste
2 teaspoons margarine (optional)

Place potato in an individual flameproof casserole and sprinkle with onion salt. Bake at 400°F. for 15 minutes or until crisp, turning to brown all sides. Remove from oven and toss with margarine, if desired. Place under broiler for 1 minute. Makes 1 serving. Serve at mealtime only.

Each serving is equivalent to: 1 serving Choice Group; 2 servings Fat (optional)

Old-Fashioned Stewed Tomatoes

2 medium tomatoes, peeled and diced
1 slice whole wheat bread, diced
2 teaspoons dehydrated onion flakes, reconstituted in 2 teaspoons water

½ teaspoon salt
Freshly ground pepper to taste
Dash basil

Place tomatoes in small saucepan. Bring to boil; add bread, onion flakes, salt, pepper, and basil. Stir to combine. Makes 1 serving. Serve at mealtime only.

Each serving is equivalent to: 1 cup Vegetables; 1 serving Bread

Stuffed Tomatoes

Cut a thin slice from top of a medium tomato. Use this top slice as a lid for stuffed tomatoes, or dice the removed slice of tomato and use as part of the stuffing. With a spoon, scoop out, dice, and reserve the pulp of the tomato, leaving a firm shell; invert to drain. Prepare desired stuffing, combine with diced tomato pulp, and pack firmly into the tomato shell. This can all be done several hours ahead.

How to Cook Stuffed Tomatoes

Oven-Baked Tomatoes—Arrange stuffed tomatoes in a shallow baking pan; add a little water and bake at 375°F. for 15 to 20 minutes. Don't overbake. Tomato shell should be firm and the stuffing hot and bubbly.

Top-of-Stove Stuffed Tomato—Arrange 2 to 4 stuffed tomatoes in a saucepan; add 3 tablespoons water. Cover and cook at medium heat for 8 to 10 minutes. If water evaporates, add a tablespoon or two as necessary.

Fillings for Stuffed Tomatoes

Rice Filling—For 2 medium tomatoes, in bowl combine ½ cup cooked enriched rice with scooped-out diced tomato pulp. Season with salt, pepper, and basil. If desired, ½ teaspoon margarine, melted, or vegetable oil may be added to each stuffed tomato just before serving. Makes 1 serving. Serve at mealtime only.

Each serving is equivalent to: 1 cup Vegetables; 1 serving Choice Group; 1 serving Fat (optional)

Spinach Filling—For 2 medium tomatoes, in a bowl combine ½ cup well-drained cooked chopped spinach seasoned with salt, lemon juice, and poultry seasoning with scooped-out diced tomato pulp; ½ cup cooked, chopped mushrooms, bean sprouts, or green peppers, seasoned to taste, may be substituted for the spinach, alone or in combination. Makes 1 serving.

Each serving is equivalent to: 1½ cup Vegetables

Meat Filling—For 2 medium tomatoes, in a bowl combine 4 ounces diced cooked chicken, lamb, or liver with scooped-out diced tomato pulp. Season to taste. Makes 1 midday meal serving.

Each serving is equivalent to: 1 cup Vegetables; 4 ounces Poultry, "Beef" Group, or Liver

Fish Filling—Remove top slice and pulp from 10 cherry tomatoes, leaving a thin shell. Transfer pulp to bowl and combine with 4 ounces drained canned tuna, 1 tablespoon mayonnaise, and salt to taste. Spoon as much as possible into tomato shells; replace top slice. Arrange on a bed of watercress. Surround with remaining filling mixture. Sprinkle with finely chopped fresh dill. Makes 1 midday meal serving.

Each serving is equivalent to: ½ cup Vegetables; 4 ounces Fish; 3 servings Fat

Pimentos

Pimentos or roasted peppers, packed in vinegar or water, may be purchased in cans or jars. Once opened, they spoil quickly. Place canned peppers in an airtight container. If desired, drain packing liquid and replace with water; add ½ teaspoon vinegar and ⅛ teaspoon oregano for each 1 cup water. Cover tightly and refrigerate. They will last for a week. Use as desired.

Sweet-Sour Red Cabbage with Apple

To help retain its bright color, add vinegar or lemon juice when cooking red cabbage.

6 cups shredded red cabbage
1½ cups water
⅓ cup cider vinegar
Brown sugar substitute to equal ¼ cup brown sugar

1 teaspoon lemon juice
1 teaspoon caraway seeds
3 medium apples, pared, cored, and sliced

In a saucepan combine all ingredients except apples. Cover and cook over medium heat for 20 minutes. Add apples, cook 30 minutes longer. Divide evenly. Makes 6 servings.

Each serving is equivalent to: 1 cup Vegetables; ⅙ serving Something Extra (⅙ teaspoon caraway seeds); ½ serving Fruit

Cinnamon Spice Spread

Serve this with Raisin French Toast (see page 47) or try it on Baked Fresh Fruit (see page 337).

2 tablespoons margarine
Artificial sweetener to equal 4
  teaspoons sugar or to taste

2 teaspoons cinnamon
Dash each ground cloves, nutmeg,
  and ginger

Combine all ingredients in a small bowl or cup. Divide evenly. Makes 2 servings. Serve at mealtime only.
    Each serving is equivalent to: 3 servings Fat

Sweet Maple Spread

Great over pancakes (see egg section, page 48).

1 tablespoon margarine, melted
Brown sugar substitute to equal 1
  teaspoon brown sugar

Dash maple extract

Combine all ingredients in a small bowl or cup. Makes 1 serving. Serve at mealtime only.
    Each serving is equivalent to: 3 servings Fat

Mock Béarnaise Sauce

Delicious over poached eggs, fish, broiled steaks, or hamburgers.

2 tablespoons imitation (or diet)
  margarine
1 tablespoon mayonnaise
1 tablespoon tarragon vinegar
¼ teaspoon dehydrated onion

flakes, reconstituted in ¾
  teaspoon water
⅛ teaspoon chopped fresh parsley
2 to 3 drops imitation butter
  flavoring

Melt margarine in top of double boiler over boiling water. Stir in remaining ingredients. Cook, stirring constantly, until heated. Divide evenly. Makes 2 servings. Serve at mealtime only.

Each serving is equivalent to: 3 servings Fat

Pesto (Basil) Sauce

Stir Pesto into ⅔ cup hot, cooked enriched macaroni or spaghetti or ½ cup hot, cooked enriched noodles. Also served on sliced tomatoes or over poached fish.

½ cup chopped fresh basil
1 ounce grated Parmesan cheese
1 tablespoon vegetable oil
1 teaspoon chopped fresh parsley
  (optional)

½ garlic clove, minced
½ teaspoon salt
Freshly ground pepper to taste

In small bowl combine all ingredients or place in blender container and process 30 seconds; let stand 1 hour before using. Makes 1 midday meal serving. Supplement as required.

Each serving is equivalent to: 1 ounce Hard Cheese; 3 servings Fat

Pimento Dressing

1 cup pimentos
2 tablespoons cider vinegar
2 tablespoons prepared mustard

Artificial sweetener to equal 4
  teaspoons sugar

Combine all ingredients in blender container and process until smooth. Divide evenly. Makes 4 servings.

Each serving is equivalent to: ¼ cup Vegetables

Tangy French Dressing

This is a bonus, as it's made without oil, but you may wish to add some at serving time.

½ cup tomato juice
1 tablespoon cider vinegar
1 packet instant chicken broth and
   seasoning mix
1 teaspoon dehydrated onion
   flakes

¾ teaspoon Worcestershire sauce
½ teaspoon prepared mustard
Dash each garlic powder and
   cinnamon

Combine all ingredients in blender container and process. Divide evenly. Makes 2 servings.

Each serving is equivalent to: ¼ serving Bonus (¼ cup tomato juice); ½ serving Something Extra (½ packet broth mix)

Baked Fresh Fruit

Baked fruits add variety to your meals. These go well with fish or meat.

8 medium apricots, 4 medium
   peaches, or 4 small pears
½ cup boiling water
¼ cup brown sugar replacement

2 teaspoons lemon juice
¼ teaspoon ground cloves
¼ teaspoon nutmeg
¼ teaspoon ginger

Cut fruit in half and remove pits or cores. Arrange in shallow baking dish, hollow side up. In small bowl combine remaining ingredients and sprinkle over fruit. Bake, uncovered, at 400°F. until fruit is tender—about 20 minutes for apricots, 30 minutes for peaches, 45 minutes for pears. Divide evenly. Makes 4 servings.

Each serving is equivalent to: 1 serving Fruit

Broiled Fresh Fruit

Watch fruit carefully to avoid scorching.

**4 medium apples, cored and sliced
¼ inch thick, or 4 medium
peaches, pared, pitted, and
sliced, or 2 medium bananas,
peeled and halved lengthwise
1 tablespoon lemon juice
½ teaspoon coconut or walnut
extract (optional)**

In bowl toss fruit with lemon juice. Arrange on broiler pan. Broil until tender, turning once. Allow about 5 minutes for apples and bananas, and 6 to 8 minutes for peaches, or until fruit is tender. Sprinkle with extract before serving, if desired. Divide evenly. Makes 4 servings.

Each serving is equivalent to: 1 serving Fruit

Tips on Gelatin

1. One tablespoon of unflavored gelatin will mold 2 cups of liquid and solids combined.
2. For easier unmolding, rinse mold in cold water or spray with a release agent before adding gelatin mixture.
3. If gelatin mixture becomes too firm to fold in solid ingredients, place bowl containing gelatin mixture in a bath of hot water 2 inches below rim of bowl. Stir until desired consistency, add ingredients, and place in mold. Chill.
4. Allow 2 to 3 hours for chilling of gelatin (less if gelatin is liquid, more if it contains solids).
5. Unmolding—Gently run a knife along the inside edges of the mold. Dip base of mold in a bath of hot water. Turn serving plate upside-down over mold and invert both mold and plate. Shake mold and plate and, if necessary, cover inverted mold with a warm towel until gelatin loosens. Remove mold.

Gelatin Dessert Whips

In small saucepan sprinkle 1 envelope unflavored gelatin over ½ cup flavored dietetic soda. Allow to soften. Heat, stirring to dissolve gelatin. Transfer to blender container and add 1½ cups of the same-flavored dietetic soda. Process until frothy, pour into mold, and chill until firm. Unmold and garnish with 2 servings fresh fruit, if desired. Divide evenly. Makes 2 servings.

Each serving is equivalent to: 1 serving Something Extra (½ envelope gelatin); 1 serving Fruit (optional)

Gelatin Pick-Me-Up

In saucepan sprinkle ½ envelope unflavored gelatin over ¾ cup tomato juice. Heat to dissolve gelatin. Add a dash of aromatic bitters. Serve hot. Makes 1 serving.

Each serving is equivalent to: 1 serving Something Extra (½ envelope gelatin); ¾ serving Bonus (¾ cup tomato juice)

Mint Jelly

In small saucepan sprinkle 1 envelope unflavored gelatin over ½ cup lemon-flavored dietetic soda. Heat, stirring to dissolve gelatin. Stir in 1½ cups lemon-flavored dietetic soda, artificial sweetener to equal 2 teaspoons sugar, 1 teaspoon mint extract, and a few drops green food coloring. Refrigerate until firm. Serve with roast lamb. Divide evenly. Makes 4 servings.

Each serving is equivalent to: ½ serving Something Extra; ¼ envelope gelatin)

Best Whipped Topping

1 teaspoon unflavored gelatin
1 tablespoon water
½ cup evaporated skimmed milk

½ teaspoon vanilla extract
Artificial sweetener to equal 4
    teaspoons sugar

In medium bowl sprinkle gelatin over water, allow to soften. In small saucepan scald milk and add to bowl. Stir to dissolve gelatin. Chill. Add vanilla and artificial sweetener and, using an electric beater, whip until mixture stands in peaks. Divide evenly. Makes 4 servings.

Each serving is equivalent to: ¹/₆ serving Something Extra (¼ teaspoon gelatin); ¼ serving Milk (2 tablespoons evaporated skimmed milk)

Easy Whipped Topping

⅓ cup nonfat dry milk
⅓ cup cold water
Artificial sweetener to equal 12
    teaspoons sugar

2 teaspoons lemon juice
½ teaspoon vanilla extract
Dash nutmeg

In bowl combine all ingredients and, using an electric mixer, whip about 10 minutes or until mixture stands in peaks. Use immediately. Divide evenly. Makes 4 servings.

Each serving is equivalent to: ¼ serving Milk (¼ cup skim milk)

Coffee and Tea Breaks

Coffee "Brandy"

Combine ½ cup boiling water, artificial sweetener to equal 2 teaspoons sugar, 1 teaspoon instant coffee, ½ teaspoon brandy extract, and a twist of lemon rind in a demitasse cup. Makes 1 serving.

Iced Coffee

Pour 1 cup freshly brewed coffee into ice cube tray; freeze until solid. Divide frozen coffee cubes into 2 tall glasses. Pour 1 cup chilled coffee over cubes in each glass. Serve each portion with ¼ cup skim milk and artificial sweetener to taste if desired. Makes 2 servings.

Each serving is equivalent to: ¼ serving Milk (¼ cup skim milk)

Variation: Combine all ingredients in blender container and process until ice is crushed. Divide evenly into 2 tall glasses.

Chocolate "Rum" Sherbet

Combine ¼ cup chocolate-flavored dietetic soda, ¼ cup freshly brewed coffee, and ½ teaspoon rum extract in freezer tray. Freeze until slushy. Serve in a chilled sherbet glass. Makes 1 serving.

Hot Mint Tea

Combine 1 cup boiling water with 1 teaspoon dried mint leaves or 1 tablespoon fresh mint leaves. Steep 15 minutes. Strain and add artificial sweetener to taste. Makes 1 serving.

Mint Sherbet

Pour Hot Mint Tea (see preceding recipe) in freezer tray; freeze until slushy. Serve in a chilled sherbet glass. Makes 1 serving.

Coping with the Cocktail Hour

Get your kicks by looking in the mirror and enjoying these party-pleasing beverages.

Banana "Daiquiri"

Pour 1½ cups cream-flavored dietetic soda into ice cube tray; freeze until solid. Transfer cubes to blender container or food processor. Add 1 medium banana, sliced, ½ teaspoon rum extract, dash banana extract, and artificial sweetener to taste; process until slushy. Divide evenly. Makes 2 servings.

Each serving is equivalent to: 1 serving Fruit

Caribbean Cocktail

1 packet instant chicken broth and   **1 cup tomato juice**
   seasoning mix   **½ cup orange juice**
¾ cup boiling water

In a small pitcher, stir broth mix in water to dissolve. Add tomato and orange juice. Divide evenly. Serve "on the rocks." Makes 2 servings.

Each serving is equivalent to: ½ serving Something Extra (½ packet broth mix); ½ serving Bonus (½ cup tomato juice); ½ serving Fruit

"Champagne" Fizz

Combine 1 cup dietetic ginger ale, ¼ teaspoon vanilla and ¼ teaspoon sherry extracts in ice cube tray; freeze until solid. Transfer cubes to blender container or food processor; process until slushy. Divide evenly into two champagne glasses. Makes 2 servings.

Cherry-O

Combine 1 cup cherry-flavored dietetic soda and 1 cup dietetic ginger ale. Pour into ice cube trays and freeze until solid. Remove cubes, place in blender container, and process until slush consistency. Serve in champagne glasses with short straws. Divide evenly. Makes 2 servings.

"Crème de Menthe" Frappé

Combine 1 cup cold water, ¼ teaspoon peppermint extract, and a few drops of green food coloring in a tall glass over crushed ice. Makes 1 serving.

Horses' Neck Highball

Combine 1 cup club soda, dash aromatic bitters, and a dash lemon juice in a tall glass. Add ice cubes and garnish with a twist of lemon or lime rind. Makes 1 serving.

"Margarita"

Pour 1 cup citrus-flavored dietetic soda into ice cube tray; freeze until solid. Dip 2 glasses in water; place in freezer for about 5 minutes or until frosty. Dip rim of glasses in lime juice, then salt. Set aside in freezer. In blender container or food processor combine frozen soda cubes, ¼ cup lime juice, and artificial sweetener to equal 2 teaspoons sugar. Process until slushy. Divide evenly into prepared glasses. Makes 2 servings.

My Mai Tai

When you're serving Hawaiian Veal (see page 157) or Polynesian Beef (see page 169), you'll want to sip on this Hawaiian specialty.

½ cup grapefruit juice
½ teaspoon rum extract
⅛ teaspoon orange extract

Artificial sweetener to equal 2
    teaspoons sugar (optional)
Mint sprig to garnish

In measuring cup combine grapefruit juice with extracts and sweetener, if desired. Pour into a 12-ounce old-fashioned glass filled with crushed ice. Garnish with mint sprig. Makes 1 serving.

Each serving is equivalent to: 1 serving Fruit

"Piña Colada"

½ cup water
⅓ cup nonfat dry milk
1 slice canned pineapple, with 1 tablespoon juice, no sugar added

Artificial sweetener to equal 2 teaspoons sugar
¼ teaspoon coconut extract
¼ teaspoon rum extract

Combine all ingredients in blender container; process about 30 seconds. Serve over ice cubes. Makes 1 serving.

Each serving is equivalent to: 1 serving Milk (1 cup skim milk); ½ serving Fruit

Puerto Rican Punch

¼ cup orange juice
1 tablespoon lime or lemon juice

½ teaspoon rum extract
Dash aromatic bitters

Fill a 6-ounce glass with crushed ice and add fruit juices, extract, and bitters. Stir and serve. Makes 1 serving.

Each serving is equivalent to: ½ serving Fruit

"Rum" and Cola

Combine ¾ cup dietetic cola with ¾ teaspoon rum extract in tall glass over ice cubes. Makes 1 serving.

"Sangria"

Combine 1 cup grape-flavored dietetic soda, 1 tablespoon frozen orange juice concentrate, and ½ teaspoon burgundy or other wine-flavored extract in a tall glass over ice cubes. Makes 1 serving.

Each serving is equivalent to: ½ serving Fruit

Skinny Devil

Combine ¾ cup tomato juice, ¼ cup clam juice, and a dash hot sauce in a tall glass. Add ice cubes. Makes 1 serving.

Each serving is equivalent to: 1 serving Bonus (¾ cup tomato juice and ¼ cup clam juice)

Spiked Clam Juice on the Rocks

1. In pitcher combine 1 cup clam juice with 1 cup tomato juice. Serve in tall glasses over ice. Divide evenly. Makes 2 servings.

Each serving is equivalent to: 1 serving Bonus (½ cup clam juice and ½ cup tomato juice)

2. Combine ¾ cup clam juice, ½ teaspoon lemon juice, dash each of celery seed, cayenne pepper, and hot sauce. Serve in tall glass over ice and garnish with a celery stick. Makes 1 serving.

Each serving is equivalent to: ¾ serving Bonus (¾ cup clam juice)

Tomato Frappé

3 cups tomato juice
1 cup buttermilk
1 packet instant chicken broth
  and seasoning mix
1 teaspoon dehydrated onion
  flakes
¼ teaspoon celery salt
¼ teaspoon celery seed
Hot sauce to taste
Lime wedges to garnish

Combine all ingredients, except lime wedges, in blender container. Process to combine. Divide evenly and serve, very cold, in chilled glasses over ice cubes. Garnish with lime wedges. Makes 4 servings.

Each serving is equivalent to: ¾ serving Bonus (¾ cup tomato juice); ⅓ serving Milk (¼ cup buttermilk); ¼ serving Something Extra (¼ packet broth mix)

Tommy Collins

Combine ¼ cup dietetic quinine water, 1 teaspoon rum extract, 1 teaspoon lemon juice, and artificial sweetener to equal 1 teaspoon sugar in a glass over ice cubes. Makes 1 serving.

"Wassail Bowl"

In saucepan combine 4 cups dietetic root beer, 1 teaspoon cinnamon, ½ teaspoon nutmeg, ½ teaspoon ginger, and artificial sweetener to taste. Heat slightly and serve in punch bowl. Makes 4 servings.

Teen Treats

Lemonade

In a tall glass combine 1 cup water, 2 tablespoons lemon juice, and artificial sweetener to equal 4 teaspoons sugar or to taste. Serve over ice. Garnish with mint leaves. Makes 1 serving.

Fruit-Flavored Snowballs

Pour 1 cup dietetic soda in a small saucepan; cook until reduced by ½. Cool and set aside. In blender container combine 4 cups cracked ice cubes and 2 cups cold water. Process until ice looks like snow crystals. Quickly drain excess water and evenly divide "snow" ice into 4 paper cups. Drizzle 2 tablespoons cooled soda over ice and serve immediately. Makes 4 servings.

APPENDIX

WEIGHT WATCHERS® MAINTENANCE PLAN

Introduction to the Maintenance Plan

The Maintenance Plan is designed for the individual who has reached goal weight. Now you are embarking on an adventure; discovering how your body will respond to additional foods. Therefore, the Plan requires *individualization.*

The Plan consists of eight groups of foods. You will be given a new group each week. The foods *within* each group contain approximately the same caloric values. Each food is assigned a *unit* value, with each unit representing approximately 50 calories.

Here's how it works. Each week, you may increase the number of units taken daily. The first week, you may take *one* unit per day. The second week, you may take a total of *two* units per day, and so forth. By the eighth week, you may take a total of *eight* daily units. It is possible that *your* body can tolerate more foods than provided by the eight units, without a weight gain. In that case, you may *cautiously* add additional units. For example, in the ninth week, you may add nine units; in the tenth week, ten units. . . .

However, maintaining weight is a highly individual matter. Additions should be taken with a vigilant eye on the scale. If these additional foods cause a weight gain, cut back to the number of units which enable you to maintain your weight successfully.

These units are interchangeable. For example, in the third week of the Maintenance Plan, you may have either one 3-unit food daily, *or* three 1-unit foods daily, *or* a combination of one 1-unit and one 2-unit food daily.

Each week you will assume the responsibility for a new group of foods, adding them to the basic Maintenance Plan on a daily basis. What you are striving for is a *stable weight*. Therefore, you are trying to determine the number of units required to *maintain* your weight for life. To maintain the same weight, the calories provided by the foods you eat, and the calories used by your body, must *balance*. Reaching this balance is a process of trial and error. Since the final number of daily—or weekly—units will vary for each person, *you* must be the judge for yourself.

Remember: Like all of the food plans, the basic Maintenance Plan is designed for the proper distribution of caloric intake among proteins, carbohydrates and fats; thus allowing for optimum nutrition.

A word of caution. Too often high calorie foods are highly concentrated sources of fat and refined sugar, with little nutrient content. For this reason, concentrated sources of saturated fat and refined sugar have been marked with a dagger (†). Use the foods sparingly, and with caution.

Variety, moderation and *awareness* continue to be key words.

Menu Plan

Morning Meal

Fruit, 1 serving
Choice of:
  Egg, 1
    or
  Cheese, soft, ⅓ cup or
    2½ ounces
    or
  Cheese, semisoft or
    hard, 1 ounce
    or
  Cereal, 1 ounce with
    ½ milk serving
    or
  Fish, cooked, 2 ounces
    or
  Poultry or Meat, cooked,
    1 ounce
Bread, 1 serving
Beverage, if desired

Midday Meal

Choice of:
  Poultry, Meat or Fish,
    cooked, 3 ounces
    or
  Eggs, 2
    or
  Cheese, soft, ⅔ cup or
    5 ounces
    or
  Cheese, semisoft or
    hard, 2 ounces
    or
  Legumes, cooked,
    4 ounces

Vegetables
Bread,
  Women, 1 serving,
    if desired
  Men and Youth,
    1 serving
Beverage, if desired

Evening Meal

Choice of:
  Poultry, Meat or Fish,
    cooked,
    Women and Youth,
    4 ounces
    Men, 6 ounces
    or
  Legumes, cooked,
    Women and Youth,
    6 ounces
    Men, 8 ounces
Vegetables
Bread,
  Women, 1 serving
    (if not eaten at
    Midday Meal)
  Men and Youth,
    1 serving
Beverage, if desired

Daily

  Milk, at any time
    Women and Men,
    2 servings
    Youth,
    3 servings

Fats, 3 servings
    at mealtime
Fruits
    Women, 3 servings
    Men and Youth,
        3-4 servings

(1 serving at Morn-
    ing Meal; other
    servings any time)
Add units as allowed,
    if desired.

Note: The Midday Meal may be interchanged with the Evening Meal.

In addition to the changes on the menu, make the following adjustments to the Basic Program.
3. Choice Group
Omit 1 serving of bread and select one item from this list up to 5 times weekly, if desired.
5. "Beef" Group
Select once a week, if desired, in place of one "Beef" Group selection: bologna, corned beef, duck, frankfurters, goose, knockwurst, liverwurst, luncheon meats, organ meats, salami, sausages.

GROUP 1

One (1) Unit Foods
Approximately 50 Calories

Add one of the following daily, if desired:

Appetizers

anchovies, fillets, *4*
caviar
    1 tablespoon
dip, guacamole
    ¼ cup
dip, prepared (Bleu cheese,
        clam, onion)
    2 teaspoons

ham, deviled
    ½ ounce
herring, pickled
    1 ounce
liver pâté,
    1 tablespoon
mushrooms, stuffed, *2*
roe, fish, *1 ounce*

Breads

crackers, plain, any type, *4*
crackers, plain, graham
1 (5" x 2½")
Melba toast, *3 pieces*
zwieback, 2

Condiments

bacon, imitation bits
2 tablespoons
catsup
3 tablespoons
olives, any type, *8*
pickle, sweet
1 large
relish
2 tablespoons
sauce, barbecue
2 tablespoons
sauce, chili
3 tablespoons
sauce, cranberry
2 tablespoons
sauce, seafood cocktail
2 tablespoons
sauce, tartar
2 teaspoons

Fats

† cream cheese
1 tablespoon
† cream cheese, imitation
2 tablespoons
fat serving
1 additional
salad dressing, any type
2 teaspoons

Fruits

apricots, halves, dried
5 medium or 4 large
coconut, shredded
1 tablespoon
dates
2 whole or 2 tablespoons chopped
fruit serving
1 additional
raisins
2 tablespoons

Milk Products

† cream, half and half
2 tablespoons
† cream, heavy
1 tablespoon
† cream, sour
2 tablespoons
† creamer, instant non-dairy
1 tablespoon
milk, whole
⅓ cup
† topping, whipped, non-dairy
3 tablespoons

Snacks

popcorn, plain
1 cup

Sweets

† honey
2 teaspoons
† jams, jellies, or preserves
1 tablespoon

† molasses
1 tablespoon
† sugar, any type
1 tablespoon
† syrup, chocolate
1 tablespoon
† syrup, corn
1 tablespoon

† syrup, maple
1 tablespoon

Vegetables

"Limited"
4 ounces

Note: Teaspoon and tablespoon measures must be *level*.

GROUP 2

Two (2) Unit Foods
Approximately 100 Calories

Add one of the following or any combination of foods totaling up to 2 units daily, if desired:

Appetizers

clams, cherrystone, 6
clams, steamers
1 dozen

Basic Entrée Additions

bacon, Canadian
2 slices
beef jerky
1 ounce
cheese, semisoft or hard
1 ounce
cheese, soft
½ cup
egg, cooked, *1*

legumes, cooked
3 ounces
liver, chopped
½ cup
pepperoni
1 ounce
poultry, fish, meat, cooked
1 ounce
sausage, "Brown and Serve"
1 link
scrapple
1 ounce

Beverages

brandy or cognac
1 fluid ounce

champagne
4 fluid ounces
gin, rum, vodka, whiskey
1 fluid ounce
lemonade
8 fluid ounces
liqueur
1 fluid ounce
sherry
2 fluid ounces
soda, regular, any type
8 fluid ounces
wine, table (Chablis, claret,
Rhine wine, sauterne)
3½ fluid ounces

Breads

bread, any type
1 slice (approx. 1 ounce)
bread, banana tea
1½ ounce slice
bread, date nut
1 slice
bread, pita, *1*
bread crumbs
¼ cup
bread sticks
1 ounce
cereal, any type
1 ounce
flour, all purpose
¼ cup
matzo, any type
1 board
pancakes
2 (4" diameter)
popover, *1*
roll, hamburger or
frankfurter, *1*
roll, soft, *1*

Choice Group

any item
1 additional serving

Desserts

ambrosia
½ cup
brownie
1 (1¾" x 1¾" x 1")
cookies, any type
2 medium
fudgicle, *1*
gelatin, fruit flavored
½ cup
ice, fruit
½ cup
macaroon, *1*
popsicle, *1*
sherbet
½ cup

Fats

† bacon
2 slices
† bacon fat
1 tablespoon
† butter
1 tablespoon
† chicken fat
1 tablespoon

Fruits

avocado
¼ medium

fruit in syrup
  ½ cup
pomegranate
  1 medium

Milk

1 additional serving

Misc.

borscht
  1 cup
gazpacho
  1 cup
sauce, cheese
  3 tablespoons
sauce, clam
  ⅓ cup
sauce, hollandaise
  2 tablespoons

sauce, spaghetti
  ½ cup
sauce, Spanish
  ½ cup
sauce, white
  ¼ cup
soup, uncreamed
  1 cup

Vegetables

cole slaw
  1 cup
ratatouille
  1 cup
salad, spinach, bacon and
    mushroom
  1 cup

GROUP 3

Three (3) Unit Foods
Approximately 150 Calories

Add one of the following or any combination of foods totaling up to 3 units daily, if desired:

Appetizers

egg, deviled
  2 halves
franks in blankets, *3*
melon and prosciutto
  1 serving
mushrooms, marinated
  ½ cup
shrimp puffs, *3*

Beverages

beer or ale
  12 fluid ounces
Bloody Mary
  8 fluid ounces
gin gimlet
  5 fluid ounces
highball
  6 fluid ounces

Manhattan
3½ fluid ounces
martini
3 fluid ounces
milk, coconut
2 fluid ounces
old fashioned
3 fluid ounces
Tom Collins
8 fluid ounces
vermouth, French
5 fluid ounces
vermouth, Italian
3 fluid ounces
wine, dessert (muscatel, port,
　　sherry, Tokay)
3½ fluid ounces

Breads

bagel, *1*
bread, cornmeal
1 piece (2½" x 2½" x 1½")
bread, garlic
2 slices (3" x 1½")
muffin, any type (e.g.,
　　blueberry, bran, corn)
1 medium
muffin, English, *1*
roll, hard
1 medium
toast, cinnamon
1 slice
tortillas, *2*

Choice Group

beans, refried
½ cup
potato, French fried
10 pieces (2" x ½" x ½")

potato, fried
2 ounces
potato, mashed
1 cup
potato au gratin
½ cup
rice, Spanish
½ cup
salad, macaroni
½ cup
salad, potato
½ cup
salad, 3-bean
½ cup
succotash
1 cup
sweet potato, boiled
6 ounces

Desserts

apple brown Betty
½ cup
cake, angel
¹/₁₂ of 9" diameter cake
cake, pound
1 slice (3½" x 3" x ½")
cake, sponge
¹/₁₆ of 9" diameter cake
crème de caramel
½ cup
cupcake with icing, *1*
custard, any type
½ cup
doughnut (unfilled)
1 medium
fruitcake
1 slice (3" x 3" x ½")
ice cream
½ cup

ice cream bar, chocolate
   covered, *1*
pudding, any type
   ½ cup

Fruits

cider, apple
   1 cup
juice, apple
   1 cup
juice, apricot nectar
   1 cup
juice, cranberry cocktail
   1 cup
juice, grape
   1 cup
juice, pineapple
   1 cup
salad, apple, celery and nut
   3 heaping tablespoons
salad, carrot and raisin
   3 heaping tablespoons

Milk

yogurt, frozen
   4 ounces
yogurt, plain, unflavored
   1 cup

Snacks

chestnuts, fresh, *10*
corn chips
   1 ounce

pork rinds, fried
   1 ounce
potato chips, *12 or* potato
   sticks
   1 ounce
pretzels, 3 ring, *12 or* sticks
   1 ounce

Sweets

† candy, hard, *1 ounce*
† caramel, any type, *3*
† chocolate, with or without nuts
   1 ounce
† chocolate creams, *3*
† chocolate kisses, *6*
   1 ounce
† chocolate mints, *2*
† fudge, any type
   1 ounce
† halvah, *1 ounce*
† jelly beans, *15*
† licorice
   1½ ounces
† lollypop
   1 (2¼" diameter)
† marshmallows
   5 large
† marzipan, *1 ounce*
† peanut brittle, *1 ounce*
peanuts, chocolate covered
   1 ounce
popcorn, caramel coated with
   peanuts
   1 cup
raisins, chocolate covered
   1 ounce

GROUP 4

Four (4) Unit Foods
Approximately 200 Calories

Add one of the following or any combination of foods totaling up to 4 units daily, if desired:

Appetizers

cheese puffs, *3*
clams, baked, *4*

Beverages

cocoa, hot
  6 fluid ounces
coffee, Irish
  1 serving
gin and tonic
  8 fluid ounces
milk, chocolate
  8 fluid ounces
screwdriver
  8 fluid ounces
whiskey sour
  5 fluid ounces

Breads

biscuits, baking powder
  2 (2" diameter)
pretzel, soft, *1*
scone, *1*

stuffing, bread
  ½ cup
waffle
  1 (5" diameter)

Choice Group

knish
  1 (3½" diameter)
potato pancakes, *2*

Desserts

apple, baked, *1*
Charlotte Russe, *1*
gingerbread
  2" square
ice cream cone
  1 scoop
ice cream sandwich, *1*
spumoni
  1 serving
tortoni
  1 serving
trifle
  4 ounces

Prepared Foods

These foods may be taken in addition to or in place of Basic Entrées (eggs, cheese, cereal, poultry, meat, fish and legumes). If the Entrée is omitted, add up to 3 additional units daily, if desired:

beef, creamed, chipped
½ cup
beef, pot roast
3 ounces
blintzes, *2*
chicken or turkey, baked or
    roasted, meat and skin
    4 ounces
croquette, any type
3 ounces
enchilada, beef, *1*
fish loaf
5 ounces
fish sticks, cakes, or fried fish
4 ounces

French toast
1 slice
gefilte fish
2 pieces (8 ounces)
herring in cream sauce
4 ounces
pizza
⅛ of 14"pie
salad: chicken, crabmeat,
    lobster, shrimp, with
    dressing
½ cup
stew, beef and vegetable
1 cup
taco, beef, *1*

Snacks

almonds, *22*
Brazil nuts, *7*
cashew nuts, *14*
macadamia nuts, *10*
peanut butter
2 tablespoons
peanuts
¼ cup
pecan halves, *20*
sunflower seeds
1 ounce
walnut halves
14 (1 ounce)

Soups

soup, creamed
1 cup

Vegetables

salad, Caesar
1 serving

GROUP 5

Five (5) Unit Foods
Approximately 250 Calories

Add one of the following or any combination of foods totaling up to 5 units daily, if desired:

Appetizers

egg roll, *1*
Fettucini Alfredo
   4 ounces
meatballs, Swedish, *3*
shrimp cocktail with sauce
   1 serving

Desserts

cake, coffee, *1 piece*
   (2½" x 2½" x 1½")
cake, devil's food

(2 layer) ¹/₁₆ of 9" cake
doughnut, filled, *1*
fritters, apple
   4 ounces
ice cream soda,
   any flavor, *1*
pastry, Danish with icing
   1 (4½" diameter)
peach Melba
   1 serving
roll, sweet, with nuts,
   raisins and frosting, *1*
strudel, any type
   1 piece (3 ounces)

Prepared Foods

These foods may be taken in addition to or in place of Basic Entrées (eggs, cheese, cereal, poultry, meat, fish and legumes). If the Entrée is omitted, add up to 3 additional units daily, if desired:

bouillabaisse
   2 cups
chicken cacciatore
   8 ounces
chow mein with noodles
   ¾ cup
creole, chicken or shrimp
   1 serving

goulash, beef
   1 cup
lasagna
   1 serving (6 ounces)
lobster Newburg
   5 ounces
meat loaf
   4 ounces

ravioli with sauce, *7 pieces*
sandwich, chicken salad
sandwich, liverwurst
sandwich, tuna fish
shells, stuffed
   3 (4½ ounces)
shrimp, fried
   4 ounces
soufflé, spinach
   6 ounces
steak, Swiss
   7 ounces
stew, oyster
   1 cup

sukiyaki
   1 serving

Vegetables

eggplant, French fried
   4 ounces
fritters, corn, *2*
onion rings, French fried
   4 ounces
zucchini, French fried
   4 ounces

GROUP 6

Six (6) Unit Foods
Approximately 300 Calories

Add one of the following or any combination of foods totaling up to 6 units daily, if desired:

Appetizers

soup, French onion au
      gratin
   1 serving

Beverages

eggnog
   8 fluid ounces

Choice Group

beans, baked, with tomato
      sauce
   1 cup
potato, stuffed baked
   whole (6 ounces)
rice, fried
   1 cup
sweet potato, candied
   6 ounces

Desserts

chocolate mousse
  ½ cup
compote, dried fruit
  1 cup
cream puff
  1 medium
éclair
  1 medium
parfait, *1*
turnover, fruit, *1*

Fruits

plantain
  1 medium

Milk

yogurt, fruit flavored
  1 cup

Prepared Foods

These foods may be taken in addition to or in place of Basic Entrées (eggs, cheese, cereal, poultry, meat, fish and legumes). If the Entrée is omitted, add up to 3 additional units daily, if desired:

chop suey with meat
  1 cup
coq au vin
  8 ounces
hash, beef
  1 cup
pepper, stuffed, *1*
pork, sweet and sour
  1 serving
sandwich, bacon, lettuce and
    tomato

sandwich, egg salad
sandwich, ham
sandwich, ham salad
shish kebab
  1 serving
soufflé, cheese
  5 ounces
tamales with sauce
  2 (6 ounces)
Welsh rarebit on toast
  ½ cup

GROUP 7

Seven (7) Unit Foods
Approximately 350 Calories

Add one of the following or any combination of foods totaling up to 7 units daily, if desired:

Desserts

cake, cheese (with or without
    fruit topping)
    ⅛ of 10″ cake
cherries jubilee
    1 serving

milk shake, any flavor
    8 fluid ounces
pie, meringue or custard,
    any type
    ¹/₆ of 9″ pie

Prepared Foods

These foods may be taken in addition to or in place of Basic Entrées (eggs, cheese, cereal, poultry, meat, fish and legumes). If the Entrée is omitted, add up to 3 additional units daily, if desired:

bagel, lox and cream
    cheese, *1*
chili con carne
    1 cup
duck, baked or roasted, meat
    and skin
    4 ounces
egg foo young
    1 serving
eggplant Parmigiana
    6 ounces
franks and beans
    1 cup
hamburger on roll with lettuce
    and catsup

moussaka
    1 serving
omelet, any kind
salad, chef's with dressing
    2 cups
sandwich, cream cheese
    and jelly
sandwich, peanut better
    and jelly
sloppy Joe, *1*
spaghetti with meatballs
    1 cup

GROUP 8

Eight (8) Unit Foods
Approximately 400-500 Calories

Add one of the following or any combination of foods totaling up to 8 units daily, if desired:

Desserts

baked Alaska
  1 serving
baklava
  1 piece (2" x 2")
cake, frosted, any flavor
  1 piece (3" x 3" x 2")
crepes Suzette
  2 (7")

ice cream sundae
  2 scoops
pie, any type
  ⅙ of 9" pie
strawberry shortcake with
  whipped topping
  1 serving (2½" cube)

Prepared Foods

These foods may be taken in addition to or in place of Basic Entrées (eggs, cheese, cereal, poultry, meat, fish and legumes). If the Entrée is omitted, add up to 3 additional units daily, if desired:

beef, Bar-B-Q on a bun
  1 serving
beef Stroganoff over noodles
  1 serving
brisket
  3 slices
cannelloni with cheese
    sauce
  2 (6")
chicken, fried
  *1 large breast, or 1 leg
    and thigh*

chicken a la king
  1 cup
chicken fricassee
  1 cup
coquilles St. Jacques
  1 shell
crab, deviled
  1 cup
curry with rice
  1 serving
duck with orange sauce
  ½ duck

eggs Benedict
1 serving
fish, baked stuffed
6 ounces
fish and chips
1 serving
fondue, beef or cheese
1 serving
hamburger, bacon and cheese
on bun
macaroni and cheese
1 cup
manicotti
2 shells (7 ounces)
paella
1 serving
pot pie
1 small
quiche Lorraine
⅛ of 9" pie
salmon mousse
8 ounces
sandwich, club
sandwich, corned beef

sandwich, fried fish
sandwich, grilled cheese
and bacon
sandwich, pastrami
sandwich, Reuben
sandwich, roast beef with
hot gravy
sandwich, turkey
sauerbraten
1 serving
shrimp scampi, 6
spareribs, barbecued
1 serving (6-8 ribs)
turkey tetrazzini
8 ounces
veal cordon bleu
1 serving
veal scaloppine
1 serving
Wiener schnitzel
1 serving
ziti, baked
1 serving

Monthly

An ethnic meal at your favorite restaurant. *Bon appétit!*

Goal Weight Charts

The weights have been established from authoritative sources. They are called "tentative" because they give a variation for sex, age, and height. A permanent specific goal for the individual should be selected according to the amount of body fat present when the individual reaches the "tentative" goal weight.

TENTATIVE GOAL WEIGHTS
GIRLS

Height Range Without Shoes	Age in Years							
	10	11	12	13	14	15	16	17
Ft. Inches	Weight in Pounds							
3 11 (47)	48- 55							
4 0 (48)	49- 58	51- 61						
4 1 (49)	50- 61	52- 65	53- 69					
4 2 (50)	51- 64	53- 67	55- 71	60- 73				
4 3 (51)	54- 67	55- 70	57- 73	62- 76	63- 84			
4 4 (52)	58- 70	59- 73	60- 76	64- 79	67- 88	77- 91		
4 5 (53)	59- 73	62- 76	63- 79	66- 82	71- 90	78- 93	79- 94	80- 96
4 6 (54)	62- 75	65- 77	66- 81	68- 85	74- 91	79- 94	80- 95	82- 98
4 7 (55)	64- 77	68- 78	69- 84	70- 88	76- 92	80- 95	81- 96	83- 99
4 8 (56)	66- 79	71- 80	72- 87	73- 91	78- 94	81- 96	82- 97	85-100
4 9 (57)	68- 83	74- 84	75- 90	76- 94	81- 97	84- 99	85-100	88-101
4 10 (58)	70- 86	76- 87	77- 93	79- 97	84-100	87-102	88-103	90-104
4 11 (59)	75- 89	78- 90	80- 96	82-100	87-103	90-105	91-106	92-108
5 0 (60)	80- 92	81- 93	82- 98	86-103	90-106	93-108	94-110	95-111
5 1 (61)	82- 95	84- 97	86-101	88-106	94-109	97-111	98-112	99-113
5 2 (62)	84- 98	86-102	89-104	92-109	98-112	101-115	102-117	103-118
5 3 (63)	87-101	89-104	92-106	96-112	101-115	103-122	104-123	105-124
5 4 (64)	90-103	93-106	97-109	100-115	104-118	106-124	107-126	108-128
5 5 (65)	94-105	98-108	102-111	104-118	107-121	109-126	110-129	111-131
5 6 (66)		103-111	106-116	108-121	111-124	113-131	114-132	115-134
5 7 (67)		107-114	110-120	112-124	116-127	118-134	119-135	120-137
5 8 (68)			114-124	117-127	119-130	120-135	121-138	122-140
5 9 (69)			118-127	122-130	124-133	126-141	128-142	129-144
5 10 (70)				127-134	128-137	130-143	132-146	133-148
5 11 (71)				132-138	133-141	135-146	136-150	137-152
6 0 (72)					136-145	138-148	140-151	141-156
6 1 (73)					140-150	142-155	144-158	145-160

TENTATIVE GOAL WEIGHTS
BOYS

Height Range Without Shoes	Age in Years							
	10	11	12	13	14	15	16	17
Ft. Inches	Weight in Pounds							
3 11 (47)	48- 52							
4 0 (48)	50- 55	51- 57						
4 1 (49)	52- 57	53- 58						
4 2 (50)	54- 59	55- 60	56- 62					
4 3 (51)	58- 62	59- 63	60- 64					
4 4 (52)	60- 65	61- 66	62- 67					
4 5 (53)	63- 68	64- 69	65- 70	66- 71				
4 6 (54)	65- 71	66- 72	67- 73	68- 75				
4 7 (55)	70- 75	71- 76	72- 77	73- 79	74- 80			
4 8 (56)	75- 80	76- 81	77- 83	78- 85	79- 87			
4 9 (57)	79- 82	80- 84	81- 86	83- 89	84- 90	86- 95		
4 10 (58)	82- 86	83- 87	84- 88	88- 93	89- 94	92-100	95-108	
4 11 (59)	86- 90	87- 91	88- 92	93- 97	94- 98	96-104	98-110	101-114
5 0 (60)	90- 94	91- 95	92- 96	96-101	98-103	100-108	102-113	105-117
5 1 (61)	93- 97	95- 99	96-100	100-105	101-108	103-112	106-116	108-120
5 2 (62)	97-101	99-103	100-104	104-109	106-113	108-116	110-120	112-123
5 3 (63)	100-104	102-106	104-108	107-113	111-118	113-120	114-123	117-126
5 4 (64)	102-107	104-109	108-112	111-117	114-121	116-123	118-127	119-130
5 5 (65)	105-110	107-112	112-116	115-121	117-125	119-127	122-130	123-133
5 6 (66)		111-116	116-120	118-125	121-129	123-131	126-133	127-137
5 7 (67)		115-120	119-124	121-130	125-133	128-134	130-136	131-141
5 8 (68)			122-128	124-133	129-137	132-138	133-140	134-145
5 9 (69)			125-132	127-136	133-141	136-142	138-144	139-149
5 10 (70)				130-140	137-145	140-149	141-155	142-160
5 11 (71)				135-144	141-149	144-155	145-160	146-168
6 0 (72)					146-153	148-156	149-163	150-170
6 1 (73)					150-157	152-163	153-166	154-175
6 2 (74)						157-165	158-170	159-182
6 3 (75)						162-175	163-180	164-190
6 4 (76)						167-185	168-191	169-195

TENTATIVE GOAL WEIGHTS
WOMEN

Height Range Without Shoes	Age in Years				
	18	19-20	21-22	23-24	25 & Over
Ft. Inches	Weight in Pounds				
4 6 (54)	83- 99	84-101	85-103	86-104	88-106
4 7 (55)	84-100	85-102	86-104	88-105	90-107
4 8 (56)	86-101	87-103	88-105	90-106	92-108
4 9 (57)	89-102	90-104	91-106	92-108	94-110
4 10 (58)	91-105	92-106	93-109	94-111	96-113
4 11 (59)	93-109	94-111	95-113	96-114	99-116
5 0 (60)	96-112	97-113	98-115	100-117	102-119
5 1 (61)	100-116	101-117	102-119	103-121	105-122
5 2 (62)	104-119	105-121	106-123	107-125	108-126
5 3 (63)	106-125	107-126	108-127	109-129	111-130
5 4 (64)	109-130	110-131	111-132	112-134	114-135
5 5 (65)	112-133	113-134	114-136	116-138	118-139
5 6 (66)	116-137	117-138	118-140	120-142	122-143
5 7 (67)	121-140	122-142	123-144	124-146	126-147
5 8 (68)	123-144	124-146	126-148	128-150	130-151
5 9 (69)	130-148	131-150	132-152	133-154	134-155
5 10 (70)	134-151	135-154	136-156	137-158	138-159
5 11 (71)	138-155	139-158	140-160	141-162	142-163
6 0 (72)	142-160	143-162	144-164	145-166	146-167
6 1 (73)	146-164	147-166	148-168	149-170	150-171
6 2 (74)	150-168	151-170	152-172	153-174	154-175

TENTATIVE GOAL WEIGHTS
MEN

Height Range Without Shoes	Age in Years				
	18	19-20	21-22	23-24	25 & Over
Ft. Inches	Weight in Pounds				
5 0 (60)	109-122	110-133	112-135	114-137	115-138
5 1 (61)	112-126	113-136	115-138	117-140	118-141
5 2 (62)	115-130	116-139	118-140	120-142	121-144
5 3 (63)	118-135	119-143	121-145	123-147	124-148
5 4 (64)	120-145	122-147	124-149	126-151	127-152
5 5 (65)	124-149	125-151	127-153	129-155	130-156
5 6 (66)	128-154	129-156	131-158	133-160	134-161
5 7 (67)	132-159	133-161	134-163	136-165	138-166
5 8 (68)	135-163	136-165	138-167	140-169	142-170
5 9 (69)	140-165	141-169	142-171	144-173	146-174
5 10 (70)	143-170	144-173	146-175	148-178	150-179
5 11 (71)	147-177	148-179	150-181	152-183	154-184
6 0 (72)	151-180	152-184	154-186	156-188	158-189
6 1 (73)	155-187	156-189	158-190	160-193	162-194
6 2 (74)	160-192	161-194	163-196	165-198	167-199
6 3 (75)	165-198	166-199	168-201	170-203	172-204
6 4 (76)	170-202	171-204	173-206	175-208	177-209

INDEX

[369]